MOTHERS AND ?

Mothers and Education: Inside Out?

Exploring Family–Education Policy and Experience

Miriam David
Rosalind Edwards
Mary Hughes
and
Jane Ribbens

Consultant Editor: Jo Campling

150th YEAR
M
MACMILLAN

First published 1993 by
THE MACMILLAN PRESS LTD
Houndmills, Basingstoke, Hampshire RG21 2XS
and London
Companies and representatives
throughout the world

ISBN 0-333-56592-4 hardcover
ISBN 0-333-56593-2 paperback

A catalogue record for this book is available
from the British Library

Printed in Hong Kong

Contents

Acknowledgements

We all gave support to each other in writing the various chapters for this book, pooling ideas and hammering out themes. We recommend this type of collaboration to others. In particular, though, three of us – Ros Edwards, Mary Hughes and Jane Ribbens – have individually received encouragement and advice from Miriam David for the doctoral theses that we have drawn upon here. We would like to acknowledge the key role she played in those, and in suggesting we come together to write a book. Thanks also to Jo Campling for her part in realising the idea.

The research on which Jane Ribbens' chapters are based was funded by the Economic and Social Research Council, and she would like to thank them for their support. Both Jane and Ros are grateful to the mothers who took part in their respective interviews, and without whom their research would not have been possible.

Ros would also like to acknowledge her son, Dominic, who began his formal education as she returned to hers. Together their lives have illustrated many of the arguments made here. Indeed, this book comes out of all our personal and political journeys and commitments to trying to create a more female friendly future, and a more caring world.

We would like to dedicate the book to all of our children in the hope that they too will take forward our aims and accomplish a more moral world.

1 Mothers and Education: Points of View

INTRODUCTION

This book is about the various aspects of the relationships between mothers and education at different levels in the education system. In particular, we shall look at mothers of young children, either pre-school age or school-age children, in relation to various educational policies, in interaction with their children's schools and teachers, as students themselves in post-school education, such as adult or further and higher education. We shall address the various policy settings and other contexts in which mothers are situated as well as exploring their experiences and understandings.

The sub-title of our book is intended to reveal our twin approaches. On the one hand, we explore the ways in which mothers and the idea of mothering have been constructed and viewed in educational policies and practices. On the other hand, we also review the ways in which mothers have constructed and experienced education policies and practices.

The context for these approaches is the ways in which advanced industrial societies have structured the relations between families and education to ensure that all children are educated to take their place in adult society. Parental rights and responsibilities have been clearly specified by the state to ensure this. Beattie (1985), in discussing concepts and the development of parental participation in four European countries, including Britain, draws attention to the fact that:

> The Universal Declaration of Human Rights (1948) mentioned parents who, it stated, 'have a prior right to choose' the kind of education that shall be given to their children ... [but] the relationship between parents and the state as the provider of education was complex and controversial. (1985, 2)

1

The 'complex and controversial relationship' between parents and the state hinges on issues about the boundaries between 'private families' and 'public bodies' and their respective rights and responsibilities.

Nevertheless, one aspect of the relationship has been clear from that period – that of ultimate parental responsibility for children and their social, emotional and educational needs. The state does not, and does not choose to, abrogate this responsibility but rather has codified parental duties into both legislation and policies. (Crittenden, 1988; David, 1980). The partnership between parents and the state has underpinned not only education provision but the whole of what is often known as the welfare state. (Dale and Foster, 1986; Wilson, 1977; Pascall, 1986).

Parental responsibilities have not always been spelled out in gender terms in policy prescriptions. As a general description, it is fair to say that in all Western industrial societies, *mothers* are expected to take responsibility for their young children. This broad picture of primary maternal responsibility holds true regardless of women's marital status, employment position, ethnic group or social class. There may of course be some exceptions and variabilities in the nature and extent of this responsibility. We might expect maternal responsibility to be carried out and experienced differently, for example, where the daily care of the child is substantially carried out by someone other than the 'natural' mother (whether father, grandmother, a paid 'live-in' nanny or a private fostering arrangement) or where childcare is removed from the mother by some social-work agency. Nevertheless, while all these situations may offer significant insights into variable maternal experiences, these are all very much minority patterns in contemporary Western societies.

Furthermore, even where childcare is substantially carried out by another person, it may be argued that it is still the mother rather than the father who is 'held to account' for the child's character, behaviour and achievements, and in this regard, all mothers are held responsible for their children as moral beings (in Goffman's sense). One of the primary tasks of early motherhood is, arguably, for women to cope with childcare responsibilities, and this coping is meant to be both invisible and enjoyable (Graham, 1982; Ribbens, 1990).

Once the child reaches compulsory school-age, however, maternal responsibility and also authority shifts dramatically – literally overnight. It is not however necessarily diminished but circumscribed in different ways by other public bodies and agencies. As Gillian Pascall has very aptly observed with respect to British social policy:

> Embedded in state provision for children, particularly the under fives, is a peculiar contradiction. On the one hand is the domestic ideology of motherhood as an essentially private, domestic affair: children are not for sharing... On the other hand, children are the future, producers and repro-ducers. They are also a very public concern... One ludicrous outcome of this contradiction is the sudden shift, in both ideology and provision, between the ages of four and five. At four, more or less continuous maternal care is preferred, and a half-day place at nursery is good fortune. But woe betide a parent who decides thereafter that she would prefer to keep her children at home. (1986; 84)

The whole dilemma of fathers in relation to childcare and developmental responsibilities seems to be one that is becoming increasingly polarised. On the one hand, childbirth outside marriage is increasing rapidly, the likelihood of children living with their fathers throughout childhood is reducing, and the redundancy of men's involvement in procreation at all has been raised within emotive media discussions of 'virgin births' in Britain (Radford, 1991). Lone fatherhood, in contrast, remains a statistically insignificant pattern. On the other hand, increasing rates of maternal employment, and general attention paid to the imbalance of women's 'second shift' in the home (Hochschild and Machung, 1989) create increasing pressures and expectations for fathers to be involved in childcare and children's development. Nevertheless, both tendencies can be overstated, since the predominant pattern continues to be for children to live with both their parents throughout their childhood, and evidence for increasing childcare involvement by men continues to be elusive.

In this book we shall explore in more depth the ways in which public policies and practices have defined and developed maternal responsibilities for children and their schooling as well as their general education and development. We shall also look at the other side of the coin: the ways in which mothers have responded to and experienced these prescriptions in the context of familial and social changes. We then go on to review the public prescriptions for mothers through post-school education, concentrating on adult education as defining maternal and domestic responsibilities. Here again we shall look at the obverse: the ways in which mothers as mature students have evaluated and experienced their involvements in the education system for themselves and their children.

THE ACADEMIC AND THE PERSONAL

The themes of this book have grown out of our joint and several concerns with the issues of mothers and education, since we are all mothers and feminists. We came together as a group when three of us shared a supervisor, namely Miriam David, who brought us all into contact, given our shared academic interests in family and education debates. We were all working separately on questions around these themes, having come to them from our personal concerns and intellectual interests in broad questions of feminism and social research. We had all reached this common point by very different personal and intellectual routes but found major similarities in our academic endeavours and experiences. Given that this common meeting point is the start for our joint academic journey it is important briefly to explore how each of us arrived.

Miriam David has had a relatively conventional academic career as a sociologist. After school she went straight to university and after graduation, she started as a social researcher. Having completed her PhD on issues to do with educational policy, she then switched to being an academic teacher of social policy, especially in relation to education and family matters. At a personal level, she became involved in the second wave of the women's movement in its beginnings and developed an early interest in academic women's studies. This led later, when she had her two children, to a concern with the practical and the academic issues in relation to childcare and the family, building on her earlier concerns with education and the family (for further details see David, 1987; 1989b). Since then she has continued to sustain her academic and professional interests in the relations between families, gender and public policies, including education and child care. She has supervised a number of postgraduate research students on these themes as well as herself researching and publishing on them.

Rosalind Edwards is a relatively typical mature woman student. She left school at 16 with minimal qualifications, worked as a secretary, married, had children, and worked part-time, as well as becoming a foster mother. When her youngest son was born, she decided to start studying through the Open University – distance learning. She had always had an urge to go to university and be 'an educated woman'. When her son was five and went to school, so did she. She became a mature student studying for a social policy degree at the local polytechnic. She continued as a student in higher education after graduation, finally completing her doctorate. All the time she has lived much of her studies and her research. Her academic work and interests have centred around feminist analyses of education and 'the family'. One of the most daunting tasks she has faced has been in fact to achieve a peaceful coexistence between these two demanding institutions in her life – as a formal educator of others and as an informal educator of her children.

Mary Hughes also has a quite conventional career and academic background. She went from a variety of school experiences straight to university, completing a degree and postgraduate teaching qualification. She married a man who was doing a PhD and had a vague notion that she would follow him and his career around. So she began teaching liberal studies at a college of further education. At this point she discovered feminism, became active in a campaign called 'Why be a wife?' and began working for increased educational opportunities for women. Whilst working full-time and for some time financially supporting her husband she began to study part-time and subsequently gained an M.Phil. By this time she had divorced, moved to London and started working in adult education. This and her continuing commitment to feminism and academic women's studies led her to use her own situational experiences to complete a PhD part-time. She completed the degree in four years whilst working in adult education and giving birth to her first child. She now has two children and, fairly late in her career, has developed an academic and intellectual preoccupation with the personal experiences of motherhood and children's schooling. She is, at the same time, changing her career from adult education to being a mature mother-student to prepare for a new career in the legal profession.

Jane Ribbens has also had a relatively conventional career as a woman, in terms of the 'career break' type of career pattern in teaching and social research. She went from school straight to university where she completed a degree and postgraduate-teaching and social-work qualifications. She married a fellow sociologist and began to work as a social worker. On the birth of her first child she gave up full-time work and continued with part-time teaching, research and studying. Whilst her two children were under school-age she saw herself as a full-time mother fitting in a range of part-time work as a teacher of sociology 'A' level for the Open University and as a researcher as well as becoming a part-time student on a Masters course at the Open University. She then became a social researcher and began to pursue a PhD having become fascinated by the exclusion of family and mothers from sociological theory. Her academic interest has come to focus on issues of mothers and families in relation to sociology as well as education. She continues to pursue this in both research and teaching.

Our interests in mothers and education are common and similar despite the fact that we come to them from very diverse and varied backgrounds. Some of our experiences have in fact been set in the same context – that of the shifts and changes in the British education system over the last 10 to 20 years and what this has meant for mothers. Most of our children have been born during the era of Conservative government and none of them have real memories of life before Mrs Thatcher. By the time our children started school more and more was being required of us as parents and mothers in particular. Rosalind Edwards writes most evocatively and effectively of these experiences:

> I have an enduring memory. It is of tramping up and down the hill to the local primary school from my home. I would be pushing single and double buggies along this route up to

four times a day (six times when the younger ones were at school for half the day and the older ones for a full day). I spent eleven years standing outside the school gates in sunshine, wind, rain and snow. I went into the children's classrooms to help with cookery, sewing and so on. I have been to teacher-consultation evenings, school concerts and sports days, and parent-teacher association meetings. I spent a year as a parent-governor. I have had verbal and written arguments as well as mutual commiserations with both teachers and my children over what the children wore to school, hairstyles, jewellery and social behaviour.

I have read school reports, letters informing me of school holidays and activities, letters asking me for help at jumble sales and school fairs and to come and help decorate the school hall, letters asking me to pay for school trips and letters asking me to covenant money to the school. I have responded to some of them. I have joined school action groups, signed petitions and tramped the streets asking others to sign them and lobbied councillors at the local county hall in protests at education cutbacks. I have paid for extra out-of-school tuition for my children in some subjects.

At home I have listened to my children read, helped them learn spellings, worked out their maths, made costumes for their concerts and shows, looked up reference books for homework answers, signed 'good work' slips and homework timetables, washed dirty PE kits and school uniforms every weekend fresh for the next week and made packed lunches. I have bought pens, pencils, paper, rulers, rubbers, lunch boxes and educational books. I have bought grey jumpers, blue jumpers, striped shirts, plain shirts, football and hockey boots – the list is endless. I have spent hours, with fraying tempers, searching shops for black or navy shoes which were acceptable both to the school and to my children.

I could write more, but suddenly I feel very tired at the thought of it all. None of it addresses the emotional investment I have in my children. I have celebrated their educational successes and worried over their failures. I have done all the things I have listed in an effort to be a 'good' mother who cares about her children's education – and am left with the feeling I have not quite made it...

INVISIBLE MOTHERING EXPERIENCES

We have chosen to study the issue of mothers' relationships with educational institutions, through policies and practices, partly because we see them as fundamental to our understandings and comprehension of the world around us and our social positions within it. We have not been able to derive these understandings from the literature available and have therefore sought to begin the process of opening up these issues to further investigation. It is a matter of some curiosity to us that these issues have not been adequately addressed before and particularly that most feminists have not concerned themselves with these questions.

Our joint and several concerns span a variety of the social sciences including sociology, especially the sociologies of education and the family, social policy and the histories of social policy and the social psychological underpinnings of policy developments as well as academic women's studies. In none of these areas is motherhood, as distinct from womanhood or wifehood, seen as of central importance and particularly not in relation to questions of education and children's educational development.

In the sociology of the family as a distinctive area of sociological investigation there is a general lack of interest in exploring relationships with educational as compared with other social institutions and social policies and practices. For the most part, such sociologists concern themselves with either internal family functionings or gender relations. However, this has become a central area of feminist debate and concern, with a critical focus on the ways in which the family can be seen as the major site of women's oppression (Barrett, 1980; Barrett and McIntosh, 1982).

Most of the fundamental feminist and sociological work has gone into the exploration of issues to do with the family. A major text, bringing together much of the theoretical and empirical work in this area, has recently addressed all of these questions save the one with which we are now concerned. Strangely Delphy and Leonard (1992) do *not* address questions of motherhood as separate from wifehood in relation to children's care and educational development. Yet they are concerned to spell out the critical ways in which women's exploitation is structurally located in relation to the institution of the family in advanced industrial societies.

This kind of approach builds upon previous feminist work in substantive areas such as the sociology of social policy as well as academic women's studies. In the sociology of social policy great attention has been paid to understanding the development of relationships within the family both from a feminist and a non-feminist perspective. Indeed, the notions of motherhood, mothering and mothers' work as caring have taken an important place. However, much of that work has focused upon the concepts of caring in general and as related to more psychological notions of caring. Finch (1989), Ungerson (1988) and Lewis and Meredith (1989) all explore, from feminist perspectives, notions of women's work as carers but do not link this with separate notions of mothering. To the extent that they draw explicitly on more theoretical concepts they refer to Gilligan's (1982) psychological theories about gender differences and moral development.

There has also been a lot of feminist concern with dual-earner families (for example, Brannen and Moss, 1991; Lewis et al, 1992). Running throughout much of this work is the belief that shifts in gender-based family and employment roles, towards a sharing of them between men and women, may represent moves towards equality for women. The focus of the majority of the studies that have such a concern, however, is on families with pre-school children and issues of childcare. Women's work in mediating between their families and other institutions, particularly their role in their children's schooling and the ramifications of this, is hardly addressed.

Snitow (1992) has tried to summarise briefly the ways in which feminists in a variety of academic disciplines and in political activities, largely in the USA but by reference to Britain, have approached the questions of motherhood since the beginnings of the second wave of the women's movement in the late 1960s. She covers a vast literature, and although she looks at motherhood as an experience as well as the more theoretical concerns, mothering–education relationships do not get a mention. She does, however, concern herself briefly with some of the work on motherhood and childcare. For the most part the focus of her attention, as it is in the feminist literature in general, is on motherhood as an initial event and the problems in relation to women's fertility or lack of it.

Her approach reflects that of the feminist literature in general. There are very few experiential accounts of mother-hood that include reference to the mothering–education relationship. Hewlett (1987), Gordon (1990) and Coward (1992) are some exceptions, where they explore being feminist mothers in particular social and economic contexts. Hewlett has been taken to task by many feminists, especially in the USA, for her rather frank critiques of the ways in which motherhood as an experience has not been problematised by feminists. Indeed some, Faludi (1992) in particular, have accused her of being part of the 'backlash' against feminism along with Gilligan (1982) and Friedan (1981) for addressing these questions in these rather critical ways.

A very recent study, by Allatt and Yeandle (1992), addresses the question of whether it is the case that families no longer care about critically important issues of social and sexual morality, as it is now often argued in the public arena. They conducted a small-scale study of a working-class community in the north of England and found that the majority of families, and mothers in particular, were still struggling in dire economic and social straits to maintain traditional commitments to family, work and community. It is this kind of careful study of the relationship between public values and private commitments around family matters that we wish to emulate but within the particular context of education.

If we turn to the sociology of education, sociology or education there is a general lack of concern with the gendered nature of the issues of family and home–school relations, and the ways in which these are linked to power. In so far as feminists have attempted to address questions of gender in this arena they have been concerned largely with a liberal or radical feminist approach to children's differential educational opportunities.

What counts as 'education' in contemporary Western industrial societies is largely institutionalised within formal systems of schooling which are themselves underpinned by complex legislative and administrative systems. Such institutionalised ideas may at times be questioned and broadened within the academic discussion of the nature of education.

The concept may be broadened to include all forms of learning whether formal or informal, such that education becomes virtually synonymous with sociological concepts of socialisation. In this case, all forms of interaction between mothers and children may potentially be defined as 'education' work. Such a broad usage constitutes an interesting rival paradigm to that which defines 'health work' in terms that also cover all aspects of mothers' activities with their children. (Stacey and Davies, 1983). There may be tendencies towards intellectual colonisation, with rival professional discourses staking claims to an expertise that covers virtually everything about the child's family life in the pre-school years.

The implications of children's home lives for their progress within the formal school system have increasingly been discussed by social researchers ever since concerns for equality of opportunity surfaced as an issue for educational policy. This is a topic to which we shall return in Chapter 2. These implications may have been unwelcome news to some professional educators since they have meant that educational concerns cannot just stop 'at the school gate'. Educators and teachers have been required to pay some heed to what has happened to children before they arrive on the school premises, on reaching compulsory school age, and once they depart from the school grounds at the end of each day after that. In many respects life for both mothers and teachers would be much less complex if their respective responsibilities and activities with children were seen as occurring in quite separate spheres.

In recent decades, social and educational researchers as well as professional educators have devoted a great deal of attention to children's lives 'beyond the school gate' but, we suggest, this attention has been limited to and shaped by a view of education and 'the child' that has been defined from within the education system itself. This is not meant to overlook the complexities and contradictions among educators themselves as to what are the proper goals and content of school-based education. There are certain very broadly based assumptions within educational discourse, particularly derived from psychological concepts, which have not considered the possibility that these assumptions are not shared by all parents. In other words, professional and institutionalised educational discourse reflects cultural assumptions, particularly of white middle-class men (Hall, 1992).

Concepts of 'child development', 'maturation' and 'intelligence' which are crucial to educational organisations are derived from psychological discourses which reflect partial views of children and their experiences of social life, as has increasingly been argued by some psychologists in recent years (Kerchoff, 1972; Tulkin, 1975; Henderson, 1981; Harrington-Brown and Kidwell, 1982; Ingleby, 1986; Walkerdine and Lucey, 1989). Dingwall and Eekelaar suggest that certain theoretical psychological ideas get taken up because '...they give scientific legitimation to significant cultural or political values' (1986, p.67).

Laosa (1981) points out that much observational work on mother–child interactions has been directed at explaining variations in school performance between different social groups. Their implicit agenda is to discover how lower-class socialisation is deficient. Cultural circles between white middle-class/better educated mothers, middle-class white researchers and white middle-class educational institutions may all reinforce each other in their implicit evaluations and understandings of child-rearing. Laosa points to the necessity in research on socio-cultural diversity to: '...recognise and accept that human behaviour may be perceived as competent or incompetent only in the context of specific roles and value judgements' (1981, p.134). Walkerdine and Lucey (1989) are quite exceptional in trying to bring together this social psychological literature with a feminist critique in an attempt to show how particular value judgements in the public arena have been used to influence and regulate mothers in their socialisation work with their daughters. This study gets nearest, along with Dorothy Smith's research (1987a) in Canada, to our concerns and predilections. In their different ways they are both concerned to spell out the social constructions in mother–education relations from both policies and accounts of experiences. Our aim is to build upon their approaches by providing more evidence through careful case-studies of these issues. We wish to balance feminist critiques of policy prescriptions with accounts of mothers' experiences in a variety of educational settings to open up these issues to critical analysis.

ENGENDERING BOUNDARIES

We have chosen to use the concept of *boundary* to examine the relationships between mothers and education. Allied with our feminist perspective we think it is a useful concept for investigating the interface between mothers and education. In recent years there have been moves in education policy and practice to conceptualise the work of parents in general and mothers in particular in terms of notions of partnership and liaison. In schools and educational institutions educators have begun to talk more freely and possessively about their clients or consumers as 'our parents'. Similarly, through these shifting concepts and ideologies motherhood and maternal responsibilities are constructed and reconstructed in particular ways which may be experienced differentially.

The concept of *boundary* allows us to recognise that ideas and ideologies are constructed and understood in different ways by different parties to these issues. The notion of 'boundary' is one which has received particularly close attention from anthropologists (Wallman 1978; 1979), being a symbolic entity even if signified concretely. The concept is used most commonly in everyday language in relation to physical space, as something that demarcates different geographical areas. Physical boundaries may also be used very significantly to represent social boundaries, as in the famous example discussed in the anthropological literature of the Cuttleslowe wall that for many years created a physical barrier across the road which would otherwise have connected a private housing estate in Oxford with a council estate (Collison, 1963). The prevalent American mythology about the significance of coming 'from the other side of the tracks' also reveals the symbolic social significance that can attach to physical boundaries.

The demarcation of different social spaces may be signified in a variety of ways: for instance through differences of speech or dress. There may also be very significant links here which might loosely be termed psychological boundaries, for example with regard to issues of self-identity, or notions of a 'private' self distinct from a more public persona, or notions of 'me as a mother' as distinct from (say) 'me as a student'. What is implicated here are the ways in which people may work with differing understandings of individual and collective identities, such as via notions of 'us', or 'people like me', as distinct from 'others' who are not like me, and the ways in which certain criteria may be brought into play to demarcate such social boundaries.

The language of boundaries has been particularly noticeable in recent discussions of educational institutions, and in this context may particularly reflect the application of management theories (Johnson, 1989; Glatter, 1989). Hoy and Miskel (1989) suggest that a shift in management perspectives – away from seeing organisations such as schools as closed systems and towards an open systems perspective – leads to greater attention being paid to school environments:

> The open-system concept highlights the vulnerability and interdependence of organisations and their environments. In other words, environment is important because it affects the internal structures and processes of organisations: hence, one is forced to look both inside and outside the organisation to explain organisational behaviour. (ibid, p.29)

Parents constitute only one item among many which these writers include in educational environments, and mothers and fathers are rarely distinguished separately. Furthermore, within the conceptual framework developed for analysing educational environments, parents are likely to constitute a relatively poorly organised environment with a low level of clustering.

Perhaps this is a factor relevant to Johnson's (1989) observation that British schools tend to be patronising, dismissive or vague towards 'their' parents, to the extent of not even holding clear registers of who their parents are (as is now required in Britain under the 1988 Education Reform Act). This Act, Johnson suggests, is likely to lead schools to pay much closer attention to the nature and wishes of their parental body, for instance through their concern to maintain pupil numbers. Nevertheless, Hoy and Miskel (1989) discuss a number of ways in which school organisations may seek to exert some control over their environments, by managing and shaping them. It could be argued that this has indeed been a feature of parent–school relationships, where not only may schools seek to control the nature of this relationship but they may also seek to shape parents' own view of themselves, in terms of how they should define themselves as parent-educators and how they should fulfil such a role.

Schools and educational professionals want to assert their own authority and expertise, which may well be more closely questioned and scrutinised than, say doctors' claims to medical expertise and authority. From this perspective, mothers and fathers – as part of the school environment – may be seen as potentially disruptive and even threatening to internal school processes. From the teacher's point of view, life would be much simpler if s/he did not have to consider the child as a 'whole person' and recognise the relevance of his/her home-based experiences. Such attitudes appear to be communicated to mothers, as expressed in their fears of appearing to be a 'pushy mother' or a 'fussy mother'. What is not clear, however, is how far such terms arise exclusively within the context of teachers' perceptions of mothers, or also within the context of mothers' perceptions of each other within local networks that may operate with notions of competition as well as cooperation (Bell, 1993).

The notion of boundary has also been explicitly used in discussions of family life by writers and professionals who use the approach broadly described as family systems theory. Aldous (1978) suggests that family boundaries are maintained by a variety of processes, including physical residence, kinship terminology, interdependencies and values shared through interactions between family members, shared histories over time, rituals and shared intimacies.

The analysis of the family system is concerned with the analysis of two kinds of process: the process whereby the system maintains its boundaries in relation to the outside world and the processes of input and output or exchange that take place between the system and its environment. The focus would be on the various feedback loops involved in the system and its relationship with the outside world (Morgan, 1985, p.144). Morgan concludes, however, that writers using this theoretical approach rarely pay attention to the nature of the 'environment' within which the 'family system' is contained. Indeed, it is remarkable that Aldous's book, which takes developmental change in families as its central focus, is one of the very few academic books on family life which includes a discussion of family relationships with schools. It seems that not only do educational writers pay little attention to family issues, but this also occurs in reverse, with family specialists paying scant attention to issues of schooling.

In seeking to deconstruct 'family' as a social object which is meaningfully revealed through discourse, Gubrium and Holstein discuss how: 'The assumption of distinct domestic order comes with a language of boundaries ... [with] an inside and an outside which makes it altogether reasonable to distinguish its interior from its environment' (1990, p.42). While Gubrium and Holstein are very helpfully, we suggest, seeking to examine the discourse which produces 'family' as a social object, it is also clear that this discourse is one which occurs not only within professional or academic writings, but relates to concrete everyday events, since ' ...family ... [is] an object that is interpretively assembled out of experience' (ibid., p.157).

More than this, however, even as a socially constructed idea, we would argue that 'family' has real consequences for the ways in which individual people act, including their arrangements of physical spaces (such as houses) and concrete objects. For instance, the symbolic significance of providing the 'cooked dinner' for the family evening meal in households in South Wales marks the threshold between public worlds and private domestic space for family members returning home (Murcott, 1983). The different ways in which front and back doors may signify different sorts of relationships with the world outside is another example (Marston, 1991). Furthermore, it is not just a feature of professional discourse that suggests that some household members may work towards 'boundary maintenance' (Aldous, 1978), since much maternal discourse also suggests a concern with creating 'family' as an internally cohesive and externally demarcated social unit (Ribbens, 1990), and with mediating between family members and others (Graham, 1985).

In seeking to extend our thinking about family boundaries, Morgan suggests that three kinds of connection between family and outside environments may be elaborated – inclusion, overlap and network. In relation to family boundaries with educational environments, it is the first two of these that are relevant. First, inclusion, in the sense that family members jointly and actively mediate their understandings of outside environments, and indeed, act upon these environments, is relevant:

> The environment, therefore, is not simply or passively a kind of ether in which the family is enclosed and which surrounds the family. It is itself actively constructed by the family in its work, collective and individual, of making sense of the world and making sense of itself... The family and its environment not only mutually influence each other but manually construct each other.
>
> (Morgan, 1985, p.155)

In relation to educational environments, families may be seeking to act upon and affect schools, and will be developing their own understanding of the meanings of education. Morgan's second connection, overlap, is also useful, in the sense that family members belong to other social settings, and these involvements are also actively processed through the family. In relation to children as pupils, family members will also be amplifying and transforming the meanings attached to their involvements in schools.

What Wallman particularly draws to our attention, however, is that boundaries have two sides to them, and they may indeed be reactive in the sense that changes on one side of a boundary may lead to changes on the other side. In addition, people on one side of the boundary may experience it differently from people on the other side, and people on each side may have different sets of meanings by which they understand the nature of the boundary: 'Lines of difference are used in particular contexts for particular ends and are selected accordingly.' (Wallman, 1978, p.215) Mothers may for example particularly concern themselves with social and personal issues concerning the child's school life, such as the child's social relationships, or access to toilets for young children. This emphasises a view of mothers as concerned with the child as a private person. Fathers may be more likely to be involved in contacts with schools if the issue is defined as a more strictly educational one. This emphasises a view of fathers as oriented towards the child's further achievements in public settings.

Social boundaries constitute an interface between one sort of social setting and another. As such, Wallman suggests that confusion, ambiguity and danger are particularly likely to occur at such points. She suggests a number of questions that may be asked about any particular boundary item:

> What *kind* of resource is this boundary? What is it used *for*? In which (and how many) contexts is it relevant? What is its status in historical or situational time? For whom is it an asset, for whom a liability? With what other differences is it congruent or associated? What meaning does it have on the other (outer) side? (1978, p.208)

Boundaries between home and school may indeed be experienced as confusing and ambiguous, even dangerous. The ideology concerning children's welfare and interests may suggest that there is not meant to be any sort of oppositional boundary since all concerned are expected to attend to the needs of the child, and the research/policy thrust in recent decades has been towards the need for a weak boundary in order best to work for the good of the child. Yet schools are not the same places as homes; being a teacher is not the same as being a mother; being a mother is not the same as being a teacher; public social settings are not the same as private ones, at least in terms of the ways in which family is constructed (Gubrium and Holstein, 1990).

The extent to which such issues lead to the constitution of a strong or weak boundary is likely to vary between particular homes/families/mothers and particular schools/teachers, but they are always likely to be there in some degree. Mothers and teachers may also vary as to how far they want to see a clear-cut boundary between the home and school settings. Issues of authority over the child may be implicated here, and, as Wallman (1978) points out, where the balance of power is uneven between the two sides of a boundary, the weaker side may have a particular interest in maintaining a strong boundary in order to defend itself from domination. As Johnson (1989) remarks with regard to relations between teachers and parents, '...the idea of equal partnership may be no more than a fine-sounding phrase' (p.19).

The differences between home and school have been explicitly discussed by a very few educational writers:

At the heart of the business of schooling are processes which

contrast sharply with some of the key features of family life
... Families and schools are very different kinds of institutions. Although there is common ground, they have their
own, sometimes contradictory, concerns and responsibilities. Most home/school accounts contain absolutely no
inkling of any of this!

> (Atkin et al., 1988, p.11)

Some of these differences arise from the understanding of
families as 'private' and thus particularly female social settings.
Age and dependency are relevant to the definition of the
private sphere and there is some ambiguity about children in
the public sphere. Schools may be seen as part of the public
sphere of social life, although primary schools particularly
may have some ambiguity about this. There are associated
dilemmas for teachers about these ambiguities, for instance
about whether or not to give children affectionate physical
contact. Newson and Newson (1977) suggest that the roles of
teachers and parents are fundamentally different, with a
crucial contrast centring on the issue of im/partiality. While
parental duty might tend towards clear and unreasonable
partiality towards their particular offspring, the obligation of
teachers is towards reasonableness and impartiality. Newson
and Newson also suggest that parents themselves often recognise and support this obligation on teachers as a way of reducing any potential disruption from the possibly unreasonable
partialities of other parents. Similarly, Atkin et al. write:

> In considering the boundary between parenting and teaching,
> then, a key concept appears to be the nature of the relation-
> ship between adult and child. Teachers in school have to be
> professional in the sense of being impartial and fair in their
> dealings with all pupils, whereas parents are allowed to have
> an emotional bond and can afford to respond to the indi-
> vidual and idiosyncratic nature of their children. (1988, p.73)

Nevertheless, social boundaries are most usefully analysed as
semi-permeable as well as elastic (Wallman 1978), and in some
of our chapters we will examine the sorts of permeations that
cross the home/school boundary from both directions, and
raise issues about power in relation to these permeations.
Numerous policy programmes in a variety of Western indus-

trialised countries in recent decades have sought to instruct mothers as to how to fulfil their responsibility in preparing pre-school children for their future fruitful participation within the school system, which we will discuss further in Chapter 2. However, it is also clear that some understandings of 'education' and of what it means to be 'a child', may lead mothers to resist such ideas. This is not to deny that there is very widespread concern amongst mothers, across the whole variety of class, racial and ethnic groups, for their children's success within a school system that is regarded as largely holding a key, if not the only key, to their children's future prosperity. We suggest, however, that women may also at times have other considerations, not least a notion of childhood as a special time for play and fun without having to pay too much attention to the serious business of adult life. One of the things that may potentially be in dispute is the notion of 'the child' involved, as a future citizen or as a private individual. Associated with this, the arena of 'the family and home' may also constitute contested terrain – as the site for the creation and preparation of future useful citizens, or as the site for retreat from the harsh realities of adult public life (Davidoff et al., 1976; Harris, 1977):

> Feminist thinkers have had to live with a certain *inherent instability* in their categories. ...They have had to pay particular attention to boundaries, both the permeability and the limits of categories.
>
> (Davidoff, 1990, p.231)

As we have already noted we plan to use the notion of boundary to cover a range of sub-sets of concepts for our analysis. We have drawn attention to how boundary can be used to help elucidate the whole idea of family–education, home–school, mother–institution, adult–child discourses. Institutional, political and ideological discourses make power inequalities ambiguous through their very language. In particular, notions such as partnership, participation and liaison imply a level of equality that may not be as unambiguous as it sounds. Similarly the physical, emotional and intellectual boundaries between individual parents and children, teachers and educators or parents may be more ambiguous than official discourses allow.

The notion of boundary will also help us usefully elucidate

the ambiguous distinctions between public and private. In general the public sphere is regarded as associated with the male world. It is the world of paid work, politics, formal education, culture and the general exercise of power and authority. The private sphere is also associated with men, because they move between the two spheres, but the private sphere is particularly women's 'place'. It is the domestic domain: the world of the family, home, children, domestic labour. Women are said to have a special relationship with the private sphere of the family because it is the primary site of both their work and of their social and personal identity. Housework and looking after people are not just another species of work, or even just women's work, they are women's identity and part of their psyche (Oakley, 1981a; Morgan and Taylorson, 1983; Graham, 1983; Pascall, 1986). In their daily actions within the private domestic sphere women do have power particularly with regard to rearing children but it is an informal, fragile and constrained power (Elshtain, 1981; New and David, 1985; Oakley, 1974; Stacey and Price, 1981). Pateman (1983, p.286) argues that the private sphere of the family is 'paradigmatically private' and an area of relationships to which access, scrutiny and control from the 'outside' should be restricted. It is 'under cultural constraints to appear autonomous and private' (Rapp, Ross and Bridenthal, 1979, p.288). Gilligan (1982) amongst others has argued that women's primary existence within the private sphere of nurturance and self-sacrifice results in the development of a distinctive psychological personality that is inherently relational.

The public/private dichotomy and difference theory have been criticised as a tool for analysis by other feminists, seeing them as either acultural, ahistorical and asocial or that the two spheres and gendered personalities are integrally connected and related to each other. Janet Sharistanian feels that while the public/private model remains useful, its greatest drawback is:

> not any particular premise that it encompassed but its tendency to stress the separation of, or opposition between the domestic and public domains rather than their complex, multi-levelled, highly variable, and frequently shifting interdependence.
>
> (Sharistanian, 1987, p.179)

If not properly explicated the public/private model and the male/female psyche model leads to a tendency to focus attention on the two constituent parts as separate rather than connected, hence our desire to use the notion of boundary as a way of making the connections.

Boundaries between the public and the private do not just shift between cultures and over historical time, they are different for the different social groupings within that one culture or society. As Anne Phoenix (1987) has pointed out, black people are subject to the same dominant ideological forces as white people. Due to the pervasiveness of such ideologies many black people subjectively accept aspects of them because they espouse the attitudes of those who are perceived to be more powerful and do not wish to be subject to stigmatisation. To this can be added that black people and the white working classes may espouse certain aspects of the dominant ideas but impute a different meaning to them. Ideologies do not 'exert pressure from a great distance over the individual' (Brannen and Moss, 1991, p.9). People can redefine them in various ways.

The public/private split can be used in a revealing way, as we hope to show, and it can offer 'an open and flexible perspective' (Gamarnikow and Purvis, 1983, p.3), provided that it is recognised that the divisions and boundaries between the two are not only not constant but are to some extent different for each person according to the structural factors operating on their lives. In positing a difference between races and classes of women in relation to spheres it has usually been differences in women's position in the public sphere that have been concentrated upon. Conversely, the social psychological analyses have mainly concentrated on feminine characteristics as manifested in the private, domestic, personal sphere, rather than looking at the feminine psyche in operation in the public male world. While sociological studies may show the non-existence of boundaries, or the existence of them only for women of a certain race and/or class, concentration on public activity and externally observed actuality rather than women's feelings and understandings can lead to the position where a model is destroyed but still exists. In observed academically-analysed reality, a bounded private sphere may not exist, but the domain may well do so in feelings and in people's understandings and explanations of their lives. Whether or not public/private boundaries are empirically real is less important than the fact that they are real in their ideological consequences (Porter, 1983). Women may work towards maintaining boundaries, or may wish to demolish them, and this needs to be looked at in its own terms. Unless understandings are rooted in women's feelings and understandings as well as their externally observed experiences, it can only be partial. Sharistanian believes that the public/private model:

...is more, not less, useful precisely because the apparent interpenetration of public and domestic life makes tracing the real ways in which conflicts between these spheres still exist for women an even more subtle and complicated analytical task than before. (1987, p.180)

It is also subtle and complicated because it is allied with the complex notions, which we wish to address, of authority and responsibility.

The concept of authority has largely been discussed by male writers in relation to male lives in the public domain. (Edwards and Ribbens, 1991). We accept the existing notion of authority as legitimate power (Lukes, 1978, p.638). Friedman's (1973) influential discussion adds the distinction of being *in* authority – which implies a special institutional role with a particular area of command – and being *an* authority – which implies claims to special knowledge or insights. If we apply this to the lives of mothers, they may be viewed as holding authority in both senses, being *in* authority primarily by virtue of a legally and socially recognised biological link, and being *an* authority via claims to the special knowledge of their children which mothers may themselves assert in relation to rival authority claims, by fathers, teachers, childcare professionals.

While the control parents wield over small children may be experienced by both parties as a straightforward power struggle rather than an authoritative relationship, it is regarded as *legitimate* coercion by other adults: 'As with gender distinctions, the natural qualities of age justify the subordination of children to parents: ignorance, a lack of moral sense and the absence of responsibility makes them different in kind from adults' (La Fontaine 1990, p. 199).

In other words, children are regarded as subject to authority from their parents, not because they themselves surrender their private judgement, but because adults in general regard children as incapable of judgement in the first place. This implies the significance of other parties in legitimating the authority of parents, which makes 'outsiders' crucial to the authority relationship. This may be a feature of why mothers are particularly vulnerable to the scrutiny of others. La Fontaine (1990) suggests that it is easier for men to assert parental authority because male stereotypes suggest rationality and self-control, and furthermore, paternal authority is regarded as divine in origin since it is less closely associated with the natural process of reproduction. As children become older, it may well be that parents expect them to develop their own acceptance of parental authority.

Sociological discussions of authority have paid little attention to domestic issues, and where they do, to conjugal rather than parental authority. (Bell and Newby, 1976; La Fontaine, 1990). While La Fontaine suggests that both mothers and fathers exercise power over children, she, like Arendt, discusses parental authority in relation to fathers (La Fontaine, 1990; Arendt, 1969, p. 93). Hood-Williams (1990) uses the umbrella term of 'family patriarchy' but does not separately distinguish maternal authority.

It is also very striking how, in legal discourse, concepts of authority and responsibility have shifted with the advent of the Children Act 1989 in Britain and elsewhere in Europe. (Eekelaar, 1991a). Bainham makes the point: 'The change in terminology reflects the view of the Law Commission...that the parental position vis a vis a child is more accurately described as "responsibility"...' (1990, p. 17)

Yet this shift in language occurred just at the point where mothers finally achieved complete legal equality with fathers, with the removal of the anachronism of married fathers having the legal status of parental guardian. All mothers are defined by the British Children Act as having automatic parental responsibility, but while all fathers may be defined as parents, they have automatic parental responsibility only if the child is born within marriage. For children born outside marriage, fathers can acquire parental responsibility through the agreement of the mother or by court order. Without parental responsibility the father will not have certain legal rights in relation to the child (Bainham, 1990).

While the concept of parental 'authority' has declined in significance in some European countries, as Eekelaar (1991a) points out, the concept of parental 'responsibility' has two meanings, first, duties and power which parents *owe* to children for the latters' benefit, and second, *freedom* to bring up children without interference from the state (1991a, p. 39). The discourse, in other words, is moving towards a consideration of how these concepts interconnect in concrete practices and experiences. Some now argue that arguments for parental authority can only be derived from their connection with parental obligations:

> ...the only right parents have [in regard to the upbringing of a child] is simply a consequence of the obligation (for that upbringing). This would amount to a moral claim against unwarranted interference in carrying out their duties and for adequate support from the society.
> (Crittenden, 1988, p. 68)

A further consideration must also cover gender implications of such ungendered notions as 'parental authority'. The issue at stake is whether responsibility is viewed as something that has been delegated from a wider chain of authority or as arising from the independent basis of a mother's own special relationship with, and knowledge of, her child. Belenky et al. (1986) provide some examples of how women may need reassurance from others before they come to assert their own maternal authority: 'Whomever a woman finds to turn to ... the significant educational action is the reassurance and confirmation that 'maternal authority' provide her that she, too, can think and know and be woman' (1986, p. 620).

It is also possible that maternal authority has been overlooked as it is not the same as patriarchal authority. Elshtain hints at this:

> Children, however, exhibit little doubt that their mothers are powerful and authoritative, though perhaps not in ways identical to fathers... Parental authority, like any form of authority, may be abused, but unless it exists the activity of parenting itself is impossible. (1989, p. 63)

It may be that maternal authority is manifested in subtle and muted ways, both within and outside the household. Exploring mothers' experiences of these boundaries is one of the issues discussed further in Chapters 3 and 4.

Yet another sub-set of concepts in relation to the notion of boundary that we will explore is that of vocational and non-vocational, especially in relation to education. These concepts are often used ambiguously, particularly with regard to women's unpaid activities within the home or domestic sphere. Another way of discussing women's home-based work is to view it as a 'vocation', in the sense of it being a moral and social commitment rather than something which is seen as requiring financial reward. Indeed, the reward might, in fact, derive from mothers' authority rather than responsibilities in the sense in which we have just discussed gendered notions of parental authority. However, in official discourse, in this case educational discourse, the notion of non-vocational, or rather 'leisure', is currently applied to those educational courses provided for women through post-school education, especially adult education, for domestic responsibilities. And, as a corollary, such non-vocational or 'leisure' courses will be deprived of resources and women's access to education may be severely curtailed. By contrast, vocational courses are also being redefined to cover special male, work and training courses in all levels of post-school education.

AIMS AND STRUCTURE OF THE BOOK

Our book aims to reveal the gendered nature of, and issues of power in, the relationships between mothers and education. We plan to illustrate these issues through a series of case studies, taking as central to them the notion of *boundary*. We will explore policy understandings and prescriptions to demonstrate how they are constructed upon public world ways of knowing and professional and social scientific agendas. We hope to show that they do not necessarily relate to the realities of women's family-based lives.

We will also explore how being a mother can mean different ways of knowing and experiencing the world from these public world points of view. On the other hand, we will also argue that unless mothers have access to place and status in the public world, as things stand they may find it difficult to make their voices heard and influence changing agendas. We show that mothers, contrary to public world perceptions, do want to make their voices heard. On the basis of our analyses of these various mother–education relations and interactions, we also want to argue for new ways of constructing public agendas to ensure wider understandings. We want to argue for new agendas that take account of mothers' experiences and realities in terms of both home–school relations and post-school education, covering adult and further and higher education. These new agendas relate to both policy and practice in education at all levels.

The book is structured as follows. In Part One, we explore mothers' roles, work and experiences as mediators for their children's education. In Chapter 2, we explore the construction of understandings through public policies on home-school relations and parental roles in education. We demonstrate just how dependent these understandings have been on social scientific evaluations, which themselves tend to be gender-blind. In Chapter 3, we explore notions of parental authority, especially looking at mothers' experiences of maternal authority in relation to young children. This is based upon Jane Ribbens' sample of mothers in South-East England and mothers' voices are frequently heard in these accounts. In Chapter 4, we explore mothers' and teachers' negotiations over their children. Again this is based upon Ribbens' study of mothers and carefully explicates the different interpretations of educators and parents over the home–school boundary. That mothers want their voices to be heard is amply demonstrated in this chapter.

In Part Two, we explore issues to do with family–education relations in post-school education. Here the focus turns upon women's roles, work and studies and experiences as consumers or as students in post-school education. In Chapter 5, we explore the ways in which policy prescriptions and understandings are based upon public world views of women's domestic responsibilities rather than their employment-related vocations. Mary Hughes looks carefully at the contradictory notions of women's family-based lives that have been incorporated into public policy agendas. In Chapter 6, we explore the different ways of understanding or knowing the world that women as mothers often have. This chapter is based upon Rosalind Edwards's study of a group of mature women students in several higher education institutions in South-East England. We investigate the boundaries between notions of university education and those of the 'university of life' and the various constructions that these mothers place upon them. In Chapter 7, we enquire how mothers value and experience higher education and how they see it as important for their own children's experiences and education. This is also based upon Edwards's sample of mother-students who recognise that, for themselves, they need place and status in the public world for their voices to be heard.

In Chapter 8, we draw the threads together and try to show what contributions we believe we have made both to theory and practice. We argue that our contributions span feminist theory and practice, as well as the more conventional academic disciplines of education, sociology and social policy. We also show that we hope to have made a methodological contribution through our use of qualitative research methods and around the intriguing notion of boundary. Most important, however, is the argument that there are different ways of knowing and understanding the world, from different points of view, places and positions, that affect public agendas. We want to argue for mothers' ways of understanding and interpreting the world to be included in public agendas for their own sakes, those of their children and their education, and for a richer and arguably more moral world.

Part One
Women as Mediators: Mothers and Schools

2 Home–School Relations
Miriam David

Educate a man and you educate a person,
Educate a woman and you educate a family.
Ruby Manikan, 30 March 1947,
from the *Bloomsbury Dictionary of Quotations*

The above quotation illustrates the expectations about the gender roles within families and the relationships between families and the education system as they were assumed to be almost 50 years ago. Women's education was to be for the purposes of becoming mothers and the mainstay of the family in terms of childcare, childrearing and children's education: the 'private' world of the family. Men's education was for the 'public' world of work and politics: a 'person' or 'citizen'. In other words, social expectations assumed a sharp sexual division of labour in the 'private' world of the family and the 'public' world, reinforced at least implicitly by the education system. These social expectations were framed publicly: they were not necessarily those of the women or mothers themselves.

In this chapter, I want to explore the ways in which these assumptions about the partnership between families, especially 'mothers', and education were built into both the form and development of modern, post-war systems of education through law, policies, social research and subsequent social practices. I will leave discussion of how social practices through mothers' own activities themselves developed, to the discussion in the next and subsequent chapters. Over the 40 to 50 year period, since the Second World War and the framing of modern welfare states and education systems, there has been a gradual shift in the form of the partnership between families and schools. In this chapter, I will focus on British developments, although similar processes have been at work in other countries, particularly in North America and Australia, but also much of Europe.

The changing boundary has been from one which emphasised the role of professionals – teachers and educators – in
preparing children for their adult roles with all their built-in
assumptions of gender differences in the family to one which
has emphasised the role of parents, especially mothers,
implicitly if not explicitly, rather than professionals. However,
the boundary changes have not been unilinear. From an early,
post-war emphasis on the roles of both the professional educator and the educational system itself as the key to children's
educational and social development there grew a much greater
emphasis on the role of parents in the educational process
both at home and in school. This shift was from a partnership
in which professional educators were more dominant than
parents in 'child-centred' education to a partnership in which
parents became rather more equal with professional educators
in their involvement and participation in children's education.
More recently this emphasis has been replaced with a concern
for *parental control* or dominance of the educational process.

This is particularly the case in the political arena, where issues
of the role of parents as consumers/customers and/or citizens
are now high on the public policy agenda. This can be illustrated in Britain where the Conservative government published a
Citizen's Charter which included as a key element a Parent's
Charter for Education and early legislation centred on this by
giving *parents* the key role in educational decision-making over
types of schools. Parallel changes in forms of teacher training,
such that the professional, college-based element is to be
reduced in favour of more school-based training, add to the
stronger role to be afforded parents in educational decision-
making on school governing bodies at the expense of professional educators and educational politicians and bureaucrats.
Although the parental role is changing, so too is that of the
professional educator. Brown (1990) has referred to this shift
as one from the ideology of 'meritocracy' to 'parentocracy',
which nicely encapsulates the notion of parent power.

This changing balance in the partnership between family/
parents and education or home and school has come about
partly through changing political values and partly through
the role that various social scientists – and social science
disciplines, particularly psychology and sociology – have
played in the process. It may also have altered through the

ways in which mothers themselves have become involved in the processes of education. I want to explore the ways in which policy-makers and social scientists together have developed strategies around the *concepts of parental participation in education or home-school relations.* I want to show how the boundaries between parents – especially mothers – and schools have altered through these various processes. The end-result has been more complex relations between families and education, but with an *increased* emphasis on the role of *mothers* as key educators, both at home and at school, in their children's development. These processes have occurred in most advanced industrial societies but I will illustrate my argument with evidence chiefly from Britain, or rather England and Wales, and the ways it borrowed from the USA (as Silver, 1990, especially has noted). There is also evidence from Australia and Canada on which to draw as well as some other European countries.

A parallel process of change during this period of time, however, has been that of the form and characteristics of family life, again centring on the role of women, and mothers in particular. The changes have focused on mothers' role in paid employment, either as professionals or other kinds of 'workers' especially in service industries, and mothers' marital or familial situations. Developments in maternal employment, especially of mothers with young children – either pre-school or in early childhood education – have begun to occur more systematically since the late 1960s in most advanced industrial societies. The form, however, has varied, with mothers mostly in part-time employment in Britain, and mothers in more temporary but full-time employment in parts of Europe and the USA (Melhuish and Moss, 1991; Moss and Melhuish, 1991). Interestingly, many mothers have become or are in the process of becoming professional educators, teachers of young children especially.

At the same time, and partly related to these shifts in maternal employment, there have been major changes in the form of family life. The key changes have been the increasing rate of divorce and/or marital breakdown, including formal and legal separations, and the increasing rates of both lone parenthood and remarriage (Coote et al., 1990). More recently, there have also been shifts in the rates of marriage and cohabitation, such that a large proportion of children are born 'illegitimately', albeit to mothers who may be cohabiting with the father or who may register the child in the father's name, too. There has also been a bifurcation in the age of such kinds of motherhood to young, teenage motherhood and older, separated or divorced mothers.

The impact of these various and complex changes in family life is that a large minority of children experience a variety of 'family worlds', including a period of time in a lone-mother household, with step-parents, step-siblings, half-siblings and a range of sets of grandparents. The traditional family of two 'natural' parents with mother primarily responsible for rearing the children in partnership with the education and other social services, is now no longer the 'normal' pattern, although it may still be the majority form. There are now a variety of other forms which essentially give mothers more sole responsibility for the care and education of their children. I want to explore whether or not these kinds of changes in the form and nature of motherhood have affected the changing partnership between families and education, and in what ways. Whether schools accommodate to changing familial patterns and more variable family or parental responsibilities will be considered in so far as there is evidence available.

These changes in family life, especially the role of mothers in employment and in responsibility for child-rearing, have inevitably been affected by parallel changes in education and social policies. These policy changes have tended to increase women's expectations about their roles in paid employment and in the kinds of family life that they might want. In other words, there has been an interaction between changing expectations about educational and economic opportunities and family life. I want to argue, along with Epstein (1990) and Lareau (1989) that these changes in family life have not been taken into account by teachers, school systems and policy-makers, creating a situation which in effect reproduces in a more complex form social and educational inequalities. Moreover, the fact that many of the key teachers are themselves mothers or potential mothers as Hamilton and Griffiths (1984), Lightfoot (1978), Merttens and Vass (1987), Manicom (1984) and others have noted makes for even more complex and contradictory home-school relations. In particular, it raises the question of the ways in which the partnership implies a kind of policing role between 'professional' mothers as teachers and other 'amateur' mothers (David, 1985). However, although changing expectations have, in all probability, influenced mothers' roles both in school and at home, whether as professional educators or as mothers *per se*, there has been very little research in this area. Lightfoot (1978) remains one of the few researchers to consider the question of the way in which women teachers in early childhood education become 'the other woman' in a young child's life. Best (1983) has also considered some aspects of these issues in her 'cohort' study of a group of elementary school children. However, they are not germane to her analysis.

Curiously, however, there has been very little feminist analysis of these processes, despite the wealth of literature on motherhood itself both as an experience and an institution (Rich, 1977). Most feminists have been concerned to explore the nature of motherhood as an ideology (Phoenix, Woollett and Lloyd, 1991), as a social institution in relation to the care of children (New and David, 1985; Hewlett, 1987) or as an experience (Gordon, 1990) or to explore the broader implications in relation to the concept of caring (Finch, 1989; Ungerson, 1988). The notion of care has received considerable attention in relation to social services in the feminist literature (Dalley, 1988; Maclean and Groves, 1991). And many feminists have looked at the 'darker side' of motherhood in relation to child care, and child abuse and sexually violent men (Hamner and Statham, 1987; Hamner and Maynard, 1987; Kelly, 1988). Others have also looked at the more general issues to do with maternal employment (Joshi, 1989) and family changes (Kiernan and Wicks, 1990).

The two exceptions to this are, however, Smith's exploratory feminist methodology and work on mothers and education, reprinted as *The Everyday World as Problematic* (1987a) and a fascinating if polemical reanalysis of a study of mothers' and daughters' relationships at home and at nursery school, which attempts to show the ideological construction of motherhood through social practices and regulation in relation to socialization and education. Walkerdine and Lucey (1989) provide a most trenchant account, through their critique of one psychological study, of how social psychology was used by educationalists to develop the ideology of motherhood. We shall have occasion to return to this study, as an important feminist analysis of the underlying social processes.

POLITICAL/POLICY CONTEXT FOR THE HOME–SCHOOL PARTNERSHIP

The post-war social-democratic political consensus that developed in Britain and to a lesser extent in most advanced industrial societies was about the role that the state should play in providing forms of social welfare, including education, to sustain economic growth. Most such societies developed intricate systems of state social and economic supports for education, health and welfare, providing mainly public social services, free at the point of provision. In particular as regards education, they developed universal and compulsory state systems for all children for at least ten years of schooling. However, there was scarcely any agreement on the age at which children should start to attend school, and the ages varied from about three to seven years old. There was agreement, however, that schooling should be provided by professional educators.

As we have already noted in Chapter 1 there was also agreement that the primary responsibility for children – their education, their health, their care – lay with the family. It was both a parental right and parental responsibility to choose an education for their children, either at schools provided variously by the state, religious authorities or private bodies, or at home. It also remained a parental right and responsibility to care for their children at times other than when in school. The *boundary* between families or parents and education or other public institutions was not clearly specified.

Indeed as others have shown, there was a clear ideological specification not only of the family *per se* but also of mothers' and fathers' rights and responsibilities. Wilson (1977), in considering women's role in relation to developments of the British welfare state, pinpointed the ideological presuppositions. Land (1976; 1983) has highlighted the construction of the ideology through her careful analysis of the formative Beveridge report (1942). The report on *Social Insurance and Allied Services* specified clear roles for men as 'bread-winners' and women as economically dependent wives and mothers. Although more recent feminist analyses have pinpointed the ideological under-pinnings, especially in terms of gender, there has been much less consideration of these issues in terms of race. They have tended to be subsumed in burgeoning class analyses of the developments of the welfare state. There are some notable exceptions. Miles and Phizacklea (1984) tried to draw out the particular assumptions about race in British post-war develop-ments, whilst Barker (1981) has also viewed these develop-ments within an ideological framework. Williams (1989) however has been almost unique in trying to bring together an analysis which combines issues of class, gender and race in looking at social policy developments in the post-war period in Britain.

Riley (1983) has looked in most detail at how the ideology of motherhood was constructed in Britain especially through the work of social psychologists. In particular, she looked at the work of Bowlby (1953) who developed notions about the proper roles of mothers in relation to very early childcare. His concept of 'maternal deprivation' was particularly crucial to the subsequent development of social and early childhood education services. Bowlby argued strongly that children needed their mothers' close and constant care to develop normally. However, he based his ideas on studies of young children and babies who, because of the war and/or the exigencies of the war effort, had been forcibly and unfortu-nately separated from their mothers when tiny (New and David, 1985). Bowlby extended these ideas generally to notions of childcare and his ideas were taken up not only by a whole range of people working in the areas of health and social services in Britain, but internationally. Indeed his original monograph was republished as *Child Care and The Growth of Love* by the World Health Organisation in 1951. It was used by developmental and child psychologists throughout the Western world and formed the ideological and theoretical basis for forms of childcare. The ideology underlying it confined mothers to the home in normal circumstances, when they had children of pre-school age, to bring them up in the privacy of their own homes. Only children in home circumstances deemed to be inadequate or socially and economically deprived were to be provided with alternative, and out-of-home care. No explicit consideration was given to issues of race within the analysis of home circumstances, although they may have been entangled with the broader categories of social class and poor socio-economic conditions.

These ideas formed the ideological basis on which education, health and welfare services were developed in the immediate post-war era. They were used to justify what Beattie (1985) has referred to as the particular 'complex and controversial' relationship between parents and the state, especially prescribing a particular role and set of standards for *mothers* with young and pre-school children in the privacy of their homes. Where children were selected for out-of-home childcare in Britain in day nurseries, criteria used related to the adequacy of the care provided by their mothers, with the paucity of home circumstances as a central criterion.

However, in developing a formal education system, it was assumed that mothers did not have the appropriate skills to teach their own children the 3Rs. The formalized system, distinguishing between different levels, related to age, nevertheless was built upon the assumption of the need for professional educators – the teachers – as opposed to 'amateur' mothers. Mothers, however, were assumed to be available to support children in their transition to, and involvement in, schooling. But the Western education systems were built on the assumption of different activities and skills of mothers, and/or parents, and teachers. It has become a commonplace to discuss this form of the education system by talking about 'the school gate' as the symbolic boundary between home and school. Indeed, many schools are said to have had notices announcing that 'no parents are permitted beyond this gate'.

In other words, mothers were seen to be totally responsible for early child care and for children at each end of the school day and throughout the school holidays. However, their responsibilities stopped almost magically at the 'school gate' when teachers, usually women, often themselves mothers, took over these responsibilities. A legal term – *in loco parentis* – has also been used to describe these duties of teachers are to be seen – *in place of parents* (Shaw, 1978; David, 1980).

Included in this set of assumptions, therefore, were the

ideas that mothers 'cared for' children and were responsible for their daily and routine care and socio-emotional development. Fathers, however, were not assumed to have the same set of routine responsibilities. They were to be 'gainfully employed' as the 'breadwinners' on behalf of their families (Land, 1976). On the other hand, school teachers were not seen as alternatives to parents, but rather were seen to provide skills that the majority of parents could not – either in terms of time or ability – provide for their children. The 'school gate' symbolised that distinction between home and school, family and formal education.

In developing this system of education, most post-war governments became committed to implementing the principle of equality of educational opportunity – the notion that children should be provided with education on the basis of their intellectual merit or academic abilities rather than their home circumstances. Indeed, it was often noted that children's home circumstances differed considerably in terms of socio-economic opportunities. Some families were extremely privileged whereas others lived in the extremes of poverty. Initially these socio-economic differences were seen as broad issues of social class; later they were developed into more complex questions of distinctions within and between socioeconomic circumstances.

In attempting to implement the principle of equality of educational opportunity, or providing *all* children with access to educational opportunities, many governments involved the help of social scientists, be they sociologists or psychologists. Indeed, some of the social science applied disciplines such as developmental and social psychology, social administration or policy, and sociology, especially of education and/or social stratification and occupational mobility, began to develop in concern with these strategic policy issues. Many social scientists were called on officially or in an unofficial capacity to evaluate policy strategies and their processes of implementation.

One aspect of these social developments was a consideration of how effective particular policies were for ensuring that children were availed of educational opportunities regardless of home backgrounds of parental privilege or parental poverty. In the 1950s, the focus tended to be on secondary education, systems of academic selection, and the interface with the labour market, with an emphasis on boys' educational and economic opportunities rather than those of girls (Halsey, Floud and Anderson, 1961). Indeed, this blossomed into a major academic set of specialisms in the 1960s and beyond with concerns for the complex processes of social, economic or occupational and educational selection and mobility (Halsey, Heath and Ridge, 1980).

Another set of strands to these policy-related considerations arose from the agendas of psychologists and sociologists in their research studies. Social psychologists began to develop a set of concerns about both the social bases of child development and the corollary of social disadvantage, which at least in the American context included consideration of race rather than class (Silver, 1990). The idea of 'cultural deficits' or the cycle of deprivation was heavily influenced by these considerations. Sociologists in Britain undertook a variety of different kinds of study. Initially, sociologists, in concert with medical and health researchers, embarked upon a series of cohort studies. A wide range of data on children's health, education and emotional developments was collected. The first cohort study took a sample of all children born in one week in 1946. Two subsequent studies by the National Child Development Studies replicated this data collection for children born in one week in 1958 and 1970. All three studies collected follow-up data at specific ages of the children, so that a wealth of data on children's development is available. The one which was to prove most influential was the 1946 study, which formed the basis for the collation of a massive data base which was used to study a range of social phenomena.

A critical study from this first cohort analysis, entitled *The Home and the School*, was of the relations between children in primary schools and their families but it tended to ignore gender differences in parenting. Douglas (1967) looked at the primary school experiences of the cohort in relationship with their families. One of the key findings was the importance of 'home background', as a proxy variable for social class, in influencing children's educational development and achievements, in particular in terms of reading as a critical form of children's early educational development. Douglas's study pinpointed the differential effects of home backgrounds on educational performance but only considered them in broad social class or 'material' terms rather than issues of gender. This study formed a critical influence not only on research studies but also on policy developments. As Bastiani (1987, p.91) has noted, this kind of study and its influence on notions of 'compensatory education' for children of poor home backgrounds influenced subsequent, especially statistical, kinds of research, which themselves influenced policy.

However, the biggest single influence on policy developments and the particular approach in Britain was that of the Plowden report, which was published in early 1967. Plowden was the last of the official enquiries for the government of the Central Advisory Council for Education. Its concern was with primary school children and how to develop strategies to ensure their effective education. In that respect, the kind of thinking and issues that were explored borrowed heavily from the kinds of issues that were developing in the USA at that time (Silver, 1990). In the early 1960s, both in the USA and in Britain social scientists, and particularly social and developmental psychologists, developed special interests in children's educational development, especially about cognitive and language acquisition and reading. A whole series of research studies were developed to consider these issues, focusing on both the home and the school. Twin concerns emerged out of these initial studies: one was with the effects of children's material home circumstances on their ability to learn and the other was with parental attitudes and expectations about their children's schooling (Banks, 1976).

Official reports were commissioned in both the USA and Britain to explore these issues further. In the USA, however, the concern focused more on particular aspects of children's socio-economic circumstances, especially race. In Britain, the focus centred more on broad indicators of social class, defined in terms of environmental and home circumstances. Nevertheless both countries alighted on questions about children who came to be seen as socially or educationally disadvantaged, which to some extent implicitly or explicitly included issues of race.

The Plowden committee came to the conclusion that two sets of remedies would deal with the problems that they had highlighted – one was to try to involve parents in their children's education, especially through the school, and the other was to provide extra resources to schools in areas deemed to contain socio-economically disadvantaged children, to overcome these disadvantages. For example, it was stated that: 'one of the essentials for educational advance is a *closer partnership between the two parties to every child's education*'. This subsequently became known as the 'Plowden triangle'. In other words, the twin strategies were, as the Americans first coined the phrase, to 'compensate' children for their prior deprived circumstances either through school or through educating their parents so that they could then help their children. In particular, social analysts developed the notion of the cycle of disadvantage, the idea that social and economic deprivations could be passed on from generation to generation (Valentine, 1968). It became important for social scientists to consider social and political strategies that might break the cycle, and provide social or educational compensation for children from such home circumstances.

Lady Plowden, the chair of the committee, noted in her evaluation of the effects of the report twenty years on that she considered the emphasis on parents to be innovative and yet crucial (Plowden, 1987). She felt that it was now, in the late 1980s, an accepted fact or a given that parents should be closely involved in their children's education. In the late 1960s, it was considered quite revolutionary because the emphasis then was on education as a professional activity and set of skills. However, at that time middle-class parents were felt to take an active interest, if not involvement, in their children's work at school. That is to say they were regarded as holding views and attitudes about education that were consonant with those of the school teachers and professional educators. There was no dissonance between home and school, whereas in the case of working-class children, it was felt that there was a gulf or great divide between the attitudes and values of the home and those of the school. One of the central tenets of the Plowden report was to bridge the gulf between home and school for working-class or socio-economically disadvantaged primary school children.

The second central tenet was to provide additional educational resources for children not from the working classes in their entirety but those deemed to be in particularly adverse home circumstances. The strategy here was twofold and involved the close interests of social scientists – it was to define educational priority areas, in terms of social indicators of localities around schools. Additional resources would be provided to schools in those areas especially to support the teachers. In addition, there were to be a number of 'action research projects' to evaluate the effectiveness of the particular local strategies, which might also entail the provision of pre-school or nursery facilities, or education social workers to work on the identification of the parents of social disadvantaged children. Indeed, the Plowden report recommended additional pre-school educational resources to be set in train, in the form of a programme of nursery education. The aim here was to facilitate the entry of disadvantaged children into compulsory schooling. However, they did not recommend that only socially disadvantaged children should be the beneficiaries of such education. Rather, the programme should entail the principle of 'social mixing' so that disadvantaged children would 'learn' from their association with their middle-class peers. The assumption was that social disadvantages could be overcome by changes in social attitudes of either parents or their children.

Despite the fact that not all of the Plowden committee's proposals were translated into policies and implemented, the report marked a major watershed in both thinking and practice around parents and education, or what has been called home-school relations, or the Plowden triangle. New thinking and practice blossomed both in relation to primary schools and the developments of a range of services and facilities for pre-school children or in the area of early childhood education. Initially, attention focused upon children from disadvantaged home circumstances, with consideration being given both to educational support services in school and to their parents at home. This was developed within local authorities in terms of defining EPAs and through the specific action research projects as forms of social evaluations. One of the most important of these was the development of social indicators for defining areas of socio-economic disadvantage and 'need'. A most sophisticated and complex social index was constructed for the Inner London Education Authority, by key members of their Research and

Statistics branch. This included for the first time in Britain an indicator of race, through the use of the notion of immigrant status. It also included the notion of lone-parenthood status. Nevertheless, a variety of different types of educational intervention were tried, tested and evaluated through the Educational Priority Area (EPA) action research (Halsey, 1972). These borrowed from and were heavily influenced by the developments in educational strategies, such as Headstart and Follow Through and the Community Action Programs in the United States, as Silver and Silver (1991) amongst others have noted (Higgins, 1978).

The model for most of the various home–school strategies and provisions remained that of the middle-class mother, who devoted her time and attention to the education and up-bringing of her children, exclusively rather than being involved in other activities. Moreover, it was assumed that her skills and interests were consonant with those of the school and the teachers. In any event the vast majority of nursery and primary school-teachers were themselves women, and often already mothers.

The notion of parental involvement that underpinned the various developments was not, in fact, ungendered. Essentially it was about maternal involvement and the 'proper' role that mothers should play in their children's upbringing, care and early childhood education. However, in the policies and prac-tices that developed out of the Plowden report and its allied developments, the ideas were implicit rather than explicit. They were rarely alluded to in gender terms although the different parental roles expected of mothers and fathers were in fact clear. Curiously, in the aftermath of Plowden the notion of parental participation became ungendered, having been more clearly gendered before the specification of particular 'educational' roles for mothers, especially of socially disadvan-taged children. Hitherto, as the quotation at the beginning of this chapter indicates, the role, at least of more educated women, was more clearly enunciated. It is also a curiosity that there was a shift in language at the time when women and especially mothers were beginning to be more involved out-side the home and family in a range of 'public' activities and in changing family circumstances.

The shift in language from being explicit about gendered

parental roles to becoming more gender-neutral occurred not only in official arenas and policy proposals but also in the kinds of social research which were conducted to evaluate and justify the policies. It was not only the use of the term 'parent' that became a commonplace in these various arenas. It was also the even more ambiguous or vague term 'home', as a proxy for family roles in relation to school. However, the term 'home' was initially used not only to refer to the activities of mothers as 'housewives' or 'homemakers' but also as a proxy for discussing material or socio-economic circumstances of families. In other words, home background also referred to 'household' income or wages and was a way of trying to find an indicator of broad socio-economic class. In the literature that blossomed from the 1960s, there were complex notions which all attempted to highlight family factors and their influence upon children's development. Nevertheless, the assumption in all of them was of differential roles within the family for mothers and fathers. So although the notion of 'home' might also refer to home background, defined as household income, it was almost invariably assumed that this was earned by the male householder/breadwinner as husband and father and that the wife/mother was responsible for the daily care and maintenance of the household, especially the children.

In any event, as these ideas became more developed in both research and practice in the 1970s and 1980s the gender differentiation of parental activities was more obvious, without being better explicated. Indeed, by that stage, mothers had begun to develop their own strategies and 'provisions' because of the lacunae increasingly evident in state social and educational provisions. In the early 1960s, the state had in fact, in a cost-cutting measure, further reduced its already limited provision of nursery education (David, 1980). As a result, a middle-class mother bereft of state support for her early childrearing activities, had advertised in *The Guardian* to develop a cooperative scheme of childcare and education on a voluntary basis. Out of this informal initiative emerged the Pre-Schools Playgroups Association, which became a voluntary organisation of mothers who organised small, local and informal groups for the purposes of looking after their children together on a very part-time basis (New and David, 1985). The aim was to develop their young children's social skills. The organisation mushroomed and by the end of the 1970s was receiving some measure of state support and recognition. Moreover, Lady Plowden had taken over as chair of the national organisation, changing her commitment from state provision of nursery education to more informal, voluntary and private parental cooperative provision.

In the 1970s nursery school provision was extended for all three and four year olds on a part-time basis but also with the notion of parental involvement through Conservative government policies initiated by Mrs Thatcher as the then Secretary of State for Education (David, 1980). Similarly, schools began to involve parents more in their routine curricular and extra-curricular activities. There were also parallel developments in social services provision, shifting from an entirely professional model of nursery provision to the idea of family centres. These were often modelled not only on British notions of parental participation but again borrowed from the American experience of 'parent-child centers', where parents were instructed in the skills of parenting (Grubb and Lazerson, 1978).

THE ROLE OF SOCIAL SCIENTISTS IN DEVELOPING HOME–SCHOOL RELATIONS

Many of these initiatives relied heavily on the work of both sociologists such as Bernstein (1970, 1972, 1974) and psychologists in their studies of children's development and the social and structural influences upon it. From an initial focus on language and cognitive development, this was broadened to include reading and, later, numbers and mathematics. However, the assumptions about how children learned were also, in the process, broadened from an initial concern with cognitive processes to how social relationships and didactic 'play' might facilitate the process. As Walkerdine and Lucey (1984) have shown through their critical appraisal of much of this literature and research mothers became more 'regulated' through the expectations about how to bring up their young children.

Walkerdine and Lucey (1989) set out to re-analyse the study

conducted by Tizard and Hughes (1984) which itself was a culmination of much of the social psychological work on child development that had occurred in the 1970s. Tizard and Hughes were interested in exploring children's language development by comparing young children at home and at school. They chose a very 'selective' sample to highlight their ideas: the sample consisted of a number of working-class and middle-class mothers of daughters who attended nursery schools and those who did not. They compared and contrasted the ways in which the daughters acquired verbal and linguistic fluency through their conversations with their mothers at home and their teachers at school. Tizard and Hughes reached the conclusion that girls learned to speak more fluently and eloquently through their activities with their mothers than through their associations with the nursery teachers. The study was then used as an argument for the lack of necessity for nursery schools, despite the fact that the study did not attempt to highlight the various ways in which children developed socially and educationally through nursery schools. Tizard and Hughes' findings were unsurprising in many respects. They replicated many previous such studies, including many of the Oxford Pre-School studies (Bruner, 1980). What was, however, surprising was the focus explicitly on just mothers and daughters.

Walkerdine and Lucey used the study as the occasion for a much wider critique and analysis of the ways in which mothers were expected to educate their children, but especially their daughters, at home and at school. Their feminist polemic is very important in pointing out the ways in which social and developmental psychology have been used in the service of increasing expectations on mothers about how to bring up their young children. As they point out, mothers have been expected to 'educate' their daughters in a variety of respects, still emphasising class differences, through an increasing emphasis on their 'work' at home, although designated as 'play'.

Walkerdine and Lucey are almost unique in the ways in which they have revaluated the work of psychologists in changing the role expectations for mothers, despite the fact that this has not appeared to be explicit in the literature. However, Walkerdine and Lucey's critique is, in fact, not only confined to the work of psychologists. They also look at the ways in which official thinking has been influenced by psychologists and other social scientists, in the period since the Second World War.

Similarly, recently Smith (1987a) has demonstrated through her feminist analysis the ways in which gradually expectations about mothers' work in preparing children for school have grown. She cites an array of examples from the Canadian literature. Curiously, although Smith's work has been influential in terms of feminist research methodology it has had relatively little influence on other studies of families and education or on the crucial elements of mothers' work either in relation to children or education.

However, most of the research studies that have been conducted in the late 1970s and 1980s have remained with a traditional, non-feminist paradigm and have focused more on parents' than on mothers' roles and involvement from the point of view of the school (Bastiani, 1987; Macbeth, 1989). In fact, neither Bastiani nor Macbeth considers, at all, the differential role of parents from a gender point of view. They both analyse and prescribe a new developmental role for parents, relying heavily on past research and practice, but without fully explicating gender differences in parenting. In Britain, they are both at the forefront of the debates about improving home-school partnerships or developing contracts to ensure a clearer set of relationships. Their prescriptions in any event draw from previous evidence of research studies about 'home influence on education'. Indeed, in 1984, in an essay for the European Commission, reviewing the array of evidence on parents and education, Macbeth wrote:

What we *can* (*sic*) say is that a very large number of studies in different cultures has indicated that *parental attitudes* have an influence on children's attainments, even if we cannot put an exact value to that influence: there is a relative dearth of contrary evidence; in-school factors seem to be related to these *home factors*. At the very least, home seems to influence school performance and it would appear that a strengthening of partnership between home and school could improve the quality of children's learning. (1984, p.185 [my emphasis])

It was on the basis of his review of the range of research evidence, that Macbeth began to develop his views on the appropriate nature of the partnership between parents and schools. From that point, his views began to change to one that prescribed a more quasi-legal partnership, in the form of signed 'agreements' between parents and schools. However, these agreements put the onus more on parents to accept the school's rules than on teachers to be flexible in relation to parents' relationships with schools. In other words, Macbeth's approach has been to formalise the boundary so that parents have a more 'educative' function and support role as defined by public agencies. Indeed, he goes further than merely prescribing a set of formal roles for schools and families; he suggests the use of formal sanctions by educators to exclude children from schools if their parents refuse to sign their compliance with school rules. This was done not only on the basis of his own research but that of other studies which appeared to confirm his initial findings of the European review in the early 1980s.

By this stage, it had indeed become a commonplace to argue that parental interests and involvement improved the quality of children's schooling. This evidence was further built up, particularly for primary school children, and in the area of pre-school provision. For example, Wolfendale (1983) demonstrated through reviews of research as well as her own studies the importance of help at home to children's early development, and especially reading fluency. Wolfendale focused especially on children's early educational development and the impact of parent participation. Through this study she developed twin principles of 'reciprocity' and 'advocacy' by both parents and teachers, which would lead, in her words, to 'mutual involvement, mutual accountability; mutual gain'. Wolfendale thereby hoped to strengthen home–school relationships in line with Plowden's recommendations about what has become known as the 'Plowden triangle', as noted above.

Similar work by Tizard and colleagues (1988) on children in infant classes in the inner city, including children from ethnic minority backgrounds, demonstrated the potential benefits of drawing parents into the learning process. They reported that 'parents had a big influence on the level of pre-school attainments' and that 'those children with a head start tended to maintain it on the whole'. They also confirmed an earlier finding that parents were working more with their children at home, in educational terms. In other words, they present evidence of how parents have taken up the kinds of initiative offered by schools and tried to respond in the ways in which they had begun to relate to their own children's learning. However, all this research is reported in gender-neutral rather than gender-specific terms.

This work has been further elaborated and demonstrated by studies on parental involvement in primary education for the National Foundation for Educational Research. Jowett (1990) has carried out a large-scale investigation which has tried to highlight the various points at which parental help becomes crucial for children's learning. She argues, however, that schools have not always developed appropriate practices and have, on occasion, missed opportunities for further development. Again, her perspective is very much school and education-oriented; she is concerned about how to achieve this most effectively. She writes:

> The NFER research points the way towards developing and maintaining effective relationships with parents beyond the formal minimum. These ambitious approaches require a delicate balancing act between what professionals wish to convey and what parents would actually benefit from and value. They also demand a commitment of time and energy that maximises the potential for enhancing contact with parents, from practitioners and from those who resource and support them at both a local and national level.
>
> (Jowett, 1990, p. 50)

This clearly sets out an educational agenda for the partnership with parents, based upon a policy-oriented research project.

A most innovative piece of action research, however, has been the work on encouraging parents to become involved in primary school work in mathematics. Merttens and Vass (1987) have pioneered school-based projects called IMPACT, modelled on the older projects on reading and language development, and known as PACT (Parents, Children and Teachers). What has been particularly innovative about the IMPACT project, however, is the attempt by professional educators to develop materials for parents to use from their school-based learning at home. In this case, the research project has been used not to bring parents into school but to take 'school' back into the home. The argument has been that parents do not automatically 'know' how to help their children with their notions of numbers and mathematics, whereas it is more likely that they are able to 'help' with reading. Merttens and Vass cite evidence from other studies to confirm their point.

This kind of action research, whilst premised on the assumption of improving home–school relations in the interests of children's learning, demonstrates the way in which the perspective taken is that of the school. However, Brown (1991) has developed an insider and sympathetic critique of the IMPACT work, showing how the very concepts themselves such as dialogue and participation may lead to the reproduction of traditional class-based relationships between parents and school. Brown writes:

> In addressing the question of the social reproductive effects of projects such as IMPACT I have focused initially on the nature of the boundary between home and school in terms of specific identities that are made available within these sites. Through teacher discourse particular legitimate identities are offered to parents, in relation to which parents are positioned. All this acts to problematise the setting up of the form of dialogue between parents and teachers that might have the kinds of transformative effects on teacher practice envisaged ... It also alerts us to the need to attend to questions of relative power in different context when considering relations between home and school.

He goes on to conclude that:

> We are in an area in which there are no easy answers and which will stretch the capacity of teachers as reflexive practitioners to the full as we are led towards *questioning the nature of the boundary between home and school* and thus the very nature of schooling. (1991, p. 14. My emphasis)

Few researchers have taken up this kind of critique and pointed to the ways in which new educational methods have a major impact upon family life and particularly both mothers' and children's ways of relating to each other. An interesting but cryptic paper by Ulich (1989) in German (personal translation) has argued that these kinds of development cause stress in the family and, moreover, transform family relationships into ones that are more like those of the school than traditional inter-personal relationships. He interviewed a small number of parents and secondary school children to explore the meanings, significance and impact of these expectations on families and to assess the effects. He did not reach very sanguine conclusions from this study.

Ulich points to the ways in which the boundaries between home and school or family and education have been altering through the changed expectations of teachers. In particular, he highlights the fact that families perforce are becoming more educational institutions. Mothers are increasingly expected to play a more didactic role in their children's upbringing, emphasising the educational content of home-based activities, as well as supporting the work of the school. Ulich writes from a rather critical position which is sympathetic to feminism.

Lareau, on the other hand, writing from a more dispassionate social research perspective, with an emphasis on class analysis, has also reached similar conclusions. She has investigated, in two elementary schools in California, the ways in which teachers' expectations have an impact upon parents' involvement in these schools. Her sample, curiously, was an entirely white one, but socially mixed, so that she could compare middle-class and working-class families. Her interest lay, however, in understanding how families felt about and responded to teacher expectations about parents' involvement in their children's education. She explored both the positive and negative effects of such involvements. Calling her book – rather instructively – *Home Advantage*, with the sub-title *Social Class and Parental Intervention in Elementary Education* (1989), she argues that particular kinds of home, namely the middle-class ones, tend to help children more than those of the working class. Although Lareau concentrates on mothers in both her interviews and analysis she does not emphasise gender issues in the conclusions. She prefers to locate the key issues in class analysis, rather than one which highlights the impact on gender roles. She does however, draw attention to the fact that teacher expectations may make for increased difficulties in the context of massive changes in family life, which as we noted above, have more of an impact on mothers' roles in the family than on fathers' activities, in particular in relation to childrearing and childcare. Indirectly, therefore, Lareau alerts us to the complex patterns of relationships that are likely to emerge between families and education in home–school partnerships given these contextual factors. Nevertheless, her perspective tends to downplay the complex patterns from a feminist perspective. In a more recent paper (1992) she has tried to re-analyse her data by highlighting gender issues. Her overall analysis, nevertheless, remains firmly rooted within an education and public policy context, rather than one that highlights feminist questions.

Inadvertently in some cases, directly in others, the changes in educational context can be seen to have had something of a major influence on mothers' and children's lives in relation to school. Despite the lack of an incisive feminist analysis, the picture that emerges from these small-scale studies is of mothers' lives in relation to their children's care and education being radically altered from the past.

A similar picture emerges from the studies conducted on pre-school provision or early childhood education. We have already noted some of this evidence from the reappraisal by Walkerdine and Lucey of the study by Tizard and Hughes. Scott's study (1990) of maternal involvement in pre-school services in the Strathclyde region in Scotland provides us with similar evidence of an emphasis on the work that mothers are expected to do to support their children. It also shows how some mothers, especially those involved in paid employment, experience difficulties in this context.

Both Lareau and Scott, from totally different regional contexts, also point out that some, especially working class, mothers do not perceive a value in their involvement at school nor do they know what is expected of them at home. These studies give the impression, again, that the changing boundary is for the most part education and public policy rather than parent or mother-led.

This kind of approach is also to some extent confirmed by the typologies of parent involvement which have been created by social researchers attempting to devise developmental classifications of the changing nature of home–school relation-

ships. Indeed, all the typologies refer only to the relationships
between parents and their children's schools, and not to other
aspects of the education system. They are all, therefore,
concerned to specify, both historically and contempora-
neously, the ways in which parents have been expected to get
involved in their children's schools. Thus they all refer not
only to the general contextual ways in which parents prepare
children for school, both in terms of pre-school and around
the school-day, but also to curricular and extra-curricular
activities at home and at school, especially on a volunteer
basis, and the developments in concepts of citizen or
community participation in school or educational decision-
making.

The most analytical and discursive of the typologies is by
Epstein (1990), using American material. Yet it does not differ
substantially from that of Tomlinson (1991), which in part
relies on the work by Macbeth on Scotland and for Europe. A
brief 'bird's eye' view of 'aspects of parental involvement' has
also been produced by HMI, reporting on a series of one-day
visits to schools. They, too, classify types of involvement in ways
which compare well with the above typologies. All of them are
concerned to show how types of parent involvement have
expanded and become far more complex in recent years than
in the past. As Beattie (1985) has claimed, much of that has
had to do with changing political perspectives and values
about parental roles in education, from the initial emphasis
on individual contributions to a more recent concern with
collective or community decision-making. Most recently,
however, the shift to a more 'consumerist' view (Woods, 1988)
has had yet another effect on aspects of parental participation.
It too has emphasised the individual parent, but as a
'consumer' with rights to information about schools rather
than being involved in the educational process. However, the
typologies all emphasise the extent to which there has been a
shifting boundary between parents and school, making the
two more coterminous from an educational perspective than
in the past. They all are concerned to highlight the ways in
which policies and practices from the point of view of the
education system have tried to blur the boundary between
home and school by making the two systems more sharply
focused on educational issues. In other words, they all

illustrate how dominant the public policy agenda has been in framing the relations between home and school, rather than the other way round.

THE CONTEXT OF FAMILY LIFE CHANGES

Epstein and Lareau are relatively unusual amongst social researchers in pointing to the ways in which changes in family life have not been considered in this kind of educational literature. Although they are essentially educational researchers they are concerned to try to make the relationships between home and school more appropriate to their specifically American family context, given the extent of changes in family life there. Lareau has written that changes in family structure and family life have been occurring at the same time as the schools have been demanding greater involvement of parents:

> Indeed, the last few decades have seen substantial changes in the family, notably changes in women's labor force participation, family size and family structure. For example, with the increase in divorce, a majority of school-aged children now spend some time in a single-parent family ... We believe there must be a restructuring of family–school relationships to reflect the changes occurring both within schools and the larger society. Schools and families are in synergistic combination. Teachers' expectations for parental participation in schooling have escalated in the last few decades, precisely at the same time that changes in family structure have reduced familial resources for participating in schooling. (1989, p. 254)

Epstein has also commented, in a similar vein, calling for more research on the issues:

> Families are changing. The 'traditional' family of two natural parents with mom working at home is now 'untraditional' (Bureau of the Census, 1984). Most children live in other types of families – one-parent homes, reconstituted or blended families, joint-custody families, foster homes, extended families, relatives as guardians, and other variations. These arrangements cross economic lines and

are not indicative of uncaring families. And, all schools and families must understand how they can influence each other to benefit the children they share. A continuing research agenda needs to focus on questions of the effects on students of family and school programs that provide developmental and differentiated experiences for families of children at all grade levels and for the special needs of different families. (1990, pp. 116–17)

Curiously there has been very little research around these questions about the relationships between changes in families and changing expectations about schools' relationships with families. What research has been conducted upon family changes has been about issues of the impact on women's lives in the public arena, especially in terms of employment and the lack of commensurate childcare facilities, rendering women as mothers still responsible for their children's upbringing, in the privacy of the family rather than as a public responsibility (Moss and Melhuish, 1991). This kind of research has indeed highlighted the ways in which the boundary between home and public social services has been tightly drawn, essentially continuing to confine childcare to the private rather than the public sphere. In that respect, changes in family life have had no impact upon the provision of public social services.

Rockhill, in two very challenging and fascinating articles about immigrant women in the USA has shown how these special family contexts have been relatively impervious to public policy changes, especially in terms of education (1987a and b). Indeed, she has pointed to the potentially negative effects of education on these women's family lives. She has argued that provision of education for young wives and mothers in these very traditional family contexts may be both perceived and experienced as a threat and a danger rather than as a way of enhancing and developing their families. Yet at the same time these women or rather mothers have been 'blamed' in the public policy arena for not aiding their children's educational developments and maintaining them in a state of relative illiteracy.

In the context of changes in family life, which themselves place greater responsibilities on women as primarily responsible for children's care and education, changing the boundaries between home and school may only add to the burdens on such women. In this context, increases in 'parent participation' in education either at home or at school may substantially alter mothers' roles and the differences between mothers in different family contexts.

There is already some social research evidence to indicate that mothers from a variety of family contexts have been involved in different ways in the running of schools, again altering the 'political' boundary. Research on the relatively new schemes of parent-governors has found major differences in participation rates between mothers of primary school children in rural and suburban areas and from ethnic minority groups in the inner cities, as well as parents at the secondary school level (Golby et al. 1989, 1990; Keys and Fernandes, 1990). Research based in Exeter, comparing Exeter and an outer London borough, found that, amongst parent governors, mother governors predominated but especially in Exeter (Golby and Brigley, 1989). Such mothers became involved particularly as representatives of the community of mothers in the locality, expressing the view that many mothers would find participation with the schools somewhat difficult. Deem's (1989; 1990) research on school governors in a sample of home counties' secondary schools found that on the whole 'women parent-governors' (in other words, mother-governors) found it more difficult to participate than male governors (1989). However, she also noted that where such women did articulate their views in meetings they tended to be clearer and more direct than the men. But more of them found that the burdens of such office were too great to sustain and they had to relinquish it prematurely, given domestic and/or childcare responsibilities. Even in the areas of increased parental power in educational decision-making where we have some evidence, mothers are expressing different views from fathers and others about the context in which they can operate and the impact of domestic responsibilities or home circumstances.

CONCLUSIONS

In this chapter I have tried to illustrate the ways in which there has been a changing boundary between home and school which has had major implications for mothers' roles in the family and in the public arena, especially in relation to schools and educators. I have tried to show how this changing boundary has come about. It is partly from changes in public policy developments and especially influenced by changing political values, and also by the research and policy evaluations conducted by social scientists. It is also partly from the impact of these and socio-economic changes. I have briefly reviewed the ways in which the policies have developed and how the research evidence has developed to take account of these kinds of public policy development. I have also tried to argue that there have however been major lacunae in the research literature, because of the dominant perspective of educationalists and educational researchers. There has also been virtually no research from the perspectives of mothers and families on the impact and effects of this plethora of changes from public policies to school practices, as well as family life changes. It is to some of this innovative research on mothers' practices and perspectives on childrearing and relations with schools that we now turn.

3 Standing by the School Gate – the Boundaries of Maternal Authority?

Jane Ribbens

INTRODUCTION

Women take primary responsibility for the care of young children in all Western industrialised societies (as we argued in Chapter 1), yet this experience may be complex and contradictory. While women's obligations towards their young children may be psychologically and practically onerous, such maternal responsibility may also contribute a potential base for the experience of power and authority within the designated area of responsibility. In this chapter I want to consider whether and how maternal responsibility links to maternal power and/or authority in the pre-school years, and what are the implications for the mother and child at the point of school entry, including issues of 'school choice'.

One of the contradictory experiences of motherhood occurs particularly clearly at the point of school entry, when women are expected not only to accept but to desire and facilitate a dramatic shift overnight in their maternal responsibilities, (as highlighted by the quote from Pascall in Chapter 1). This shift has very significant consequences for their own lives and for family relationships. In this chapter, I will examine the nature of this contradiction for mothers' lives with their children at the point of school entry. My discussion will consider the meaning for mothers and their children of their initial encounter with this divide – the before and after of this boundary in time. The divide is based on legally defined ideas of compulsory school age, which in turn are justified by beliefs concerning the right of the state to intervene in family lives, and in particular, to insist that all children are 'educated' once they have passed their infant years (Crittenden, 1988; Johnson, 1990).

By the time children enter full-time formal education, women will have had several years' experience of coping with and caring for them. This responsibility occurs in relation to *four major contexts* during the pre-school years:

(1) a social policy and legislative context in which the care of young children is presumed to be the 'private' responsibility of their parents or legal guardians, at least unless their capacity to fulfil this responsibility is seriously challenged by 'outsiders'; this context draws our attention towards issues of 'family' authority and State authority;

(2) the household of residence, which may include simply the mother and child/ren, but may also include other adults with varying levels of significance for mother–child interaction – this domestic unit generally incorporates notions of 'home and family', as a concept which household members may actively construct and assert as an on-going social entity; this context draws our attention towards gender issues within the broader notion of parental authority;

(3) worlds of paid employment, in which mothers themselves may participate as individuals, but which exclude children and generally remove fathers from their children for substantial and regular periods of time; this context draws our attention to gendered economic issues which affect the exercise of parental responsibility;

(4) a wide variety of informal and largely female social networks that may centre on 'private homes' but also may involve child-centred activities in semi-formal settings outside the home; this context draws our attention to informal and gendered social settings which may act to support mothers in fulfilling their responsibilities and/or may serve to challenge or support any associated maternal authority.

Within these four major contexts, mothers may have variable experiences of sharing their childcare responsibility on occasions, but the women themselves will very largely regard any such sharing as determined by their own decision rather than being imposed upon them (although within a set of either taken-for-granted or resented wider constraints). The major exception here occurs in situations of marital breakdown. On the one hand, legislative history has seen mothers' responsibilities with their children receive increasing confirmation

since the late eighteenth century in Western industrialised
societies – even if this has occurred via a focus on children's
needs rather than women's rights, and has not been unequiv-
ocally to women's advantage (Brophy and Smart, 1981;
Eekelaar, 1991b). On the other hand, more recent equal rights
legislation in some countries may constitute a countervailing
tendency and serve to undermine mothers' rights over their
children by treating 'parents' as ungendered (Sevenhuijsen,
1991).

There is now a substantial body of literature concerning the
lives of women and pre-school children in industrialised societies, written from a variety of theoretical perspectives and
using research focused on mothers living in a wide variety of
circumstances. I will be drawing upon this wider literature as
well as my own particular research with a limited sample of
British mothers (Ribbens, 1990 and forthcoming). These
white women were all living in middle income, privately own-
ed houses in the south-east of England, with an eldest child
aged seven at the time of first interview (in the late 1980s).
While in some senses the women can be described as living in
similar circumstances, their conventional class classifications
by reference to husbands' occupations fall into both working-
class and middle-class categories, and their own educational
and occupational experiences are very varied. The quotes
from mothers used in the following discussion are all from
women interviewed for this study, unless indicated otherwise.

LEARNING TO COPE – MATERNAL RESPONSIBILITIES AND STATE SURVEILLANCE

The medicalisation of childbirth and the transition to motherhood have now been thoroughly documented, both as historical and continuing processes. The overall effect has been to
reduce women's sense of self-determination at a key moment
of their lives, particularly with the birth of a first child. We
have little research about women's experiences of birth other
than with their first child. It seems at least possible that with
subsequent births, the level of maternal responsibility experienced with the first child (further discussed below) may enable
women to feel better able to resist medical and quasi-medical

control. In overall terms, also, this medicalisation process is still resisted by women in varying forms of organised cooperation, e.g. between mothers and midwives, through such organisations as the Maternity Alliance in Britain.

Women may feel severe loss of control over events within the hospital setting (Oakley, 1980; 1986). By contrast, the period after returning home with the new baby may frequently be felt as a 'terrible sense of responsibility' (Oakley, 1986, p. 141). Some of the sense of accountability of new motherhood centres on the dependency of this fragile link with a new life, whose existence is hard to grasp, and whose wants can only be communicated through crying. Ruddick (1982) describes this as a metaphysical attitude, which she labels 'holding' – an aspect of 'maternal thinking' which she contrasts with the 'acquiring' aspect of scientific thought. The sense of awe involved with this maternal thinking may in itself relate to feeling responsible for this new life:

> When you start a family you really are on your own – well this is how I felt anyway. .... I'll never forget the first day home with Zoe, I'd come home and David was all delighted to have me back. I sat down, and Zoe's in her lovely crib, and she started to cry, and David looked at me – she's crying Penny, do something. And I had had a week in hospital, where if she cried I looked at the nurse, and I thought, OOOH, I've got to do something. It's really awful to realise the responsibility, and how it all comes back to *you*. (Penny, teacher)[1]

While Ruddick refers to the metaphysical aspects of maternal thought, at the same time, many maternal activities involve what may appear to be minor daily aspects of childcare. Yet these, too, can serve as a channel for the exercise and reinforcement of the sense of responsibility:

> When you get all these baby books and they say, this is what you need for your layette... and you think, oh well, I'll go and buy some vests. Then you go along to Boots and there's six different types of vest you can get. And I can remember standing and looking at them and thinking, well, what kind do I get, which is the right sort to get for a baby? And I can remember standing there in a quandary and thinking, well, I really don't know, I'll have to ask (my sister)... and then I

thought, well that's daft, just get what you think. And it sounds so silly now... (Diane, doctors' receptionist)

During the pre-school years, while precise arrangements may vary, in all Western countries there are medically based services provided for the routine screening of the care and health of this young population. In Britain, while the precise role of health visitors may contain considerable ambiguities, it is clear that the service is intended to involve surveillance (Abbott and Sapsford, 1990), and mothers do regard it in this way. It is for this reason that the mother's ability 'to cope' is crucial if she is to be able to establish her independent maternal authority and self-determination against any external and alternative authority emanating from the state. This, then, is an early and very crucial boundary which mothers may actively seek to establish around themselves and their children. By asserting the notion that this is '*my* child' mothers assert their right to a social and psychological space within which they may have maternal authority. Within my own study, the women varied in how far they deferred to health visitors' advice, but they did not suggest they were *obliged* to take any advice given if they did not see it as relevant or useful. Health visitors were seen positively as a source of help if they were not felt to threaten the mother's own authority, and did not give advice that made her feel imposed upon (Mayall, 1990). The same attitude has also been found among an ethnically heterogeneous group of mothers living in London:

> [The mothers] were now confident about their own knowledge gained mainly by getting to know the child ... This knowledge and confidence form the basis for mothers' belief that they should initiate discussion about health and child-care topics. They appreciated access to health workers, but felt it was for them to judge when to seek advice. They did not accept that health visitors had a right to give unsolicited advice. We think this is a most striking and important finding...
>
> (Mayall and Foster, 1989, p.60)

This is not, of course, to say that some mothers may not *actively seek* 'outside' professional help at times, either through contact with professional individuals, or from professional ideas to be found in advice books for parents. In my own study, Pauline (an ex-clerical worker) consulted a psychologist after feeling unable to cope with her depressed feelings, and one effect of this consultation was to bolster her childrearing authority against that of her husband (further discussed below). In relation to aspects of childrearing, mothers may also be more inclined to seek professional advice in relation to certain sorts of issues, particularly those defined as medical or physiological.

Morgan (1985) has traced in some detail contemporary tendencies towards the medicalisation of 'family' issues much more broadly. However, it is not clear how far such tendencies have been accepted by parents themselves, and this medicalisation process may itself be regarded as a dispute about the basis for independent childrearing authority within the household. In may own study, in non-medical areas of the child's social and emotional life, there was no evidence of parents seeking out professional consultations, and any problems in these areas would be talked over within their informal networks of family and friends – as Backett (1982) also found in her study of white middle-class parents in Scotland.

Within informal networks, help and advice may be obtained on the woman's own terms, without being experienced as threatening to family boundaries and maternal authority. Kate (a teacher) was prepared to be part of a parent discussion group when it involved other mothers, but she was careful to stress the importance of its non-professional identity:

> I went on a parent group course in the evening. It was through a speech therapist I knew, not part of her work but she was interested... to sort of set up parent groups to discuss problems with children... I went as a favour... she went as a mother, she didn't go as a therapist.

However, when this led on to involvement in a counselling group, Kate withdrew when she felt they did not deal with the children as she wanted, implying a conflict of authority.

Written expertise in books can be read or laid aside as the reader wishes, and might not be felt to threaten parental authority. Nevertheless, although at some point they had probably seen advice books of some sort, very few women in my study actively used books or magazines on childcare, which were generally felt to be confusing:

...they all contradict each other if you read too many of them... they tend to be on bringing up the perfect baby, very often, and there is no such thing, they are all different. I mean, what pacifies one might not pacify another nine. (Sandra, bookkeeper)

While a few women did make some use of books, this was more likely if they had hesitations or doubts about their own childrearing ideas. Books helped them to establish their own preferences more securely, giving them confidence or particular techniques rather than major new ideas. Other writers and studies on this issue also suggest that there is no straightforward causal link between advice books and the childrearing ideas of parents (Jamieson and Toynbee 1988, Kohn 1963; Stolz 1967, Urwin 1985).

HOUSEHOLDS, FAMILY RELATIONSHIPS AND MATERNAL AUTHORITY

The position of fathers in relation to this boundary of mother–child responsibility is a rather ambiguous one, since paternal involvement may be felt to be supportive or threatening by mothers. If childcare is one of the very few areas in which women may potentially experience a sense of authority, they may be very wary of relinquishing this too easily: 'When I had Anna I thought, she's mine more than Robert's ... I think I kept Robert out of Anna a bit...' (Marie, nurse).

I'll tell you what annoys me, at weekends or when he's home in the evenings, and I've allowed the kids to do something new, he'll say, 'I don't think they should be doing that'... and I say to him, 'What do you think I do when I'm here all day on my own?' You know, he's telling me what to do, and how to look after them, and I say, 'Look, I manage on my own all day. Just keep your nose out.'[2]

The issues surrounding dual parenting and the involvement of fathers are therefore complex (Ehrensaft, 1983; Radin, 1988), and it may be difficult for individual women fully to anticipate its potential costs and benefits to themselves as individuals, even if men are willing to take on more childcare responsibility (as distinct from 'helping' with the children on occasions). Despite images of the 'New Man', however, there is very little evidence indeed of any real movement in practice towards dual parenting (Bronstein and Cowen, 1988; Hoem, 1988; Lewis and O'Brien, 1987; Ve, 1989). And of course there are major constraints (particularly in the ways in which paid employment is structured) that militate against dual parenting, as well as arguably some strong intra-psychic mechanisms that perpetuate a strong gender dimension in childcare responsibilities (Chodorow, 1978).

Earlier studies of British family life suggested the continuing existence of highly segregated responsibilities for mothers and fathers in both working class and upper-middle class families (e.g. Young and Willmott, 1957; Young and Willmott, 1973). In some respects, we might thus expect that the middle-income households which were the focus for my own study would be precisely those where segregated parental roles would be *least* in evidence, and yet fathers who were interviewed spontaneously described themselves as 'outsiders' in the household, and the women's own attitudes towards fathers' involvements were equivocal. Stacey and Price (1981) have pointed to the ways in which segregated spheres in pre-industrial Western societies may have provided women with areas of some authority – even if on unequal terms. Thus, by contrast with such pictures of separate domains of authority, ideas of shared parenting and involved fathers may actually make the woman's position more complex by giving fathers a greater say in the day-to-day care of children.[3] Such ideologies will be even more complicated for reconstituted households, where the number of adults with potential claims on childrearing authority increases.

Nevertheless, where the father does share household membership with mother and children, his psychological support and recognition of the value of the mother's childcare may be significant for her satisfaction with her experience of motherhood (Boulton, 1983; Brown and Harris, 1978). Where women are operating with ideas of building 'a family' they may be even more concerned to ensure that their partners are not too marginal to family life, but are incorporated in a meaningful way within the household unit. In my own study, many mothers were less concerned about their own desires to enter or extend

their paid employment than they were about the ways in
their husbands' paid work was seen to undermine their
to build a family unit, since employment patterns were
impose too many demands on the men's time and energies.
Male social and sporting activities could also be seen as
threatening to family life by involving fathers in exclusively male
networks, and mothers might find various ways of reducing this
threat to family unity (Ribbens, 1989; 1990; and forthcoming).

Belief that fathers ought to be part of 'the family' through
shared activities, and not just via the breadwinner role, may
be associated with the notion of the children as the central
definition of what it means to be 'a family'. 'Showing an
interest' in the children, as well as sharing childcare tasks in a
more mundane sense, may be regarded as a major family
'project' (Morgan, 1975) that the parental couple can share
together. Backett's (1982) detailed study of middle-class
mothers and fathers in Scotland examined how they negotiated childrearing together, and she revealed the extent to which
parents develop various and complex mechanisms for sustain-
ing a vision of childrearing as a joint activity despite realities of
unequal responsibilities. There are likely to be notions here
that parental authority ought to be shared to some extent, and
that children should be shown a 'united front' to prevent this
authority from being undermined. The phrase, however, is
instructive, since it implies not only the desire for agreement
between parents, but also the likelihood that this may be 'a
front' and difficult to maintain in practice.

Ideas about involved fathers, and the need to show a united
front, pose some difficult dilemmas for mothers if their own
childrearing ideas differ from those of their husbands. Nevertheless, of the 24 mothers interviewed in my own study, only
three referred to such issues as problematic for their own
sense of responsibility and authority with their children. Two
of these women discussed how they had at times felt constrained by their husbands' views:

> I do find I'm very confident with them looking after them
> when we're on our own. When it comes to holiday times
> when we're all together a whole week, I do lose confidence a
> bit, because I'm aware that Derek is there. (Sally, ex-
> librarian)

In the first years of motherhood, Pauline had also found differing childrearing ideas to be problematic even when her husband was not at home. Pauline did not find early motherhood easy, and her feelings of depression led her to see a psychologist:

> ...we had this big thing with the telephone, Susie used to continually play with the telephone... Mike used to say 'Watch she doesn't play with the phone', so I used to spend all day making sure she didn't do it, because I don't feel they can live by one rule through the day ... but my psychologist said, 'What is the problem, is she doing any harm?' 'Well no...' '...you're getting annoyed with the baby because it's something that she's doing that doesn't upset you but upsets your husband'. And you know, he got me thinking that way which is why I think Mike didn't really like me going [to see him].

By the time her children had reached school age, Pauline had come to express less concern about differences of childrearing views, preferring to follow her own ideas during the daytime when her husband was at work – 'I've got my own set of rules during the day; you do, you get more lax with them' – 'We're like two separate circles and this is my domain really'. When her husband enters her world with the children at weekends she feels 'it's a bit of an imposition'. Women may thus experience authority with their children simply because men are not there (Boulton, 1983, and see Boh, 1989, on maternal authority in Norwegian fishing families). Shirley (a computer operator) was the third woman to discuss the difficulties that arise from differing childrearing ideas with her husband, but she commented:

> He feels that whatever he says, I'll overrule it if I don't like it... Some of it's true, I do feel sorry for them and then I let them go and – which is not right. If he's made like one rule, I shouldn't overrule it, I know I shouldn't, but then some of the things I think are so trivial, is life really worth it for all the hassle you get afterwards? But I do agree that I shouldn't do it, but it doesn't always stop me I'm afraid.

Mothers are thus likely to be constantly mediating between fathers and children, and maintaining a delicate balance of priorities between them. Backett (1982) has also shown how this mediation extends to the ways in which mothers construct fathers' knowledge and shape fathers' understandings of their children. Indeed, where children suffer abuse from their fathers, mothers are likely to be assessed as having failed them precisely in this respect of a failure to mediate and stand between the child and the father (Hooper, 1991). Consequently, unless the mother is able to demonstrate her willingness and ability to put herself in a mediatory position and protect the child from the father, she is likely to see her maternal authority removed completely, even though mediatory responsibility may require her to actively seek the break-up of 'the family' by removing both herself and the child.

Furthermore, maternal mediation within 'the family' may also extend to other household members, as in sibling relationships: 'The mothers' goal of ensuring that children's behaviour fitted into their family context was their primary aim... Mothers monitor, keep track of and structure not only individual children, but also the relationship between their children' (Munn, 1991, pp. 170, 174).

In my own study, women placed considerable value on any signs of affection between siblings. Note how Jacky mediated this affection in the following incident:

> It's lovely, Antony and Grant were just cuddling each other this morning out there. I think Grant had fallen off the stool... he went up to Antony and put his arm round him and I said, 'Oh are you going to cuddle your brother?', and so they both did. Antony stopped what he was doing and he stood there and he cuddled him and he gave him lots of kisses, which I thought, oh that's lovely. (Laughs). They're probably beating the daylights out of each other ten minutes later, but it's nice to have those moments, to know that they are there for them (Jacky, ex-nursery nurse).

Where sibling relationships were difficult, women could be preoccupied by their efforts to try to maintain some sense of family harmony, and they discussed in detail their disappointment if siblings were seen to quarrel too vehemently or constantly. Even where children often quarrelled, mothers might assert that underneath brothers and sisters did 'really' care for each other, and they looked for indications to support this assertion, as well as explanations for why harmony was not always apparent:

> They argue quite a lot, bicker. I don't think they mean it, but I'm sure they just do it to wind me up. And they certainly succeed sometimes. But I think that deep down they like each other really! (Shirley)

MATERNAL AUTHORITY IN CONTEXT: SOCIAL CONTOURS OF EMPLOYMENT, KIN AND LOCALISED NETWORKS

The tendencies and patterns discussed above, with regard to women's experiences as mothers, will of course vary between women living in different material circumstances, or with different individual characteristics, or membership of different sorts of communities and ethnic groups. Women's variable expectations towards maternal employment and paternal involvement in childcare may relate to class differences between women in the likely equation of any ensuing potential costs and benefits that may accrue to them, e.g. according to the women's own opportunities within the labour market (Boh, 1989; Knijn, 1989). For mothers struggling to survive financially, their own maternal authority and priorities may be completely undermined by the necessity to use any form of childcare they can obtain, regardless of their desire to use it or their evaluations of its quality.

The interlinked significance of maternal employment and motherhood may not be uniform for all women. The predominant professional and policy discourse, at least since the Second World War and the political application of Bowlby's work (discussed by David in Chapter 2), has viewed maternal employment as inevitably in conflict with childcare responsibilities. Yet for some women, employment may be seen as a valued part of motherhood, contributing towards the fulfilment of childcare responsibilities (Collins, 1990). What does seem to be clear, however, is that increasing rates of maternal employment in industrialised societies do not seem to be changing the underlying pattern of maternal responsibility and authority within families. Even where both parents are in full-time paid employment, alternative childcare is still largely seen as the responsibility of the mother, both to arrange and to pay for (Brannen and Moss, 1991; Femiola, 1992; Hochschild and Machung, 1989).

Maternal employment has been rising within industrialised European countries. Boh remarks: 'never before have so many married women and mothers with young children gone out to work, which in turn required a reorganisation of their family life' (1989, pp. 266–7). Nevertheless, within the EC overall, less than half (44 per cent) of women with a child under ten were employed in 1988, although with considerable variations between individual states (Moss, 1990). These national variations arise partly because the actual patterns of employment open to women vary nationally (see David in Chapter 2). Overall, however, there is still a predominant tendency for women to seek to balance out their employment commitments in such a way that they may also fulfil what they regard as their family commitments, and meet their maternal responsibilities (in whatever way they understand these) (Boh, 1989). Even when mothers are in full-time employment they are likely to be working fewer hours than fathers in full-time employment (Moss, 1990).

The regularisation of time during the day through widespread coordination of hours of work in any particular industrialised society (except of course, for shift-workers and home-workers), leads to the removal of full-time employees from the private home and localised settings where childcare is based in the pre-school years. In the context of a highly gendered labour market, this has the effect of creating a predominantly maternal space (Bell and Ribbens, 1993) in which women exercise authority with their children with little male interference, and generally an unchallenged recognition of the authority of each mother with her own child. Nevertheless, the involvement of other *mothers* in the care of individual children may also vary between different sorts of communities. Collins (1990) for example, suggests that black women are particularly likely to have a different sort of experience of childrearing, since they are more likely to be operating with notions of childcare as something that may be shared between women within the black community. In this way, black women may be challenging assumptions about children as the 'property' of individual parents. Collins does not, however, discuss how this may affect the individual woman's sense of authority with her own child. Nevertheless, such notions of sharing childcare responsibility are likely to be restricted strictly to within the boundaries of the black community:

> ...Other mothers – women who assist bloodmothers by sharing mothering responsibilities – traditionally have been central to the institution of Black motherhood.... Organised, resilient, women-centred networks of bloodmothers and othermothers are key in understanding this centrality. (Collins, 1990, p. 119)

Such experiences of shared parenting within particular ethnic communities are of course likely to be affected by migration (Mayall and Foster, 1989; Werbner, 1988).

While possibly working with rather different notions of how to 'share' their childcare, white women may also routinely use childcare support from female relatives (particularly grandmothers) (Daniels, 1980), or from other mothers via 'swapping' arrangements during the pre-school years, as well as using a variety of more organised pre-school facilities such as playgroups, nurseries and nursery classes. Although based on informal understandings, some of these swapping arrangements may be highly regularised, with strict notions about reciprocity and some careful calculations to ensure a balancing out of any childcare help given and received (Bell, 1993). This may be most explicitly seen in the operations of babysitting groups.

Help from relatives may require even more delicate negotiation, since there is unlikely to be any reciprocity involved, and there may be a greater tension around childcare authority, e.g. between mothers and grandmothers. It is for this reason that grandmothers may be sensitive to the need to maintain a finely judged distance, especially in the very early days of new motherhood (Cunningham-Burley, 1985). It remains to be seen, however, whether the introduction of the Children Act 1989 in England, which has given some legal recognition to the 'rights' of grandparents, leads to any shift in everyday understandings of the 'proper' balance between maternal and grandmaternal authority.

Despite widespread popular (and sociological) presumptions to the contrary, there continues to be evidence for the significance of female-kin links in contemporary Western societies (Finch, 1989; Warnes, 1986). In my own study, where the maternal grandmothers were still living, all were in regular contact, and for the majority this occurred at least weekly. This is not to say that there were not also tensions in these relationships. Besides the maternal grandmothers, mothers-in-law and sisters were also often mentioned as important sources of female company, sometimes leading into complex networks of cousins.

These informal links between mothers, and between mothers and female kin, may constitute a very significant social context for both women and children during the preschool years, which may have both enabling and constraining implications for mothers' lives. Their significance can be seen in terms of the implications for the women themselves, and for their households and communities, as well as issues of social policy and social theory (Bell and Ribbens, 1993). The social links between children, and those between mothers, may intertwine in complex ways (O'Donnell, 1985; Tivers, 1985; Urwin, 1985), and the great majority of women in my study described themselves as living their daily lives in the context of extensive networks of other women and children. For some women, networks that were not kin-based might arise from ante-natal groups. For others, non-kin links particularly developed at the time their children were first assumed to need peer-group relationships, so that they were taken to mother-and-toddler groups and other semi-organised settings where women and children can meet together. Once such contacts were made, for many women they signalled the end to the isolation and uncertainties of early motherhood, and led to the establishment of complex networks of acquaintances and friendships that continued to evolve around the children's involvements in playgroups, schools and leisure activities.

Such networks may have both enabling and constraining implications for women's lives (Bell and Ribbens, 1993). For the mothers in my own study, these webs of localised relationships could constitute a very important resource, whether used for practical help such as childcare support and information, or in an apparently non-instrumental way for sociability. Perhaps it is not surprising, then, that the women also showed much concern for their children's own social interactions within these networks.

The existence and significance of such networks for the lives of women with children has now been documented in a wide variety of settings in Western industrialised societies (reviewed in Bell and Ribbens, 1993). In this regard, Lydia O'Donnell described the American mothers she studied as 'social agents':

> What sets being a social agent apart from the broader concept of network building is that it highlights not what individuals do to build a personal network for themselves, but what they do to connect and link others, their spouses and children, to the world beyond the nuclear family (1985, p. 121).

While O'Donnell's discussion serves to draw our attention to the wider social significance of mothers' apparently insignificant social interactions, the term 'social agent' begs the question of how mothers see their own authority within these interactions. How maternal responsibility relates to authority has been a subplot within the discussion so far in the present chapter, but it requires explicit attention in its own right to consider the potential source of legitimation for any authority mothers may feel they derive from their childcare responsibilities.

MOTHERS OF YOUNG CHILDREN: RESPONSIBILITY WITH OR WITHOUT AUTHORITY?

Motherhood is a very complex experience for women, as feminist writers have struggled to describe and disentangle (see reviews by Segal, 1985; Stacey, 1986; Tong, 1990). Maternal responsibilities may indeed at times constitute an overwhelming burden, but they may also at times provide a welcome and novel experience for the exercise of *authority* as women:

> When I look back, I was young and had always been told what to do...
> [Did it make you feel nervous at all, being responsible for her, or unsure of yourself?]
> Perhaps at first. No, I think all that Nicola did was allow

me to assert myself. I think she was good for me, I think that's what she did. (Diane)

This may indeed be a major reason why women do not refuse childcare *responsibility*, as these mothers in the USA suggest:

> If they get any bad habits, I want to have given them to them...I want to be solely responsible for their growth. I want control over it in that sense. (Mother quoted by O'Donnell, 1985, p. 72)

> I like the challenge of coordinating everything and trying to have things run relatively smoothly. Having the kids do their homework, getting them bathed, and having them get out the door to school, looking nice – like I said, it's a tremendous feeling of power. I like to be in charge and to direct everything and I just think that's a big challenge... To think that you can take those little minds and mould them. I really, truly enjoy that an awful lot. (ibid, p. 160)

To summarise, then, I am suggesting that from the time a mother brings her baby home from hospital, to the time the child enters school, the predominant pattern of childcare in Western societies places the mother in a pivotal position with regard to taking responsibility in relation to her child both within the household and in mediating between the child and others (including state services; Graham, 1985). During the preschool years, women are expected to take the primary childcare responsibility, and are likely to find this easier to fulfil if they also have a clear sense of their own authority as mothers. Not all mothers of pre-school children will have the resources or circumstances to be able happily or easily either to fulfil this responsibility, or to exercise any associated authority, but this is the overwhelming expectation of mothers in contemporary Western societies. These expectations to some extent emanate from wider social arrangements and State services and policies, but they also often accord with mothers' own views. What may well be in daily dispute, however, is whether the mother feels able/is expected to exercise her maternal responsibility on the basis of her *own ideas* and authority, or by *deference* to someone else's ideas and authority ie whether she experiences her authority as 'professional' or 'delegated' (see Chapter 1).

School entry is likely to be experienced by most mothers as the first point at which they significantly lose the control of their children's care, and are *obliged* to hand over their maternal authority to another adult. Furthermore, in my own study there was little evidence that the women had seen their own role as mothers in the pre-school years as being concerned with educating their young children. Rather, they discussed the details of their children's pre-school lives primarily in terms of their involvement in complex sets of relationships, either as family members or as participants in social exchanges within the locality. In this view of the child, s/he is not seen as a disconnected individual but as someone who is already deeply embedded within intricate webs of social ties. Yet it is also clear that all this is expected to shift dramatically at the point when the child enters school, when the home and neighbourhood cease to be the sites for the child's major daily activities.

I shall explore next whether and how anticipations of their children's future school lives were relevant to the mothers I interviewed in the pre-school years, before going on to consider any control they exerted as to which primary school their children entered. Tensions concerning maternal authority/responsibility in relation to the educational system, as well as within the household and local community, will be examined throughout these issues.

ANTICIPATIONS OF 'EDUCATION' IN THE PRE-SCHOOL YEARS

The very definition of what counts as 'education' (see Chapter 1) may be the first and most fundamental indicator of how any particular mother views the boundary between home and school. Does she, for example, define education in terms of learning that occurs in school, or does her definition come closer to the more inclusive sociological concept of socialisation (discussed in Chapter 1)? The first implies a very clear boundary between school-based knowledge developed within the public educational system, and everyday knowledge based within domestic and localised settings. Indeed, is education seen by mothers to require a different way of knowing than that pertaining to everyday life in informal interactions (see

Edwards in Chapter 5)? Between these two expectations – of clear-cut difference *or* seamless continuity between home and school based knowledge – there may also be further variability as to how far the mother regards herself as able and wanting to be involved in developing forms of knowledge that will assist her child's progress within the school-based system of knowledge.

Yet all of these potential differences of meaning surrounding the child, the family and education may never be made explicit but may rest as dormant yet significant sources of tension between the parties concerned with the individual child. In the interviews for my own study, such differences might initially be indicated by variations in how soon the mothers mentioned schools or education in recounting their child's pre-school years to me. Some women spontaneously referred to such issues early on, but others did not raise them until their semi-chronological account reached the time when the eldest child started school.

In line with existing research (Atkin et al., 1988; Newson and Newson 1977), most of the women I interviewed took a view of education as something that occurs within schools and is defined by schools. Where they expected to engage in 'educational activities' in the home, both the content and the timing of such activities was constructed by reference to school definitions and timetables. There was very little evidence of any prevalent concern by these women that they should themselves use the pre-school years to prime their children ready for the start of an educational race to come. Many of them, indeed, did not feel they had the necessary skills to do this, or perhaps the available time. Hilary (an ex-secretary currently working as a partner in her husband's business) was already aware, from her experiences with her older child, of what she would be asked to do by way of teaching her daughter once she started in the formal learning situation. Furthermore, Hilary showed some confidence in dealing with the educational system, but she still hesitated to anticipate the school schedule:

> She's starting at playgroup at the school next September and they all start off on the Roger Red Hat [reading] scheme, and so before that I might do some of the words that are in the tin, that she has to learn before she can go

onto the first book. I might start on that, but when? I don't think so yet, because she would begin to learn those words and then I would be ahead of the scheme and then I'd really have to go and get the books and do it seriously...

Furthermore, some women expressed doubt as to how far schools approve of any home teaching (a doubt that may be well founded: Cleave et al., 1982). While some mothers had disregarded this and gone ahead anyway, others believed the teachers wanted to keep such educational work for school:

> Everybody said you shouldn't push them too much, and they do at school, they prefer to teach them in case you teach them the wrong way. So I haven't really encouraged her to read.
> [Is that something the teachers have told you?]
> Yeah, well sort of gossip really...best to leave it to the school. (Susan, nurse)

The strongest form of preparation for school, which most of the women saw as appropriate in the early years, was attendance at an organised group without the mother, such as nursery or playgroup.[4] Many of the women referred to playgroups as 'playschools' (which is not the terminology used by the Pre-School Playgroups' Association in Britain), and the different emphasis of this term is significant, highlighting its organisational aspects:

> They're quite good for discipline [at the chosen playschool], which I definitely wanted for Simon. You know, they have to get into lines, go to the toilet and all this, sit with their legs crossed, and it's very well organised. (Susan)

Such groups were thus seen to be particularly helpful in assisting children to become accustomed to being apart from their mothers, and taking part in organised group activities.

APPROACHING THE GREAT DAY: HANDING OVER OR LETTING GO?

The precise *timing of entry* into school life was discussed by some women as the first major source of tension with the school system, even within the private sector (see the example of Christine's son in Chapter 4). There may be complex bureaucratic reasons for the particular timing of a child's school entry, which may only partially depend on chronological age. Rosemary (an ex-bookkeeper) felt she had very little notification of the date for her son's school entry. Yet she assumed she had no choice but to go along with this decision, although this was experienced as very traumatic for herself as well as her son:

> It was awful because I didn't know; I was in a dreadful state really... I just had a letter from the school.... I had three weeks to prepare him to go to school. I felt dreadful. I felt that the school was taking my baby away from me. It was awful, I felt dreadful at the time because I didn't know if it was worse preparing *me* for *him* to go to school, or him.

Rosemary understood this shock to have been something that arose from legal requirements that did not fit in easily with the particular school's timing of entry that year:

> she just explained to me that because he was five on the day they go back to school in September he's legally bound to come into school at Easter...
>
> [What would you have liked to have had more time to do with him before he went to school?]
>
> Just to prepare him I think. Just to say that he's going to school. And I would have gone up there more, I would have walked by the school and shown him the children in the playground and I would probably have taken him up there after school...Alex likes to be familiar with the place.

Rosemary thus indicated various ways in which she would have liked to *prepare the child for entry* into the school system, and she attributed the eventually happy outcome of his first day at school to his experience of playgroup:

> So he did like it afterwards, he realised he wasn't going to be shut in, he wasn't going to be hounded at, it was just another place to go and play, like playgroup.

Mothers commonly described a variety of means to smooth the transition between the two worlds of home and school, including the use of playgroups as discussed above. Amy (a teacher) regarded her whole childrearing approach as a good preparation for school life:

> All the children are alike...Zoom! Straight into playgroup and the same with school... And I think that's because they had great security when they were little, that they weren't frightened.

Teaching children numbers and reading before starting at school was also sometimes discussed in terms of helping them make the transition into school, by providing some *continuity in the experience of 'school work'*. Cleave et al. (1982) also found that parents paid attention to independence-training for their children to ease the transition into school. As school entry approached, then, continuities between one situation and another were worked at actively by mothers, to enable the child to settle well at school.

DECIDING ON A SCHOOL

In my own study, four major approaches could be discerned in mothers' accounts of how they had 'chosen'[5] schools for their children: (i) as an assertion of maternal/paternal 'educational' decision-making; (ii) by reference to continuity between home and school experiences; (iii) by reference to closeness to home; and (iv) by an assessment of the child's needs as a particular individual. I shall use this framework for my present discussion of choice of primary school, using the detail from my own qualitative interviews with mothers alongside findings of the few other studies which have been carried out concerning choice of primary school. These other studies have used larger samples but generally more structured research methods, and have rarely differentiated mothers' views on school choice from fathers' preferences. There appears to be very little American research on the topic, perhaps because the possibility of parental choice of school has so recently emerged as an option in the USA (Cross, 1989). There is also considerable variability between European countries as to how far parental choice of schooling has been viewed as desirable and encouraged within State educational systems, from the high level of diversity funded by the State in the Netherlands, to the historical tendency towards central control of education in France (Glenn, 1989; Macbeth, 1984). The background to the English educational system has been very different from many other Western countries, with greater diversity occurring through the historical establishment of schools through localised initiatives.

Very few of the women I interviewed had considered the possibility of *private education* as a choice. Christine (an ex-university laboratory technician) was therefore approached for inclusion in the research specifically because she had chosen private education, Ellen (an occupational therapist) was included because her children attended a private Steiner school, and Emily (an ex-secretary) because she had decided not to send her children to school at all (all discussed further as case studies in Chapter 4). No one, however, had considered using a boarding school.

Within the state system, most of the women in my study felt that they did have some choice of school for their child, and for many this represented the most *powerful point of contact* with a school, when they might be able to seek any continuity they expected between home and school values. Choice of school was also the point at which fathers were most likely to be involved in decision-making and contact with the school, e.g. in visiting schools formally before putting a child's name down. Occasionally there might be an outright conflict of ideas between mother and father on the subject, which might be resolved in either the mother's or father's favour. Some men, however, were described as leaving such decisions entirely up to the women. Even where a father was involved in the decision, the mother might have paved the way for this, by making some initial investigations of her own (e.g. Margaret, see below). The mother might also be seen as having more relevant knowledge through her involvement in local networks – 'I suppose it's down to me more because I hear more from other mums' (Susan). It is very notable that studies concerned with parental choice of school have not so far paid any attention to the question of *which* parent takes the primary role in this decision, or how mothers, fathers and children negotiate the decision between them. In Walford's study (1991) of secondary school children in City Technology Colleges's, however, it can be seen that the young people

Walford quotes also frequently referred to their mothers' influence in school choice even at this later stage of education.

(i)   Educational decision making

Margaret (a university administrator) had made her choice of school after considerable investigations:

> I had made my living at looking at Polytechnics – when I was validating courses – looking at Polytechnics as whole institutions, so I regarded myself as... somebody who had had a fair crack. And it was in the time before the HMI reports were published, but I actually got copies of all the HMI reports when they weren't readily publicly available... I went round all the Middle schools as well – much to their horror – I spent days doing that.

The decision about her daughter's schooling may be regarded as an assertion of Margaret's *own definition* of what constitutes *good education*. Some women thus discussed school choice in terms of their view of what they consider to be the appropriate educational approach and environment, and yet many of the women interviewed did not have such confidence in their own ability to decide on educational issues.

The only national British survey of parental reasons for choice of primary school was that conducted for the Plowden report, and this found that only 7 per cent of parents specifically mentioned educational standards. Other studies have also found that specifically educational considerations do not seem to play a great part in parental choice of primary school, at least within the state system (Adler et al., 1989; Hughes et al., 1990, Nault and Uchitelle, 1982; Petch, 1986). It is hard to know, however, whether this is because educational issues (narrowly defined) are not considered important at this stage of schooling, or because parents do not feel competent to make judgements between schools on these sorts of grounds.

(ii)   Continuity between home and school experiences

Not surprisingly, the women in my sample who were most confident about their own definitions of educational needs were those who had spent most time themselves in the educational system. Other women, however, might feel confident about the sorts of non-educational experiences they wanted their children to encounter at school, and sought to ensure *continuity* between home and school values.

While Emily has kept her children outside the school system to avoid compromising the childrearing values she has developed in her family life (discussed further in Chapter 4), Christine and Ellen have explicitly chosen private education in order to be able to ensure that the school mirrored the values of the home.

> I feel no matter what kind of education you choose, it should fit in with your home life... You can't have a child brought up in a certain direction at school and follow a totally different pattern at home, in some ways that would cause conflict. You've got to think along the same lines as the teachers and the teachers should think along the same line as the parents...(Ellen)

Continuity between home and school values might be sought in other ways also, e.g. through *religious values,* or in terms of similar sorts of *caring* – 'Right from the Head down, it's disciplined but it's tempered with love' (Kay: ex-office worker). Jo looked to school life to be a continuation of the general experience of family life, rather like *large families.* She chose a small village school because it felt like 'one happy family', which was enhanced by the inclusion of different ages in one class. Some women looked for a high level of *discipline* in school to mirror their home values:

> We believe it's better for them to start off in private schools, to gain the foundations of knowing what work's about, being polite to parents and teachers. We've got old-fashioned ideas... (Veronica: an administrator)

Larger-scale studies have also found religious issues to have some significance for parental choice (Central Advisory Council for Education, 1967; University of Glasgow, 1986), particularly for choice of a non-local school or for parents using private education (Darling-Hammond et al., 1985). Considering the significance of religious issues historically, however, such issues are clearly declining in importance for policy debates about parental choice (Glenn, 1989). The more pastoral aspects of school life and 'school atmosphere' are also significant factors in more recent studies (e.g. Hughes et al., 1990, Nault and Uchitelle, 1982; Petch, 1986). While it is difficult to know quite what is meant by 'school atmosphere', this does seem to imply that parents are concerned at this stage of a child's school life to consider the child's needs in broader terms that just educational and academic success.

(iii) Closeness to home

The significance of proximity to home emerges as a vital factor in all studies of school choice, whether at the primary or secondary level (e.g. Central Advisory Council, 1967, Nault and Uchitelle, 1982; Petch, 1986; Stillman and Maychell, 1986; University of Glasgow 1986). Furthermore, zoning as a method of allocation to schools occurs to some degree in all EC countries (Macbeth, 1984). In rural areas, attendance at the local school is likely to be the only practicable option for many parents. With younger children, particularly, safety and convenience factors are likely to be considered important, and this is indeed found to be a major consideration for large proportions of parents (Central Advisory Council, 1967; Petch, 1986; University of Glasgow, 1986). A recent study by Hughes et al. (1990) in the West of England revealed that parents would normally expect to send the child to the nearest school, unless there were strong reasons to give them a push to look further afield. Only 15 out of 141 parents voluntarily send their child to a non-local school without there being negative reasons present for avoiding the local school. This finding echoes that of a major Scottish study concerning the relative importance of 'push' factors for parents who reject their district school (Adler et al., 1989). Nearness to home is also an important consideration even when parents are choosing a school within the private system (Fox, 1985).

What exactly is being valued by parents when they refer to the importance of closeness to home, however, is more difficult to establish, although some studies do treat safety in travelling as a distinct consideration from proximity to home (Petch, 1986). Furthermore, there may also be important differences in the meaning of proximity to home according to the degree of choice parents have exercised as to where they live in the first place.

In this respect, it is very important to remember that almost all the women in my own study lived in owner-occupied housing. Among this group of women, school was often particularly viewed as an *extension of the local community*, which for most women was highly valued, and had been the basis of their childcare activities in the pre-school years (as discussed earlier):

> ...you can put them down if you want them to go to another school and then you normally get them accepted... but this school has a good reputation so I was quite happy. It's literally just across the road and all his friends are local so I think that's quite important really. I've grown up with all my friends and... I still see them and I think it's quite nice. (Susan)

For many, the overriding consideration (assuming the basic level of education was satisfactory) was that the child should attend *the local school*. Margaret (discussed above as having made a very active investigation of schools) implied that this sort of decision was just made as a matter of convenience: '...most people seemed to be just going to the nearest place'. Yet women who sent their children to the local school did not seem to view their decision in this way, nor a decision made by default. Rather, their preference seemed to relate to their strong concerns about their children's social acceptability and membership of local peer groups and networks. These concerns extended from the friendships developed from the child's earliest years, and from the pre-school groups attended, and intertwined later on with all sorts of out-of-school experiences and activities. Continuity between home and school might thus also be seen in terms of *continuities mediated by peer groups and communities*, and this continuity between the two was itself actively sought by mothers.

(iii)   A school to suit the individual child

A few parents made it clear that they chose a school to suit the specific nature of the individual child, but interestingly, all these cases concerned a child who was seen to have special needs through some form of disability or medical condition.

Hilary's son suffered badly from eczema, which she felt set him slightly apart and lead to concerns about his social acceptability. She specifically chose a local school for him because she believed this would help him to integrate into local networks, as well as enabling him to be near home in case of illness at school:

> We just chose the village school because we thought it wouldn't matter if he was ill in the dinner-time, because then he hasn't got that far to go, also he would know a lot of people in the village and he wouldn't be that boy who sometimes looks a bit funny who goes to a different school out of the area...

On the other hand, she suggested that a different sort of individual child might need a different sort of choice:

> I suppose if you've got a smart child you might tour round the schools and think which one would be pushing them best academically...

Social acceptability had also been an important consideration for Kate's daughter who had Down's Syndrome. Kate's approach seemed to have been to keep her in a mainstream school by trying to avoid the attention of the educational authorities, but using what professionals she could find who would be on her side and help her in obtaining the goals she wants for her daughter. Thus she had been able to send her to a small village school that was vertically grouped. This school had been suggested by the nursery school teacher, and Kate gave quite a graphic account of how she expected to have to negotiate a place for her daughter:

> I went into [the school] cold, having heard about it... I just went in and said, could I see round... and she took me straight round the school, without knowing about Suzanne at all! [Gasps] I was hoping to speak to her first and she took me round the school, and she discussed the maths scheme and the English scheme, and the reading scheme. It wasn't until she'd done the tour that I could then explain the situation, and she immediately said, "Well I've been meaning to do something like this for a long time".... We

had a very good educational psychologist...she got us in here, and helped us set up work schemes...I don't really know that [the County Education Office] know that she's there...

This aspect of choice of school is difficult to discern within the larger-scale quantitative studies of parental choice, although Johnson and Ransom (1980) discuss how some parents made a 'child-focused choice' in the selection of secondary schooling. Other studies also refer to the 'happiness of the child' as an important consideration (e.g. Petch, 1986) but it is difficult again to know what is being judged by parents here. Is happiness being considered by reference to the individual characteristics of the child, or by reference to the atmosphere of the school, or something else again? The significance of having older siblings already at a school, however, points to a strong pattern of younger children following in their siblings' footsteps, rather than parents sending individual children to different schools (Johnson, 1990).

Indeed, there are a number of ways in which the quantitative studies raise as many questions as answers about how parents do actually regard the choice process. Besides the lack of clarity about what exactly parents are prioritising when they cite proximity as a major consideration (as discussed above), there is also ambiguity about what parents actually mean when they refer to having heard 'good reports' of schools, or that schools have 'good reputations'. A recent study of primary school choice in Scotland concluded:

> Emerging clearly... from the open-ended responses is the importance of the local network, both specific individuals who act as informants and the more abstract grapevine, the pool of information which accumulates over time from a variety of non-specific sources and provides the 'stock of knowledge' on which parents base their commonsense understanding. (Petch, 1986, p. 36)

None of these studies differentiates between mothers and fathers in this respect. What is highly likely, however, is that the information that flows between mothers (either of the same generation or between generations) is crucial to the ways in which children are placed within particular schools (Bell and Ribbens, 1993), as well as within particular pre-school provisions (Blatchford et al., 1982). In this sense, mothers of pre-school children may be exerting some influence at the point of school placement not just through individual preference but also collectively.

CONCLUSION

At the point of entry into the compulsory education system, the child and her/his mother have been largely functioning as a unit, often as part of a 'family', a unit for which the mother has been largely responsible on a daily level, which she has played an important part in creating, and in which she will have invested a great deal of time and effort and often a large part of her own individual identity. She has done this work with very little recognition, either from herself or society at large, but she has done it largely within an informal but extensive and complex world of other women and children. In her study of mothers living in London, Boulton concluded:

> Getting on for two-thirds of the women experienced a sense of meaning and purpose in their lives as mothers. They felt their children needed and wanted them and they invested their personal hopes and dreams in their children. Their children therefore gave them a purpose to which they were deeply committed and in pursuing this purpose they experienced their lives as meaningful and worthwhile.
>
> (Boulton, 1983, p. 204)

There may of course be considerable variations within this general description, (as I have tried to indicate in this chapter), but school entry is likely to be experienced by most mothers as the first point at which they significantly lose the control of their children's care, and are *obliged* to hand over their maternal authority to another adult – generally another female. Most of the mothers in my own study did express a sense of having exerted some control over which schools their children attended. Yet, in line with other studies of primary school choice, very few of the women discussed here used this influence by reference to 'educational' considerations in the narrow sense of school achievement. Furthermore, there was little evidence that these women had seen their own role as mothers in the pre-school years as being concerned with educating their young children. Rather, they discussed the details of their children's pre-school lives primarily in terms of their involvement in complex sets of relationships, either as family members or as participants in social exchanges within the locality. In this view of the child, s/he is not seen as a disconnected individual but as someone who is already deeply embedded within intricate webs of social ties, and it was this understanding of the child as a social being that informed most of these women's ideas about school choice.

Nevertheless, school entry is the moment at which the child as *an individual* is compelled to cross the boundary from 'home and mother/family' to enter other social settings, under an alternative authority. Again, in entering school – as with leaving hospital – there may be legal underpinnings (*in loco parentis*) of the notion that the care of children has been 'handed over' to the school authority until they leave again at the end of the day. Yet the reality for most children is that, while they do leave behind their mothers and families as they enter the school premises, they do not leave behind other informal social ties, whether of kinship or friendship. For very many parents, perhaps the majority, integration and social acceptability within these local networks are very important considerations when it comes to the child's entry into school life.

This is not to say that school entry is seen simply as an unwelcome imposition, since almost all mothers believe that 'education' in the school system is a 'good thing', and many may feel a sense of relief at being relieved of responsibility for their children for substantial portions of time. It is however, to say that there may be many tensions about how the *transfer of parental authority* to the school is accomplished. In contemporary Western societies this is largely in practice a question of the transfer of *maternal* authority. While women may vary in how far they seek to control the conditions under which this transfer occurs, there are very few women for whom this will not represent a major shift in their life style and identity as mothers, as well as introducing a major new arena for continuing maternal mediation. This is the issue to which I shall turn next.

NOTES

1. In identifying particular women from my study for the first time in my discussion here, I shall not refer to their husbands' occupations but to their own main occupational experience.
2. This quote is left unattributed as it led to some discussion between the woman and her husband when they read their write-up together.
3. Images of the 'New Man' may thus provide a new legitimation such that 'having secured the heartland of the public world, men are now moving in on the private' (White, 1990, p. 17).
4. It was a feature of the sampling method used that most of the women in the study had sent their children to playgroups (which is the overwhelming expectation and pattern in this geographical area). There is also a very low level of nursery provision in the areas of study. For a discussion of organised pre-school facilities on a national level within Britain see Cohen, 1990, and for a European discussion see Melhuish and Moss, 1991, and Moss, 1990.
5. The concept of 'choice' has become increasingly significant as an aspect of political rhetoric and social policy generally, as well as educational policies specifically, especially in Britain. An examination of the possible meanings underlying this concept, however, is beyond the scope of the present discussion.

4 Having a Word with the Teacher: On-going Negotiations across Home–School Boundaries
Jane Ribbens

INTRODUCTION

In the previous chapter, I considered the existence and meaning of maternal responsibility/authority in the pre-school years, and discussed the presence and significance of a major geographical, temporal and social boundary that occurs at the point where young children reach compulsory school age. In this chapter, I will continue past the point of school entry, to consider how this boundary is experienced by women as an on-going feature of their lives and their children's lives during the primary school years. Morgan (1985) suggests that the concept of 'boundary' in social life can be used administratively, theoretically and/or expressively. For the concerns of the present chapter, it is the expressive sense of family boundary that is central, i.e. 'those boundaries to which people actually make reference and which are meaningful to them in their everyday lives' (ibid, p.153).

Additionally, I am focusing on the expressive sense of family–school boundary as viewed *from one side only*. I am explicitly taking the perspective of individual mothers during the early years of compulsory schooling, considering how this boundary looks to them. To what degree do they perceive this boundary to exist, and what issues does this raise for mothers? How do they approach this boundary within the unequal relationship that arises within the context of compulsory schooling? This chapter thus examines maternal perspectives of the home–school boundary within daily life, apart from any wider political rhetoric of parentocracy (Brown, 1990; David, 1992).

This political rhetoric may have power because it does resonate with parents/mothers' feelings of powerlessness over their children's lives in relation to state bureaucracy, in an area which is seen as crucial to their children's future life-chances. In reviewing educational policies in Western industrialised societies, Glenn concludes:

> Struggle over parent choice in recent years has been less a matter of the conflicting claims to loyalty of Church and State as rival powers ...than of the resistance of individuals to the claims of the State to know what is good for everyone and in particular for their children. (1989, p. 209)

The respective claims of state and parents over children's lives have received some attention from political philosophers in recent years (e.g. Crittenden, 1988; Scarre, 1989), raising key controversies about how we are to interpret the value of 'family' life for children. What has not so far been considered is how these issues have particular significance for women's lives as mothers, and the ways in which women deal with such tensions in their everyday role as mediators for children (Graham, 1985; Ribbens, 1991).

Thus, while school choice may enable fathers as well as mothers to exercise some parental power (if school choice has some reality), mothers may be living with such tensions and working out daily how to deal with them with their children – from how to deal with homework, to children's physical appearance, to decisions about whether or not 'to have a word with the teacher'. Lareau's American study found that it was mothers (especially middle-class women) rather than fathers who experienced more intense involvement in their children's school lives, and over a wider range of issues:

> mothers were preoccupied with the micro-details of their children's classroom life, including their performance in specific subjects, their friendship networks, and their overall emotional state. (Lareau, 1989, p. 90)

Indeed, it may be argued that the perceived necessity of dealing with such social and educational issues for their children, have widened and deepened gendered parental responsibilities throughout children's school years – in contrast with those (out-dated) sociological pictures suggesting that compulsory schooling has reduced the significance of family activities or 'functions' (Ulich, 1989). Where Lareau did find fathers becoming more heavily involved was in the more formal aspects of home–school links such as parent-teacher conferences, showing particular concerns with issues to do with their children's *educational* success; a pattern which I also found among the mothers and fathers in my own English study (Ribbens, 1990).

I shall first discuss these issues in relation to the women in my own study, to elaborate how we obtain different pictures and raise different issues if we view the home-school boundary from the perspectives of mothers. While these women constitute a specific sample (see Chapter 3), they are also interesting here particularly because they do *not* constitute the stereotype of 'hard-to-reach parents' (Heleen, 1988). While issues of ethnicity (e.g. Tomlinson and Hutchinson, 1990) or social class (e.g. Connell et al., 1982) are undoubtedly significant for home–school relations, Atkin et al. observe the extent to which writers about home-school relations presume that any problems can be attributed *solely* to such issues:

> But is the higher educational achievement of their children a justification for the belief that relationships with schools are unproblematic for middle-class parents? Teachers have clearly had doubts – the 'pushy' or 'interfering' parent is as much part of staffroom lore as the apathetic or uninterested one.
>
> (Atkin et al., 1988, p. 68)

Even when parents have been or are teachers themselves, they may still experience tensions in dealing with schools in relation to their own children:

> Becoming a parent helps teachers to understand more the vulnerability experienced when one's child or one's self is going to be judged by others, the feelings engendered by encounters with authority figures, the helplessness of an individual faced with a complex system. (ibid., p. 82).

Furthermore, the school is a crucial area in which maternal competence may be judged: '...since it is one of the points from which the internal practices of child care become visible to agencies outside of the family' (Prout, 1988, p. 783). Similarly, it is well known that the introduction of mass compulsory schooling at the end of the nineteenth century in

Britain was crucial in making children visible to professional bodies (e.g. Hendrick, 1992; Sutherland, 1984).

While educational professionals may expect home–school relationships to be unproblematic for such women as I interviewed, this is too simplistic a picture. Furthermore, the women themselves used variable notions of what school life and education are all about, and took different approaches as to how they might deal with the home–school boundary. I shall first examine these variabilities through a series of case studies, before briefly raising some general issues.

In the interviews with these women (which started in 1986 and in some cases continued into 1992), I did not initially ask direct questions about schools and education; these topics were discussed within the context of the overall accounts the women gave of their lives with their children up to the age of seven. Educational issues might thus arise spontaneously early on in their discussions, or they might not be mentioned at all until their chronological accounts reached the point of formal school entry. This had the advantage of allowing women to talk from their own sets of concerns, but it also provided scope for silence and avoidance, and the analysis may need to consider what is taken-for-granted within the accounts.

The case studies address two central issues, which are carried forward from the previous chapter:

(i)   do the women expect continuity or discontinuity between children's experiences at home and at school, i.e. do they view the two institutions as operating on 'contrasting principles of social organisation'? (Cheal, 1991)

(ii) do the women assert their own ideas and authority about their children's educational experiences, or do they defer to 'professional' ideas about children's educational needs? This issue raises questions of 'professional' or 'delegated' maternal authority (discussed in Chapter 1).

The six case studies address these issues in the following ways:
Janet, who regards home and school as very separate spheres and has had an uneasy relationship with her child's teachers;
Shirley, who also regards home as rather a different place from school but is anxious to tread a gentle line in relation to her children's teachers;
Kate, who expects more continuity between home and school

but asserts her own ideas by 'working the system' to her children's benefit;

Christine, who expects a distant relationship with her daughter's school, but only after buying into a school that provides continuity with home values;

Ellen, who expects a very close relationship with her daughters' Steiner school and very close continuity between home and school experiences;

Emily, who has asserted her own views of her children's educational needs by keeping them outside the formal educational system altogether. Emily's account most clearly highlights what is taken for granted by the other women about the consequences for family life of their children's attendance at school.

The last three women were all asked for interviews specifically because they had made rather different educational choices for their children from the other women in the study. It will be apparent, then, as I go through these case studies, that not only do they become *increasingly unusual* in the sense of statistical norms, but also that there is a sense of increasing assertions of maternal authority in relation to the school system. Yet this maternal authority *may or may not* imply a clear-cut boundary between home and school. Additionally, this boundary is negotiated, not only from within the contexts of home and school, but also neighbourhood and the mothers' and children's involvement in informal networks:

> [Existing] analyses fail to capture the notion of a family–school *linkage* with – to use an analogy – a small, rarely used pathway, in one community or a large, well-travelled pathway in another... Having the company of many others may shape the nature of the journey; by focusing primarily on individual travellers researchers have missed these possibilities.
>
> (Lareau, 1989, p. 6; original emphasis)

Other studies have pointed to changes over time in gendered parental attitudes towards school authority (e.g. Wadsworth, 1991). Besides the interviews with the women themselves (and some of their husbands), interviews were also carried out with some maternal grandmothers. I do not, however, have any direct material relevant to children's own activities and attitudes towards the home–school boundary.

SIX CASE STUDIES

(i)   Janet – home and school as separate spheres

Janet might be regarded as the most working-class of the
women interviewed; she was the only woman in the study who
was not living in owner-occupied housing (although she has
more recently achieved this ambition). At the time of the
initial interview, Janet, her husband, Ted, and their seven-year
old son Russell, were living with her parents in their council
house, having lost their previous tied accommodation. Ted
was working as a landscape gardener, and Janet was employed
full-time as a bookkeeper, although she gave this up in
anticipation of the arrival of their second child. Neither have
any formal qualifications from their schooldays, although Ted
obtained some agricultural qualifications at college.

Janet made it clear that she found great enjoyment in
Russell's company, with few problems in her relationship with
him, particularly in their lives in the home and immediate
neighbourhood. In other – more public – situations, however,
tensions might arise. Janet appeared to feel under greater
pressure as a mother in more public contexts, arising at least
in part through a conflict of ideas between her ideas about
childrearing and others' ideas about appropriate behaviour. It
was notable that, over several interviews, the only point at
which Janet described Russell as 'naughty', was in relation to
an incident while out shopping.

When it came to the public institution of schooling, these
tensions were also very much apparent. As with several other
mothers, Janet approves of discipline in school. Unlike many
other mothers, however, Janet does not expect a straight-
forward continuity of discipline between Russell's home life
and school life, regarding school as a *different sort of setting*
from home:

> ...I suppose [discipline's] all right at school, because
> otherwise you're going to have them bashing the teachers or
> something, throwing food around or that.
> ... I suppose some schools are very strict on discipline, but
> you don't want that at home as well, you've got to have a bit
> of leeway...

In this regard, Janet's account bears strong similarities with that of one of the grandmothers, who explicitly described the home as a haven from the different requirements of school life.

While thus holding different expectations of school life and home life, Janet stressed her concern for Russell's education, and her willingness to work with him at home in response to directions from school:

> They do a bit of reading at school and then they come home and read to us, which is nice because you can see what he's doing ... when he comes home and he can sit down and read a book ... it's nice that ... I think you feel sort of quite proud that he can actually sit down and work it out.

Nevertheless, although Janet was very keen to have contact with Russell's teachers, these contacts have at times been difficult, with outright hostility from some:

> He didn't get on with his first teacher... When I went to see her on the mothers' day the first thing she said to me was, 'Oh, Russell's a very naughty little boy. He's very good at saying no'. Well I knew that anyway...And it was exactly the same with his next teacher, Mrs M, she said exactly the same thing...

However, while agreeing that Russell is 'stubborn', Janet's view is that it is the teacher's job to motivate the child, and she expressed resentment:

> [How did you feel about these things being said?]

> Well the thing is, I knew he could be stubborn: if he doesn't want to do it, he won't do it. But then again, I felt like saying to them, 'Well, that's what you're paid to do' ... my impression was that Mrs M and Mrs S didn't like him, so they obviously thought, well why should we help him? Because the teacher he's got now, Mrs G, when it came to the open evening ... I said to Ted, I know what she's going to say – 'Russell's a very naughty boy, he's very good at saying no, I can't do this with him, I can't do that'. And what a surprise, because she said, 'Oh, I did have a bit of trouble with him to start with,' but she said, 'I squashed him and now he's fine, his reading's coming on great, he's really settling down and

doing his sums' ... he's obviously clicked with this teacher, and she will spend a bit more time with him and let him do things...

While the teachers have made their views clear to Janet, she has not vocalised her reactions to them, implying an inequality of power between them. Janet does not regard herself as playing a major educational role, even though she is willing to undertake educational tasks under the teachers' direction. In this regard, her attitude is very much in line with the more general finding that 'parents are very aware ... of the school as an institution, and the learning that takes place there as 'proper' learning' (Atkin et al., 1988, p. 34). Education is seen to be defined by teachers, largely taking place in schools. Dealing with the school thus carries much potential for tension, because even though there may be agreement about the importance of learning, there may be different conceptions of the *nature of the child* concerned, and of the *role of the teacher*. Furthermore, the role of teacher is seen as very different from the role of mother, and the home is seen as quite a different sort of setting from the school. The boundary between home and school is here quite sharply defined, with the potential for considerable tensions in mother–teacher relationships unless these are carefully managed, despite goodwill on both sides.

(ii)   Shirley – treading a gentle line

Shirley lives in the house which her grandfather built in a small village, with her husband Stephen, her seven-year old daughter Mary Rose and her son Paul aged five. Stephen works as a semi-qualified manager in a small engineering company, while Shirley herself has had part-time office work since Mary Rose was one year old. Shirley herself left school at 16 with minimal secondary school qualifications, and worked for some time in London as a computer operator, becoming a supervisor before leaving with the birth of Mary Rose.

Shirley told me happy stories of her life with the children when they were very small. In discussing their lives at home, she expressed a concern to meet her children's needs, as she understands these, with as little restriction as possible – even though her husband regards her as too 'soft'. This approach was especially given priority when they were younger. While she expects more from them as they get older, and reproves any cheekiness, she is also prepared to 'back down', and respond to their requests if she thinks they are reasonable. In moving outside the home and family, however, Shirley expressed concern with her children's acceptability to other people, and she was proud to have reports from others that her children behave well when they are out without her.

Both health and education are matters in which Shirley respects the advice of professionals, and education was given some centrality in her account. For Shirley, educational qualifications are important aspects of gaining opportunities, because employers perceive them to be important even though they may not necessarily be relevant to job performance. A child's ability level is defined by her progress at school, and this constitutes an important aspect of a child's characteristics. Shirley was also pleased to undertake educational activities at home with her children. These activities might often occur as part of the children's 'cuddle times' with her, the amount of such activities being largely determined by the children's responsiveness.

Nevertheless, Shirley defined clear limits to this goal of using education to progress in life.

> I hope that they'll do well for themselves without having to struggle ... you like to think that your children are doing quite well, and finding life not too much of a burden.
>
> I'm not saying that most people don't want qualifications these days, but if it's going to upset the children in the process, then I don't think it's worth it.

Shirley does not have daily contact with the teachers, but she goes into school on a weekly basis to cook with the children. She wants to avoid being seen as the sort of person who makes undue demands on teachers. Parents' evenings occur twice a year, and this is the point at which her husband is most likely to be involved. His other major point of involvement occurred at school-entry, since he had particular views about which school the children should attend, and his views prevailed.

Most of the contact between Shirley and the school occurs at the initiative of the school, in relation to issues defined as important by the school. In Shirley's account, school is a place where it is important for the children to present themselves on other people's terms, being well behaved and smartly dressed. However the teachers have been concerned that the children should be able to speak up for themselves in the classroom:

> [the teachers] call him Um at school, because he thinks of something, and by the time he's got up to ask he's forgotten what it was, and he goes 'Um'!

Shirley herself has initiated contact with the school at times, for example, to convey Mary Rose's considerable anxieties about school to her teacher: 'If I wasn't happy with anything that they were doing then yes, I think I could go in and talk to their teacher'. However, she described going to see the head-master as 'making waves', and at the time of the first interviews, she had not been to see him during her children's time at school, and if she were to go, she expressed little expectation of being listened to. By the time of the return interview two years later, however, she had been in once to see the headmaster, regarding the children's access to toilets during lesson times.

Shirley's apparent preference, then, in her relationship with the school, is to be helpful to the school, to help the children at home, and to see the teachers over matters that worry her without making undue demands of their time. At the same time, she does not expect to lay down the law, and wants her children to be smart and well thought of, within an institution that she regards as concerned with central aspects of her children's characteristics. Shirley's story thus exemplifies the attitude that education is very important – up to a point – and that her role as mother is to support the school in whatever ways the school prefers. This pattern was reported to be widespread among the parents interviewed by Atkin et al. (1988), accepting that the parental role should be supportive since schools know the right way of doing things.

(iii)   Kate – working the system

Kate is a home economics secondary school teacher by profes-sion, although while the children were small she worked as a part-time youth worker. She lives in a detached house in a small village with her husband, John, and three children, Paul, aged seven, Suzanne, aged five (who is the child with Down's Syndrome referred to in Chapter 3) and Philip, aged four. John is a graduate manager with a national construction company.

In Chapter 3 I described how Kate had made use of a parents' discussion group during the children's pre-school years, but only in so far as she agreed with the format and experienced no conflict over her children. Similarly, she is happy to read books about childrearing if she can take or leave the advice on her own terms. She is thus happy to hear professional advice as long as it is not intrusive and does not threaten her maternal authority.

There were some difficulties when Kate's first son started formal education. Kate attributed these to the school, as well as to her son's 'character':

> School was a bit of a struggle to start with, sitting down and working, writing. He's a child who never likes to be shown how to do something, he always wants to be able to do it without being shown... school was a bit of a shock – to have to be shown. And I hadn't pushed it, I didn't see the point of trying to force him to write his name, or learn numbers. He was fighting all the time, and at nursery they said just leave it, it'll come when he's ready, so I didn't push it at all...

It thus appears that Kate and the nursery school were operating with a similar model of child learning – to wait for the child to be 'ready' – but this did not accord with the learning model used in the first primary school. After moving house, Paul changed to a primary school which Kate feels is more in accord with her own ideas of education, and here there has been much improvement:

> He's different, it's amazing, he enjoys it so much more, they do all the work that they did at the other school, but Mr B is very keen on social education as well... He needed a bit more of a boost really, to make it a bit more of a fun place...

Kate has sought out what she considers to be the right educational setting for each of her children, and feels she has on the whole achieved this through the state educational system. She has actively sought out different schooling for each child, an individualistic approach which may partly reflect the particular needs of Suzanne with Down's Syndrome. Suzanne and Paul attend different primary schools, while the youngest child, Philip, goes to a private nursery school which the older children have not attended. In relation to Suzanne, Kate uses the professional services available, and supplements these with her own resources, including essential private transport, and a friend who goes into the school as part of the early stimulation scheme of which Kate is the chairperson.

Kate thus has the confidence actively to seek out and assert her own educational preferences for her children, and also has the insider knowledge of being a teacher herself. Yet this has not prevented issues arising in the ways the children's lives straddle these two worlds of school and family, issues which Kate seeks to manage as she coordinates these disparate lives. One difficulty in doing this is simply her limited knowledge of what is actually happening to her children once they enter the classroom:

> They have a sort of cook-in, and the parents take turns. I enjoy going over there and seeing what's going on... And you get to know the teachers better which I think is good. I mean parents are not trying to take over, we're only there to help... I think a lot of teachers worry that parents, once they get their foot in the door, are going to start dictating to the staff...

While Kate has difficulty knowing what is happening in school, she well knows the effects of school life on family routines, giving a graphic description of her daily schedule:

> We have to be organised, I have to have all their clothes out the night before and the breakfast laid... I take Paul to school first, because he can play in the playground for ten minutes, with his friends. And then I take Suzanne, I come back here, and then I take Philip at half past nine, which leaves us with a 15-minute hanging around session... [Paul comes back from nursery] and has lunch ... It's only about an hour and a half once lunch is over, and then at three o'clock we start again.

A key childrearing concern for Kate is the learning of independence, and she experiences serious concern when this priority conflicts with the ways in which outside organisations impinge on family life in terms she cannot control. The process of getting ready to go out with the children is experienced as highly stressful, since she is keen to encourage and allow the children to dress themselves, and yet she is constrained by timetables not of her own making. Her tension in dealing with this conflict was actually identified as one of her failings as a mother, particularly because she is also concerned to treat her mothering rationally, and with detachment. Faced with these conflicting priorities she blames herself:

> I tend to be impatient, and when I'm tired I lose my temper too quickly... Even if I don't always show it, I think it's inside and it makes you like that sometimes, trying to get the energy to go out. My worst thing is trying to get them to go out, get them ready, because it takes so long, and I know myself that if I went in the other room and left them to do it, they'd probably do it in the time – even though they might be fighting over the coats, and, 'You've got my gloves'. But I'm bad there, I'm not detached enough over certain things, getting out or something.

> [Is that because you worry about getting there on time?]

> Possibly, yes... I think that's my main thing, that I do tend to be impatient... I show my impatience although I shouldn't.

There is no question that it will be anyone else but Kate who deals with such tensions. She accepts that her husband's job requires long hours away from home, and that this has to take priority even when he himself might not wish this. His attendance at school events brought praise:

> He was meant to come to Paul's school concert yesterday and in the end he couldn't make it because something came up in the office that he couldn't leave... He writes them all in his diary and tries to come as much as he possibly can. He's good like that.

Overall, then, Kate has exerted a fairly high degree of authority in her children's lives, and has actively shaped the children's lives outside the home as well as inside. Yet, at the same time, the school is a major setting limiting her authority, while the children's involvement in school has major implications for her life with them at home. Atkin et al. (1988) discuss how determined and persistent parents who pursue their children's interests very actively – even despite continuing obstacles from schools – can obtain spectacular results, but this perhaps overlooks the extent to which children's school involvements seem inevitably to create tensions within home lives.

(iv)   Christine – buying in and controlling the system from a distance

Christine is a university graduate who married while still a student, to Richard, who is now a computer manager for a banking organisation. At the first interview they were living in a semi-detached house in a rural area on the edge of an affluent commuter town, with their two children, Louise, aged seven, and Sebastian, approaching five years. Christine had not expected to find motherhood as enjoyable as she did, but described herself as unusual – 'You'll find out just how unconventional I am'. Christine and Richard have developed very definite ideas about how to bring up their children, including using private education to obtain the sort of experience they want for their daughter. However, they have not achieved the same control over the educational fate of their son, who is in a state school. Christine is thus able to make some interesting comparisons – 'private schools work in a totally different way'.

In some respects Christine believes that children have to learn to conform. She described family life as the prelude to taking your place in society:

It's important that they learn their place in the family, and then it follows on that they will then have to learn their place in society. I mean we all have to conform to a level.

However, there is also some deeply felt ambivalence about fitting in: 'As you have probably gathered, we are totally unusual weird people'. For a child to join in organised activities outside the home is seen to require some suppression of individuality. Christine wants achievements for her children, but also a complex balance between individuality and educational goals. She also looks for confidence and self-presentation skills, as useful attributes later in life, even without educational achievements.

Christine described the choice of private education for her daughter as '...a very big decision', yet there was a taken-for-granted assumption that she had the right and knowledge to make this choice, in conjunction with Richard and Louise. The reasons given for choosing private education were both educational and non-educational, including 'self-confidence, poise and polish'. Christine also wanted the strong religious influence of a convent school: 'The caring in the school is very obvious and the way children are made to think about what they do...' In the free and active choice of private school, Christine feels she has been able to ensure a *continuity in the values* of home and school:

> So the values that the children develop they take with them, and its much easier if school mirrors the way you feel because then it continues in children, much better with continuity than change.

Conversely, the school has clear expectations of the home, including an early introduction to homework, and a foundation for discipline:

> When our children started the headmistress stated very categorically ... it is, not the responsibility of the school to tame wild children.

There are thus clearly defined responsibilities for home and school, but these are seen as quite separate and firmly demarcated spheres. Mothers are very definitely not allowed into the school as helpers, unlike Sebastian's state school which asks for helpers:

> school should be school and home should be home, and for a child to see its own mum helping out at the school I don't think it separates the two enough...

With the private school, then, continuity between home and school was established, *not* by mothers' *involvement* in schools, but the initial parental *choice* of school:

> It's like buying a house, you find what suits you, so you're choosing education, so hopefully if you go into it in enough detail you've then got the right educational environment for your child.

At the same time, Louise's school quite actively negotiates with the parents, with written feedback and more frequent parents' evening than in Sebastian's state school. Christine also feels she has very free access to the teachers – 'there's no restriction whatsoever...' While not assuming she would necessarily have such a good relationship with all private schools, Christine feels she has more power in dealing with a private rather than a state school. While talking about difficulties with Sebastian's teacher she said:

> You don't get this in the private sector, you go in and say, "This is happening, what are you going to do about it?" And because you are paying you have the right to criticise, whereas in the state sector it's really very much a take it or leave it, this is Hobson's choice.

Nevertheless, in the years since the first interview with Christine, difficulties have arisen with regard to bullying in Louise's school. These difficulties have not been resolved by negotiation with the teachers, leading to Louise's removal to another private school some distance away from home.

Christine and Richard wanted private education for Sebastian, as for Louise, but after considerable negotiations with both private and state schools concerning the appropriate age for him to start school, Sebastian eventually started at a local state school. Even so, Christine feels strongly that he was too young (at four and a half) to start school, but they were obliged to send him or risk losing any control over which school he attended. At a later stage, they reapplied to the private school but he was rejected on the grounds that he would not fit into the school at that time.

After starting at the state school Sebastian did not appear to settle: 'We are having him up every night, we are having wetting problems...' In tackling these issues, there had been considerable difficulties between Christine and the class teacher at first – she felt stereotyped as 'a pushy mum' and that Sebastian was disliked by the teacher. Christine's reaction was to seek out other resources, including an intelligence assessment, and advice from a health visitor friend. As a result, she went to see her family doctor, who then referred them to a psychologist, who then liaised with the school:

She went into the school and talked to his teacher and the teacher had quite grave misconceptions about us, she thought that we were just anxious pushy parents... We were more concerned that he was happy and enjoying school.

Christine feels that her opinion as a mother did not count for much until backed up by a psychologist, and that she has lacked feedback from the school.

In turn, Christine is critical of the school for lack of discipline. Discipline, for Christine, seems to refer to organisation and clear expectations, alongside an accommodation to individual differences:

It's one of my biggest criticisms of the school, I don't think there is enough discipline... There does need to be far more order than there is, but I think Sebastian as a child needs to know exactly where he stands.

The difference in Christine's perceptions of her children's two schools may also have been affected by the fact that she experienced the private system of education first, developing expectations that were not shared by the state school:

The most important thing in most private schools is reading, because it's believed that if a child can read then they know what is being asked of them, so they understand... things are introduced much earlier.

Christine is quite happy to let the private school take the lead in Louise's educational activities at home. With Sebastian however, she and Richard have themselves taken the lead at home:

his teacher believes he is not old enough or mature enough to start on pre-reading skills at school so he's not doing word-building, he's not starting on flash cards, so we work at home with him.

Since the initial interviews with Christine, Sebastian has been officially diagnosed as disgraphic, and has started receiving a high level of support services. In addition, Christine herself by chance met a child psychotherapist, and asked him to carry out a private assessment of Sebastian. As a result, an urgent referral was made for appointments with a National Health Service psychotherapist, whom Sebastian now sees weekly. At the same sessions, Christine herself has been given appointments with a social worker, but so far has not found these helpful. She is, however, very pleased that Sebastian's special needs have been recognised.

Fundamentally, Christine is concerned to be able to have choice, providing some control over her children's school lives. She expects the values of school to reflect those of home, so that she can be happy to entrust her child to the school and then keep at something of a distance, confident that the school will give her plenty of information and be aware of her child's individual needs. With Sebastian's education she has at times felt out of control, and has not trusted the judgement of the school. This has led to a good deal of active negotiation, and the search for resources other than money to enable her to have some influence in defining the best interests of her child.

(v)   Ellen – developing a close relationship with the school

Ellen is married to a general practitioner, and they live in a mature detached house in a cathedral city, with their three daughters, aged between two and seven at the time of our first contact. Ellen herself has enjoyed motherhood, and regards childhood as a very special time, but she also works 'jolly nearly full-time' and values her career as a senior occupational therapist.

Like Christine, Ellen has used private education as a way of ensuring *continuity* between her home values and the values the children would encounter in school (see the quote from Ellen in Chapter 3). Unlike Christine, however, Ellen expects to have a very close relationship with the school rather than a distant one.

While Ellen's ideas are closely in line with those of the Steiner school teachers, she is also clear that her views do not simply *reflect* those of the school; on the contrary, she herself *sought out* a school that would support her own values:

> it just fitted in so much, as if something supernatural had dropped it into our lap, that is how we felt about it, this just must be right... we still feel very deep down that this is right.

In particular Ellen discussed her strong views about the importance of play for young children – 'precious playtime':

I really strongly believe that very young children should play, they shouldn't try and read and write so early, they shouldn't be bending their heads over books, it will come and it will come much quicker.

She also expressed strong views on the importance of learning coming from 'within the child': 'I like to see them want to learn rather than be made to learn, the motivation comes within the child'.

Ellen had not initially expected to go outside the state system of schooling, but when she visited the local state school, she felt the headmaster did not have a balanced view of children's needs – 'He had absolutely no time for the emotional side of the child'. Having heard about the Steiner school through friends, and decided to send the children there, Ellen still maintained a critical stance and wanted to know more closely what went on:

Keeping our eyes open and going to all the lectures at the school. Getting involved in committees... the meetings were during the day, so I went there and was able to hang about a little bit... And of course I took the chance to meet and talk to the teachers while I was there.

She thus feels she has been able to seek out a school to reflect her own values, and then to work closely with the teachers to develop a harmonious circle between child, mother and teacher. At the same time, the school itself has particular ideas about how pupils should spend their time at home, and Ellen feels there is a complex philosophy to learn about:

I shouldn't really tell you about Steiner education because it's so vast and I don't even understand it myself, I'm just telling you about the impression I had when I had my kids...

Ellen has learned that there are clear ideas, for example, about what sorts of toys are suitable for young children. On the whole, Ellen herself enthusiastically supports these ideas, with some minor differences of view:

Lego shouldn't really be given to a Steiner child because it's plastic, but I still like it, I'm not very rigid ... TV for instance, is out of the question. We haven't got a TV anyway so that again fitted in well with our ideas, we were against

TV right from the start and it was just nice to see that Steiner education doesn't believe in TV and computers...

Over the years, Ellen has developed great enthusiasm and admiration for the school:

> Amazing; it's amazing, we just couldn't believe that the teachers would really do what they say so nicely... The teachers are very approachable, every parent has got the teacher's telephone number and can ring the teacher whenever they need to, and the teacher would find it perfectly normal ... any problem is sorted out, is worked at with great openness between parents and the teacher, that is very important to the school ... we wouldn't have this at the state school.

This close relationship with the school, and the interconnected development of ideas between home and school, can occasionally cause feelings of difference from *other people* outside this circle:

> People might think, I don't know, because people are very conservative aren't they? Conservative – if it's not socially accepted by everybody then it's something weird...they are very reluctant to enter a certain path if somebody hasn't gone there before them...

This has also meant that at times there can be some differences of expectation between Ellen and other mothers which she may then have to negotiate with her own children. Thus when they visit other houses with televisions and a variety of manufactured toys, this can create particular pressures:

> They want to have a Little Pony and they don't understand why they can't have a Little Pony, so I tell them that they've got such and such a toy here so when they come here they can play with this toy, and when they go there they can play with her toy, and they usually accept that until a birthday comes on and, 'I don't want anything else apart from a Pony'. Then I'm in trouble, that's a problem...

In these circumstances, then, it appears that boundaries may occur in rather different circumstances, with a minimal sense of boundary between home and school, and very close contact between mothers and teachers. Instead, there may be differences and tensions between families using different sorts of schools and holding different sorts of childrearing ideas, tensions which the mother may still find herself mediating on behalf of her child, as she strives to help the child to make sense of disparate ideas and different sorts of settings.

(vi)   Emily – opting out

Emily lives in an older semi-detached house in the small rural village where she herself was brought up. She is married to Tom who is a quantity surveyor, and they had three children at the time of our first contact, all boys, aged between seven years and 20 months. Emily herself left school at 16 with some O-levels, and became a secretary in a university. Since having her children, she has had various casual part-time jobs, including care assistant and barmaid.

In a sense, Ellen (above) has found an ally in her children's Steiner school, where she could confidently send her children knowing the school shared her own strong beliefs about the meaning of childhood. Emily, on the other hand, has not found any organised setting outside her home where she feels confident about handing over her children to someone else's authority and care. Consequently, Emily's children have never attended any formal schooling and have never crossed the boundary into an alternative institutional structure.

From the earliest days of being a mother living on a modern council estate in a large town, Emily felt herself to be different from other mothers: 'Before he was even a year old, I felt I was very different to the other mothers in my attitude'. Although friends with neighbouring mothers, she also felt under pressure for being different: 'I used to get really upset and come home and cry'. This difference focused in particular on the issue of breastfeeding, since Emily was the only one still breastfeeding at three months. As a result, she responded to an advert in the newspaper for La Leche League – 'a breastfeeding support group'. This was the first in quite a long line of such moves to make contact with other like-minded parents. Thus she has also been involved with the National Childbirth Trust, a birth centre, the Pre-school Playgroups Association (PPA), and Education Otherwise, and has developed a long reading list of books on relevant topics. While these contacts were first sought out on her own initiative, they have then had a further impact in changing her own ideas. 'La Leche League and PPA were the two, I feel, important beginnings, and this sort of set me off on this path.'

Emily was very explicit about having an overall philosophy of childrearing: 'I think that my way is the right way. I can't help thinking that, but I'm sure there are other ways'. She suggested that all her concerns interlink around the idea of her taking responsibility for herself and her family, with the belief that they can learn to take responsibility also for themselves – 'It's all part of being in charge of yourself'.

This process of taking responsibility for yourself includes self-reliance in health and education. Emily's views on education first developed when she attended courses for playgroup helpers. While she approves of the PPA philosophy she feels that local playgroups do not always reflect this philosophy in practice. She feels social pressure to send her children to playgroup, but has never found a group that really takes the approach she wants. She feels she provides the same experiences and activities at home, and moreover the children themselves do not want to go.

Thus, at the expected time for moving her children outside the immediate family circle, Emily has found it very difficult to find a situation that will reflect her own values. Nevertheless, she described the decision to educate at home as having crept up on them, particularly because of her feelings about the schools in the area where they were living when her eldest child reached school age.

Emily believes it is as important *how* children learn, as that they reach certain educational *goals*, so that learning is a process that children should direct for themselves:

> I want them to be able to be free-thinking and [school] might make them, I think it's quite a strong chance, it would make them so they think that learning is a chore instead of something exciting.

The significance of her son's reading ability does not lie in the fact that he is keeping up with other children of the same age, but because it constitutes evidence that a self-directed child can still achieve the same results. It is also important to her that learning is seen as part of the whole process of life: 'I don't teach them in any formal sense ... absolutely everything they do is learning...' This contrasts markedly with the parents discussed by Atkin et al. who saw education as something where the child has to sit still and be taught:

> You've got to sit down, and she's going to actually teach you how to read, and how to write, and I said, you've got to sit still while she actually teaches you all this... (Mother quoted by Atkin et al., 1988, p. 35).

Atkin et al. also discuss how the parents they interviewed did not clearly distinguish between educational aspects of children's experience of school life, and organisational aspects that children must learn if they are to fit in. Emily, on the other hand, is also concerned about the organisational aspects of school life, as a structure of social relationships:

> I don't want them to be frightened of teachers, I want them to be able to interact, converse with people on a level rather than them being inferior; they teach them all sorts of values that I don't have ... they can make their own minds up about things, and I think that school -- it's just what I think, I don't know – I think school crushes that; teaches them all to just dutifully obey...

Emily's experience of playgroups is that in this respect they do indeed prepare children for school life:

> I see playgroups as a mini school ... my experience is that they're teaching a lot of conformity and a lot of social behaviour... That's not what I want for my children, I don't want them to have to conform to that if they don't want to...

In this respect, she feels a marked contrast between the ways in which they live their family life, and the demands that school would make:

> He couldn't have coped with the discipline of school because we've led such an undisciplined life really, with few constraints or things put upon him, that he has to do things: he could do what he chose to do.

As for peer group contact, Emily feels she provides this on her own terms:

If there is company to be found they go and find it, they just say I'm going off ... there's a play area just over the road. I give them quite a lot of freedom ... and we've always got a garden full of children so I don't think they are deprived of social contact... I suppose if I'm honest they don't play with some people ... they play with my friends' children, and my friends tend to be like me I suppose, so there is some sort of circle that they mix in I suppose...

At the same time, Emily wonders whether she should try to change outside organisations, particularly the playgroups, in line with her beliefs:

I feel in a way I'm opting out instead of getting in the system and improving it for other people; I'm opting out, but I haven't got the energy or the personality ... at the moment, I've got to think of my own family and that's what I'm doing, I'm putting us first.... I feel it's all I can manage at the moment.

By not sending the children to school, Emily has avoided their encounter with school structures and values, and has also kept her home life free from the constraints other mothers learn to take for granted, in terms of the timetabling of family life, and the effects on family roles and concepts of education: 'We just do absolutely everything you could think of, but not in any particular pattern'. Emily has decided not to compromise her family life by entering into such relationships with an outside authority. Nevertheless, she did discuss some concerns about their lifestyle, such as the intensity of the relationships within the house, her powerful position as role model, and her uncertainty about her adequacy for such a responsibility.

SEMI-PERMEABLE BOUNDARIES

Very little attention has been paid to the ways in which the child's participation in the school system permeates into family life. In this regard, Emily's story (above) is particularly striking in the way that it highlights how much is normally taken for granted about the family consequences of the child's school attendance, simply because in her circumstances these effects are absent. In this section I want to draw out some of the permeations that seep across the home–school boundary, and sketch in briefly some consequences for mothers' lives, as well as for their children and other household members. I will first sketch in some permeations that cross from school into family lives, and then move on to consider how mothers may seek to assert some authority or have some effect in relation to their children's school lives.

In considering some of the issues that children's school lives raise for mothers' mediation of family life, there are a number of themes that could be raised. There are for example, implications for the ways in which mothers socialize their children in terms of what it will mean for them to participate in formally organised public life, and questions about the significance of children's school-based identities for how they are perceived within family interactions. There are also major issues about school-based organised time in relation to family-based understandings of time. Attendance at school requires the child's punctual appearance at a particular site at a preordained and regular time dictated by the requirements of organisational coordination, and the primary responsibility for punctual school attendance is seen to fall to mothers (Gregory et al., 1984; Shaw, 1981). There may also be quite different understandings of time within the two institutions of home and school. However, I will here briefly consider just one major theme – the issue of homework and its effects on family lives.

Homework is perhaps the most apparent permeation from school to home life, i.e. when work is set from school to be completed at home. Homework seems to be very widely regarded as a necessary part of education, although there may well be disagreements and societal variations around issues such as how much, in what way, and when it should be introduced. Again, the implications for family life are generally left unremarked, since all parents are expected to support these school-defined educational endeavours without comment. The children's own views on the matter are even less vocalized although, as Atkin et al. comment in relation to mothers' attempts to 'teach' their children at home:

> The dynamics of the parent/child relationship is a factor here as many of their children resisted receiving any action that could be termed direct instruction. (1988, p. 73)

Homework did not occupy many hours amongst the seven-year old children in state schools in my study, yet even so, its impact on family life was already being felt. Homework might be timetabled in as part of the family pattern. In Kate's family this happens as part of the eldest child's time with Kate after the younger siblings are in bed: 'I do reading with him, and his homework, that's our peaceful time which works out.' Finding this time may be very difficult, however, in the midst of competing family and individual priorities. For Susan, who has three children close together in age, her son's spellings have been a particular cause for concern, so that spelling practice is regarded as important, even in the morning:

> It's one mad rush until nine o'clock... I just spend the whole hour shouting, 'Simon, will you get dressed, do this, do that', and then they're fighting most of the time, and then we have breakfast when they're all dressed, and I do spellings with Simon in the morning before he goes to school, and they don't have much breakfast and then it's to school...

In the evening, she tries to find more time for spellings, and family dynamics are affected as a result for everyone:

> We come back and have dinner, then I do more spellings with Simon and try and get the other two to do something quietly or if not Martin [the father] takes them and reads them a story in the other room and then it's bedtime...

Several times she referred to the difficulty of finding the time for him, and they have brought in additional help for his reading and spellings, in the form of an older neighbour who is also a teacher.

Sometimes the school itself initiates and closely structures the ways in which the family can, and are expected, to help with children's education at home. One of the schools in my study had a system of sending words home in a 'word tin' for children to go over with the parent/mother, and later on reading books also came home. As a result, mothers were well aware of how far on in the reading scheme their children were, and parental pleasure at a child's abilities might well be obvious. Rosemary implied that reading the book at home is a sort of performance for the parents, perhaps a form of reinforcement rather than directly teaching the child; '...and when they've read the book at school they are allowed to bring it home and read it to the parents.' This educational activity was thus generally seen as kept under the control of the school. It is worth noting, however, that while mothers might find it difficult to find the time for 'education' at home, no one complained or resisted this role in any way, reflecting their desire to be helpful in this key area of their children's lives. The rhetoric of correct and involved mothering may make it difficult for mothers to voice any associated tensions. And yet:

> Through homework the school's standards and expectations are brought directly into the family, parents – especially the mothers of younger pupils – are confronted with demands for support, above all, the parent–child relationship is impaired.
>
> (Ulich, 1989, p. 182)

Ulich goes on to discuss the evidence of stress experienced by parents in Germany as a result of their young children's homework, and in particular, he emphasises the significant implications for *mothers'* interactions with their children.

In the reverse direction across this semi-permeable home–school boundary, how do women seek to exert any control or have any effect on a day-to-day level over their children's school lives? How do they obtain information about what is going in at school, and how do they deal with issues that are seen as problematic? These questions can be delicate ones for mothers to address if they see themselves as having a continuing role as mediator for their children (as is generally assumed by both mothers and teachers). Certainly the women I interviewed varied considerably in how far they seemed prepared to assert themselves with educational authorities, and how far they deferred to teachers' opinions and felt vulnerable to their judgements – 'Her teacher said to me, "Where on earth did she come from, she's so noisy and you two are both so quiet?" I feel terrible' (Mary, ex-secretary). Cleave et al. (1982) found that the majority of infant school parents regarded 'the staff with uncertainty tinged with distrust and a sensitivity so prickly that a contact could be destroyed at a word' (pp. 101–2). Yet, given that both teachers and mothers may feel that they should be having contact for the sake of the children, who controls how this happens and towards what issues?

All the women discussed above confirm the widespread evidence that parents from a great variety of social groups do care a great deal about how their children achieve within the educational system (e.g. Connell et al., 1982; Tomlinson and Hutchinson, 1990; Ulich, 1989). Yet they have very little day-to-day control, or even knowledge, of what happens to their children within the educational setting, despite the contemporary rhetoric of parental participation (Cleave et al., 1982). As Atkin et al. point out:

> In providing opportunities for parental access, schools filter and screen opportunities for parents to see the life and work of the school, often in a very limiting way. (Atkin et al., 1988, p. 46)

For some women, the least stressful way of dealing with such potential tensions was to avail themselves of all opportunities the school provides for making contact. This approach may be seen as likely to give their children particular advantages, as O'Donnell discusses in relation to her study of American mothers:

> 'I think it's pretty well accepted that if you're going to go into the school and work, your kids are going to get priority treatment...' (Mother). Other mothers agreed that by being involved in children's schools they were able to find out about ... special programmes and activities. Additionally– and perhaps more importantly – they are able to get an eyewitness account of what went on behind school doors.
> (O'Donnell, 1985, p. 144)

In my own study, contact between teachers and parents/ mothers was very largely carried out within the parameters set by the state schools, in terms of concerts, etc. put on at significant times of year, mothers going into some schools to help with reading, cookery, etc., and formal meetings to discuss children's educational progress.

In the schools concerned, mothers did not see the teachers informally when leaving and collecting children. In their much larger British study, Cleave et al. found that this pattern was established soon after children started school:

> It was as if a boundary became established beyond which parents waited for their children... Why the waiting place became established where it did was not always clear... Boundaries in the infant schools were more rigid and remote than any observed in pre-schools. (1982, p. 100)

Consequently, for the women I interviewed, any conversation with teachers had to be deliberately sought out. While some mothers were prepared to do this, there could be anxiety and hesitation about making what amounted to a definite and deliberate decision to 'have a word' with teachers. There are parallels here with definitions of sickness and health and anxieties about defining problems as 'serious' enough to take to a doctor (Urwin, 1985). Atkin et al. also discuss the length of time that parents may take to focus clearly upon what may be felt as a 'nagging problem' (1988, p. 56), and then to decide to speak about it at school. There might thus be:

> extended and detailed introspection and cud-chewing, until a clearer understanding of the problem and a confidence in one's own efforts to challenge the school effectively begin to emerge (1988, p. 57).

Mothers may hold considerable fears of antagonising teachers, limiting their assertiveness in relation to schools.

> I was *very* aware of the power that she (the teacher) was going to have over my child, so I didn't dare push it because I knew there were a thousand and one ways she could get back through the child.
> (Teacher-parent quoted by Atkin et al. 1988, p. 75)

Blatchford et al. found evidence of such attitudes arising even in relation to nurseries:

> Parents were generally wary of doing anything they believed teachers would find unacceptable and were fearful of being out of their depth with more 'educational' demands. (1982, p. 164)

Susan described her son's school as maintaining clear boundaries with parents, keeping mothers at a distance:

> They don't actually have Parent/Teacher [Association]. That's one thing we don't really like about his school. They don't involve the parents that much. In other schools, because there are big classes, they involve the mums to read with the kids ... but they don't do anything there like that. I wouldn't mind going in and helping at all, because it benefits all the children.

While Susan had taken an active part in contacting the school when problems were identified, this was hampered by lack of communication and knowledge. Anticipating trouble from the headmistress, she took her husband along with her:

> He brought these spellings home and you just thought – crumbs, hadn't realised. You go to the school on all the open evenings and they say he's fine, and this and that, and it comes as a bit of a shock when he didn't know what letters are when you're doing spelling, so we have chased it up a bit and the school are keeping a closer eye on him…. When we went to see them about Simon we thought we're going to have a bit of fun but she was nice and understood… I thought she was going to say, 'Oh, mind your own business', but in fact she's very good, so we were quite surprised. She said come back at any time if we're worried. They don't really involve the parents but I think if you make an effort they're quite interested to talk to you and we were quite pleased we went.

When mothers act as mediators on behalf of their children at school, there is (as a minimum) a triangular relationship involved, of mother, child and teacher (with other parties also involved at times). Within this web of relationships, variable and shifting alliances are possible. A mother might thus, for example:

(i)   ally herself with a teacher in order to impose a joint perspective on the child (a 'united front') based on a shared understanding of what they consider to be the child's best interests; Ulich (1989) cites evidence to suggest that this approach can be experienced as particularly problematic by the pupils themselves;

(ii)   interpose herself between the child and the teacher in a position that protects the child while she negotiates on behalf of the child with the teacher;

(iii) stand behind the child to be supportive but expecting the child her/himself to speak up with the teacher.

The first approach, of an alliance between mother and teacher, occurred when Marie's daughter quarrelled with friends:

> I went up to see her teacher and I said, 'She's coming home crying every day.' … She said to me she hates the children

having best friends, she likes them all to mix anyway. And I said that I said to Anna, 'Why can't the three of them play happily?'

Kay also allied herself with the teacher after receiving a complaint about her son at the pre-arranged teacher interview:

> The last time I saw his teacher for the teacher interview, and he'd been through this stroppy stage and he'd started being rude to her... She said, 'It's beginning to grate, it's not on.' ... I know he does it to me, and it grates when he does it to me, but I said to her, 'I'm not having it'... I said I was going to give him a good grilling when he got home, which I did do.

Hilary's account, on the other hand, expressed shifting emphases between the second and third approaches, i.e. whether it was herself or her child that she expected to undertake negotiations with the school, to assert his needs. In this incident she expected the teacher to respond to her request and recognise her son's particular difficulties around the question of asthma and eczema, and then act as an ally with the other pupils:

> One particular child said something to him, but it sorted itself out ... this girl just didn't have her facts straight, the minute she was told it was all right.

> [You explained it to her did you?]

> Yes. She was in another class. And if it was problem I would have probably gone and seen his teacher and asked her to explain it to the group of children including this girl perhaps...

However, Hilary also believes that children should take responsibility for themselves, and thus also expected her son to speak up about his needs for himself:

> We went to school and I said, 'He is very allergic to [fungi]', and she said, 'I've got one on the table over there'. And I said, 'Matthew, why didn't you say?', and he said he didn't feel he could. But I think he should learn he can go up to his teacher and say, 'Look I know this is nice but could you put it in a plastic bag or something,' and help him to help himself a bit.

Where mothers are not so happy with the outcome of contact with teachers, they may take independent action to *increase the resources available* to deal with a perceived difficulty, e.g. by paying for tutoring help, or developing organised weekend schools. Resources may also be mobilized by mothers as a way of increasing their power in negotiations with teachers, as in the example of Christine (discussed above). Within all this, while all parties may express their overriding concern with the needs of the child, what is the nature of the child and her/his needs itself becomes contested terrain, alongside differing views about the nature of families and schools as social units. Mothers themselves may feel quite torn between these different sorts of expectation:

> The parents are always faced with the conflict of trying to cushion the harshness of school, so as to alleviate the emotional and physical strains on their children; at the same time they themselves exert pressure on their children – often against their will or feelings – so as to keep all opportunities open for them'.
> (Sass/Holzmuller 1982, 8f, quoted by Ulich, 1989, p. 181)

The case studies described in this chapter reveal the extent to which home–school contact occurs on terms set by the schools themselves, even though the women have taken a variety of approaches towards their children's schools. Parental involvement in schools is quite carefully managed in ways that teachers may not consciously recognise – both in terms of tasks and people who are allowed in. Lareau suggests that this in itself is a factor which keeps (middle-class) fathers particularly at more of a distance from day-to-day interactions with the school:

> A few fathers spoke explicitly about the problems they had deferring to teachers' control of the classroom ... mothers were more likely than fathers to reveal doubts and anxieties about their right to challenge teachers' decisions... [Middle class] fathers did not express similar feelings of anxiety about their interactions with teachers. Some said plainly that teachers did not intimidate them. Nor did fathers appear anxious or withdrawn in their visits to the school.
> (Lareau, 1989, pp. 91–3)

For some of the fathers, however, this unwillingness to defer to teachers' authority meant they did not feel able to have close and informal contact, e.g. by helping out in classroom activities. Mothers, on the other hand, may have felt that continuing

informal contacts with teachers depended upon their willingness to display some deference, or at least not to challenge
teachers – as is exemplified by all the women discussed above
from my own study, whose children were in state schools and
who all felt a need not to be seen to be challenging the
school's authority in their contacts with them. As Kate
remarked: 'I mean parents are not trying to take over, we're
only there to help...'

It is clear from existing policies and current rhetoric
throughout Western industrialised societies, that ideas about
parental choice are generally focused on the choice of school
in the first place, and do not extend to parental choice about
aspects of the child's experience within the school itself,
except in very limited ways (Macbeth, 1984; Raywid, 1985).
The mothers I interviewed had little control over the particular individuals who would take charge of their children, and
did not feel able to ensure that they have handed their children over to the care of someone who would use this authority
in ways of which they approved. The *possibility* of discrepancies
between mothers' own expectations, and the ways in which the
school exercised its authority and responsibility, held the
potential for considerable tensions:

> Altogether there can be little doubt that most parents and
> pupils have quite considerable problems with school today ...
> because it has become simultaneously more important, more
> difficult and more stressful. (Ulich, 1989, p. 181)

Children's entry into formal education and subsequent
school life is described as a very significant boundary that has
to be crossed, beyond which the mother has very little control.
The mother's concerns with '*the family*' unit receive very little
recognition from the school system, except perhaps in terms of
according priority to siblings if there is competition for places
in a particular school. Indeed, Macbeth (1989) suggests that
'the school exists, in part, to *separate* the child from the family'
(p. 12). Furthermore, while the teacher and the mother may
share the focus on the child as '*an individual*', they may not
share their perceptions of the nature of this individuality and
what education of the individual may mean. Unless the mother
feels able to trust the teacher and the school, she may experience considerable anxiety at her loss of control. While there
may well be variations in how maternal responsibility has been

exercised in the pre-school years (e.g. whether or not substitute care has been provided), as Pascall (1986) makes clear, formal school entry is the first major transition from the private into the public sphere. The mother perceives that the child has to be *compulsorily* relinquished to the authority of the teacher, and yet feels unsure as to whether she can safely entrust her child to this different institution, and to the judgements of others. If she feels critical, she may work to exert some influence, without herself being labelled a 'pushy' mother. There are thus complex issues here about responsibility, control and authority between mothers and teachers.

Children enter school as individuals outside the family unit, involving a dramatic reduction in maternal supervision and authority compared with the pre-school years. While some women may seek to assert their own definitions of children's needs within the school system, and may mobilise various resources in order to do so, children's lives at home are also substantially affected by their experiences in the school setting in ways that may be quite taken for granted. While the boundary between home and school is very significant, influences may cross it in both directions. This particular boundary between home and school, however, is not one where women feel the same degree of control as the boundaries they themselves negotiate and cross in the more informal and semipublic settings of pre-school childcare.

CONCLUDING REMARKS

In this chapter and the previous one, I have been seeking to explore the nature of the home–school boundary as it is experienced by mothers, in the light of the different sorts of expectations that may occur in homes (the private arena) and schools (the public arena). These different expectations may be conceptualized as 'contrasting principles of social organization' (Cheal, 1991) or as different 'ways of being' (Edwards and Ribbens, 1991). I have sought in this discussion to indicate some of the complex and variable tensions that may surround the definition and negotiation of the home–school boundary in contemporary Western societies.

These are issues that will be examined further in Chapter 7, in relation to Ros Edwards' research with mothers whose own educational experiences are continuing during their children's own school years. Yet the discussion in this chapter is intended to show the extent to which there are (probably inevitable) tensions inherent at the interface between home and school lives, regardless of the social class or educational qualifications of the mothers/parents. Even amongst parents who were themselves teachers, Atkin et al. (1988) describe the extent to which they varied in their degree of assertiveness with schools. Only some felt able to assert a high level of power in relation to the school, drawing upon a sense of personal power (although what this is based upon is itself a further question). Many other teacher-parents, however, like the mothers interviewed in my own research, felt the need to 'maintain a low profile' or 'tread a fine line'.

Finally, however, we must return to the theme from which I began this discussion of mothers and primary education in Chapter 3 – how do issues of maternal authority relate to issues of maternal responsibility? Thus we must take care to consider that asserting control in relation to a child's schooling may not just be an issue of empowerment for mothers. 'Parents can make a powerful case for *not* becoming actively involved in their children's schools' (Atkin et al., 1988, p. 65; emphasis added). In the previous chapter I suggested that maternal responsibility can potentially lead to power and authority, but equally, the exercise of power and control in relation to education can itself be translated into a maternal responsibility and become a source of new obligation. The political aspects of our language are very apparent here – at what point does 'empowerment' become 'responsibility', and 'responsibility' become 'duty'? Women themselves, as well as educators, are likely to have their own (variable) views as to how far they wish to exert such power in relation to their children's schooling and take on such maternal responsibilities. While Emily (discussed earlier) has been able to resist much publicly-based authority by keeping her children outside the school system, this has also greatly increased her maternal responsibilities, which many women might find an insupportable source of personal limitation.

At other times, language will be used in ways that gloss over the potential tensions between home and school, mothers and teachers, most centrally, through unexamined but highly political notions of 'children's needs' (Woodhead, 1990). While such glossing over may enable tensions to be obscured, I have tried to show through these two chapters that homes are indeed regarded as different sorts of social units from schools, such that 'the child' at home may be conceived differently from 'the child' at school.

Furthermore, mothers are operating within different sets of considerations from teachers. Then there is the further question of where and how mothers and teachers situate 'education' within all this. All of these are issues that research has hardly begun to address, which await further investigations. These questions are of great significance not only for the lives of children, mothers and educationalists, but also for our more general understanding of what it means to be a member of society in contemporary industrialised Western countries.

Part Two
Women as Consumers: Mothers and Post-School Education

5 Home Base: Policy on the Education of Women as Adults
Mary Hughes

This chapter is concerned with the development of policy in post-school education. In particular, I illustrate the general argument by taking adult education as an example of educational provision for adults as distinct from further and higher education. (See for example Blunden, pp. 153–62, in Acker et al., 1984; Thomas, 1990) Women have been accorded a different status to men both in policy and practice by both default and design. Adult education has been referred to as a 'women's service' (Keddie, 1981). Traditionally, it has confined women's horizons to the home. I will argue that it is a service for women but not a service of women. I will consider, in particular, whether adult education for women has really been non-vocational and a leisure-time activity as it has been assumed commonly to be. In addition, I want to consider the meaning of adult in the term adult education in relation specifically to women.

Adult education has a problematic status in terms of social policy because of the difficulty of defining precisely what it is and what its purpose is. Adult could appear to refer to the status of the person studying whereas the terms further and higher education appear to refer to the stage and content of the education process. Consequently it could be argued that it encompassed any structured learning situation for adults. Some adult educators would probably say that much of the content is similar to some of the courses offered by further and higher education but that the ethos and environment is different, being geared to the specific learning, psychological and social needs of individual adult students. This would include, for example, flexible timetabling at local sites with good transport facilities and childcare provision (see Sperling: 1991, 119–213). I am not saying that these kinds of issue are not addressed by the other two sectors but that they have been of particular relevance to adult education students, often women and mothers who do not have the practical or psychological freedom that would pertain to younger students. I would argue that in recent years adult education, particularly in urban areas, has led the educational field in addressing issues of equal opportunities and access, sometimes referred to as the hidden curriculum.

There has been considerable debate as to whether adult education is something that is undertaken largely by choice and is 'provided solely for the individual's benefit, untainted by other considerations – or at least that considerations about the individual benefits are much more prominent' (Finch: 1984:91). Thomas, in arguing that higher education has been largely excluded from consideration by educational sociologists, suggested that this was in part because it was not compulsory. She added, 'it is perhaps difficult to argue that something which is a matter of choice can in any sense be repressive' (Thomas, 1990, 6–7).

A comparable argument could be made for adult education but Finch has suggested that whilst in theory it has a strong commitment to the ideal of individual self-improvement it also has the potential for fundamental change. She identified, however, a 'profound tension' between 'personal development' and 'social purpose' in public policy. Social purpose being seen as the maintenance of an uncomplaining and conforming populace. 'The case of adult education therefore supports the general conclusion that "individual's benefit" rationales for education seldom get translated into public policy unless they are linked with justification which relate to "society's benefits".' (Finch, 1984, p. 94).

This being so, Griffen has argued that because adult education has not received a massive amount of public funding, unlike the school system, being referred to by one writer as the 'poor cousin' (Newman: 1979), it has not been the object of contending public policy models or ongoing ideological struggles to the same extent. Consequently, it 'has not much been conceptualised or theorised in terms of its socialising functions, or its function in respect of social control or social mobility, the production of the work force, the domestication and reproduction of labour, and so on'. (Griffen, 1987, pp. 136–7).

Thompson has suggested that:

The extent to which adult education contributes to the trans-
mission of values and attitudes which reflect the interests of
dominant groups in society is a condition of adult education
which is, as yet, under-researched and largely ignored by
adult education.

(Thompson, 1980, p. 24)

She has also contended that: 'Most adult educators would
argue that their practices are not equivalent to those of the
school ... and as such do not merit the same kind of scrutiny'
(Thompson, 1983, p. 61).

I suggest that this may be the defensive reaction of educators
who feel somewhat marginalised from the educational system,
not being entirely clear of its purpose and status. I would argue,
nevertheless, that adult education is a part of the total education system but in some ways has been seen as an adjunct to it,
or as it was referred to in one article, as 'always an awkward side
show in the apparent view of ministers'. (THES, 13 March
1992) I want later to unpack why this should be so. As the
Alexander Report on adult education in Scotland noted, it:

is influenced by broadly the same factors as influence the
rest of the educational provision. In addition, the character
of school education has a considerable influence on all post-
school education as regards the foundations on which it has
to build and gaps it may have to fill.

(Scottish Education Department, 1975, p. 19)

Keddie wrote:

Historically, the mission of adult educat.ion was informed by
a desire to reach those in society who had benefited least
from the influence of education. Although this remains an
element in the contemporary adult educator's ideology, the
emphasis has shifted so that it is now a matter of taking a
better kind of education to those whose previous education
has been misconceived.

(Keddie, 1980, p. 46)

As Westwood has argued many working-class people have been
alienated by the school system and have consequently been
less keen than their middle-class counterparts to take advantage of the choices offered by adult education, which they have
perceived as being part of the same system:

Adult education has a social class bias born out of the defeats
of the school classrooms and its organisation, in terms of
classes, courses, teachers and its physical location within
schools, colleges and universities which represent to the
majority of people a reproduction of school practices.

(Westwood, 1980, p. 37)

Initially, state adult education was seen as a continuation of
day-school provision for those young people and adults who
had not had adequate initial schooling. It was not conceived as
having a remedial function. It offered the same curriculum as
the schools and was regarded as a precursor of further education and vocational training. The corollary was that there was
less of the latter for girls and adult education assumed a
vocational role for them, I will argue, in a way which it did not
for boys and young men, for whom it began to focus on leisure
and hobby activities. I will return to this point latter in this
chapter. Alongside this instrumental type of education was a
concern to develop the concepts and ideas of citizenship with
a concentration on the liberal arts. This was traditionally the
field of the universities and voluntary organisations but also
became a part of state provision. Gradually, adult education
for women who formed the majority of students, although
maintaining largely the same curriculum emphasis, began to
be equated with a safe and comfortable leisure or recreational
activity. What had initially been targeted at the working classes
began to be taken over by more middle-class students who had
probably had a better experience of the schooling system and
recognised the benefits of education.

From the 1970s there was a move in Britain and in other
developed countries to provide a remedial type of education
for those who had been failed by initial schooling or for whom
English was not their first language, for example. There was
also an increasing recognition that a front-end model of education would never be sufficient preparation for people living
in an increasingly complex and changing world. It was at this
stage that adult education began to develop stronger links
with other parts of the post-school educational sectors and to
provide clear points of entry and progression routes into further and higher education.

With the increasing emphasis and concern for vocational

training in recent years in all developed and developing countries there has been an attempt both to colonise those parts of the adult education service which support this move into the area of further and higher education and to denigrate and to make even more insecure in policy and funding terms those parts of the adult education service which do not appear to complement directly this kind if provision (Merriam and Cunningham, 1979; Ogelsby, 1991a, pp. 159–61; Ogelsby, 1991b, pp. 133–44; Lichtner, 1991, pp. 154–67; SCUTREA, 1990; Titmuss, 1981; Williamson, 1991, pp. 211–27).

The concentration on further education and training has become particularly acute in England/Wales because of the realisation that English/Welsh young people are lagging behind their counterparts not only in developed countries but also in some parts of the Third World in the quality and quantity of this provision. The Further and Higher Education Act 1992 will separate what has been traditionally conceived as non-vocational and leisure adult education in terms of both providers and funding from more vocationally orientated and instrumental education. This will lead to much of what has been traditionally regarded as the staple diet of adult education being even more marginalised and insecure in terms of both funding and status, remaining under local authority control, whilst the rest will form a part of an independent further and higher education sector. This will have a detrimental effect on educational opportunities for many women, particularly those who are mothers of dependent children.

LEA [Local Education Authority] classes attract a larger proportion of women than men in their thirties ... They are particularly important for younger married women, who are at home caring for children, and have few other learning opportunities...To separate further education from local authority provision and only to provide financial support for specified areas of mainly vocational and qualifying provision is likely to seriously damage opportunities for women, many of whom use such opportunities as a way of keeping in touch, returning to learning and thence to paid employment as their children grow older. (Sargant, 1991, p. 12)

It has been suggested that 60 per cent of the adult education provision in Islington, a part of London, could be hived off leaving an unviable LEA service.

ADULT EDUCATION – A WOMEN'S SERVICE

Adult education has been referred to as a 'women's service'.
(Keddie, p. 50 in Hughes and Kennedy, 1985) Taking a feminist
perspective I want to examine what this means in both practice
and policy and to unpack some of the commonly held assumptions about adult education. In particular, I want to examine
the notion that it is a non-vocational and leisure-time service for
adults and to suggest that as far as women students in particular
are concerned this has often been a misnomer. A misnomer
which has contributed to its marginal and expendable status.

Adult education has been called a 'women's service' because
there are more women students (approximately 80 per cent
in LEA provision) and more women staff (approximately 60
per cent) than men. Yet Mee and Wiltshire found that in
English LEA provision there were 87.3 per cent male organ-
isers and only 12.7 per cent women – nearly nine men to every
woman. By organiser they meant someone who had responsibility for planning a programme (Mee and Wiltshire: 1978:
59). In 1986 the International Council for Adult Education
did an evaluation of the service internationally, an evaluation
found still to be true in 1990:

> It would appear that the structure of the adult education
> movement still remains firmly in the control of men. That is,
> men occupy a disproportionate number of positions on
> boards or executive committees and as secretary-general or
> executive directors of ICAE's member associations at all
> levels. Men tend to be the fund-raisers and power brokers of
> the movement. (International Council for Adult Education,
> October/November, 1990)

Whilst it may have become a service for women it can in no
way be described as a service of women. Obviously, women
could vote with their feet and stay away if what is provided is
not what they want and we must assume that for those women
who do attend they are getting something positive out of the
experience. But we must also question how much choice
women students feel they actually have in changing the
curriculum offer or any other part of the service. I will argue
that, traditionally, adult education has been permeated by the
dominant ideology of separate spheres for men and women
which has led to a large imput of a domestically orientated

curriculum as the backbone to its range of activities. This has tended, I suggest, to reinforce the boundary between the home-based lives of women and the outside world. Additionally, adult education has largely had a different purpose and place in the lives of women than it has had for men. It has been compatible with and directly relevant to mothers in a way which is not apparent to men as fathers. I suggest that, for women as mothers or potential mothers, adult education has complemented to some extent their vocation or duty as homemakers and preservers of home life. In addition, it has sometimes supported their paid work in servicing others, either as domestics, particularly in the early part of this century, or in other parts of the paid labour market. It has emphasised and supported women's servicing role and I would argue offered to women surreptitious vocational training. I use the word surreptitious because I believe that this aspect has rarely been made explicit in policy or practice.

It has been common for girls, particularly but not exclusively those of lower ability, often a euphemism for working-class girls, to have a large injection of domestic subjects in their school timetable, this being in preparation for and anticipation of their future roles of wives and mothers. How useful this has been has been questioned (Turnbull quoted in Purvis, 1991, p. 29). I suggest that historically, adult education has also been seen to have a role to play in this process of domestication. In part, it has mirrored and reflects the debates and practices within the domestic curriculum of the schools. I believe that this is partly because the role of an adult woman is very different from that of a man. Adulthood has not been equated for girls with a move outside of the home environment to the same extent as it has for boys. I would argue that there is often a less clear demarcation or boundary between the roles that girls and women undertake than between those of boys and men. Whatever else a woman does she is expected to assume primary responsibility for organising and running a home and bringing up a family. One result of these factors has been the development of a sex-segregated curriculum offer within what is officially described as a comprehensive and co-educational adult education service.

One reason for the emphasis on a domestic curriculum may be the lack of women in policy-making and management positions but it may be more fundamental than this. It has come to be a service for women whose basic roles have not changed even when they have assumed wider responsibilities. Even the Ministry of Education wrote in 1956 in a pamphlet on the evening institutes, which still remain a common organisational model for the delivery of adult education in England:

> The evening institute has not, in times past, been one of those institutions which breed educational revolution, nor does it appear likely that we may expect any such to emerge in the future.
>
> (Ministry of Education, 1956, p. 3)

HAS ADULT EDUCATION FOR WOMEN TRADITIONALLY BEEN NON-VOCATIONAL?

> 'The judgement as to whether a subject is vocational or non-vocational is made by learners, who know what they want to learn and why they want to learn it. Examples of this are two of the most popular subjects, foreign languages and computer studies.'
>
> (Sargant, 1991, p. 14)

The traditional ethos of adult education for women has been clearly vocational as it related directly to their vocations as unpaid mothers, housewives and carers. I think that women would see this connection more clearly than men, who would be more ambivalent. There has always been some credence given to the idea that women who did not undertake *paid* work but who stayed at home did not in fact work but lived to some extent a life of leisure. I will return to the concept of leisure later in this chapter.

Vocational education or training has often been narrowly skill-based and connected with a specific paid job. It has frequently been part-time and undertaken both within and outside work time. Domestically orientated non-vocational adult education fulfils all these criteria except that women do not get paid for their work or their training.

Despite being a voluntary activity and unconstrained by external examinations and syllabuses there has been a surprisingly large common core curriculum in adult education institutions. Mee and Wiltshire found that three-quarters of the

22 761 courses they examined in LEA provision were basically similar (Mee and Wiltshire, 1978, p. 41). Their research showed that the curriculum was divided into four broad categories.

1. *Craft and Aesthetic Skills*
    (i) Courses related mainly to personal care and household economy (33.6 per cent).
    (ii) Courses related mainly to leisure-time enjoyment (19.5 per cent).
2. *Physical Skills*
    (i) Courses related mainly to health and fitness (9.3 per cent).
    (ii) Courses related to leisure-time enjoyment (14.8 per cent).
3. *Intellectual and Cognitive Skills*
    (i) Language courses (10.9 per cent).
    (ii) Other courses (5.8 per cent).
4. *Courses for Disadvantaged Groups* (6.1 per cent).
                                    (Mee and Wiltshire: 1978: 32)

The largest type of provision, one-third, was concerned with female domestic arts and crafts, beauty culture, car maintenance, cookery, dressmaking, flower arrangement, gardening and soft-furnishing. This was and is also the staple diet of the Townswomen's Guilds, the Women's Institutes and other voluntary women's organisations which provide classes. Whilst new subjects have been added to the programme this large percentage of domestic subjects appears to still remain, for example, in London in 1968–9, 189 different subjects were offered but one-third of the 3 238 classes were in domestic crafts. The next largest related to health and fitness helping to ensure not only that women were physically fit to do all that was required of them but that they would also remain attractive to the opposite sex. Purvis wrote:

> Yet, despite these contrasts with the past, the most popular of the range of courses for women students in adult education today include those subjects so familiar to historians of women's history, namely various 'homecrafts' such as dressmaking, cookery and cake-icing. It would appear that women's choices in adult education are still constrained by ideas about their femininity. (1991, p. 129)

In the last ten years the number of women studying domestic crafts in a formal setting has fallen considerably, probably partly because of the increasing emphasis on vocational training for paid work, although there is a clear difference between working and non-working women. The latter study more of the former than working women. (Sargant, 1991, p. 14) However, working-class women are twice as likely to study home-based skills as the upper-class group. (Sargant, 1991, p. 55). Sports and physical activity are less studied in a formal sense but are increasingly popular as leisure-time activities. Domestic subjects and sports still figure largely in women's informal learning and leisure time activities.

> It would appear that people are redefining some activities as leisure rather than as learning. In other instances, it is not clear whether the repositioning as informal learning is due negatively to a decrease in formal provision or whether it is due positively to an increase in the possibilities of alternative methods of learning and choice of delivery systems.
>
> (Sargant, 1991, p. 16)

Sargant indicated that many subjects of informal learning are instrumental in their use and are often related to vocational purposes. (1991, p. 64) Whilst there are obviously less classes for domestic instruction than there were previously it may also be that women realise that they do not need formal instruction in what is in essence a natural vocation, preferring to learn on their own or more probably through family and friends. Could it also be that women have less time for their own education, being busy with that of their children?

There is no doubt that adult education in the early part of this century for women and girls (after they left school at fourteen or earlier) was clearly meant to train them for their jobs as wives and mothers and for work as domestic servants. These were in short supply, and often thought inadequate. It provided a similar function for women to further or technical education provided to boys and men.

Women were considered crucial to the maintenance of a happy and healthy family life, the key to the nation's future prosperity. Consequently they needed to be trained for what, ironically, was conceived of as their natural vocation. Surely one should assume they would already be proficient in this role as it was a part of their 'feminine' nature? Adult education for women was seen, pragmatically, as vocational training. Devereux, writing of the adult institutes established for women in London in 1913, stated clearly that: 'the work of the women's institutes in the domestic and needlecrafts was not regarded as non-vocational. Certainly the women's institutes were not regarded as non-vocational institutes at that time' (1982, p. 68). The same point was made by Bertha Sokoloff:

> While the men's provision had a clear structure of vocational and non-vocational education, *the early women's institutes blurred the lines*, and in handling domestic training, laundry work and needlework, often taught skills which women found directly useful in paid work as well as the language, literature, drama, dancing, art and general education, which were regarded as more for personal enrichment.
>
> (Sokoloff, 1987, p. 75; my emphasis)

Even the Russell Report in 1973 recognised that women had the potential to earn money from skills acquired in adult education classes:

> There are arrangements in some parts of the country for women students of dress subjects from local adult institutes to take courses which will develop both their subject knowledge and their ability to teach to the point where they, in turn, become part-time adult tutors.
>
> (DES, 1973, para. 336)

The boundary between education for work or for personal enrichment was, as Sokoloff states, blurred. Gradually, as women came to have fewer children and were maybe relieved of some of their domestic drudgery with the introduction of labour-saving devices in the home leisure, or free non-obligated, time became more of a reality for some women. The domestic curriculum was offered to them as recreational, non-vocational activities. They were also given the odd more light-hearted class in, for example, drama, dance or singing to sugar the pill of a rather unexciting diet. There was a move away from a concentration on the 'make do and mend' type of classes with an increasing emphasis on taste and design; what I refer to as the keeping up with the Jones's syndrome. There were classes in, for example, designer dressmaking, *cordon bleu* or hostess cookery and interior decoration.

If after the Second World War officially women with young children were not expected to work outside the home, even if reality was somewhat different, a rationale for this had to be provided. Homemaking had to become both a science and an art with an emphasis on higher standards, on the homemade, on the unique and on the intricate. A government pamphlet on Further Education in 1947 had the following comment:

> Too often in the past there has been a lack of imagination in planning programmes of this kind, and indeed for women's classes generally. They were too often limited to the traditional craft classes in needlecrafts and cookery, and to first-aid and home nursing ... There are opportunities in cookery classes, for example, for discussion on the planning of a balanced diet. Dressmaking is a subject that can cover the whole complex and important art which produces the well-dressed woman, and can include guidance in buying materials and considerations of style, design and colour to suit the individual, as well as the prosaic but ever necessary make-do-and-mend. Classes in housecraft and home management give scope for a wide variety of interests: repair and decoration to fabric and furniture, planning good colour schemes, the best organisation of domestic equipment, family budgeting, the planning of the day's work and leisure. Health classes, besides covering the usual home nursing syllabus, can consider the needs of different ages in regard to nutrition and clothing, while in the programme of a class in child study, discussion of the physical and psychological development of children may well be varied with some practical work, for example, in making children's clothes and toys.
>
> (Ministry of Education, 1947, pp. 51–2)

Although there was still a place for the more basic classes, essentially for those deemed to be 'disadvantaged' or deficient, in reality working-class women had been replaced in adult education classes by women of the lower-middle and middle classes, the former being turned off education by their experiences at the hands of the schooling system (see Westwood, 1980). They also had less time and money to engage in these kinds of activity. These classes were being, and continue to be represented as women's interests, as recreational activities and as a corollary non-vocational. In 1960 a report for the National Institute of Adult Education (NIAE) was arguing that, 'women's subjects are commonly and properly considered a part of liberal adult education' (Groombridge: 1960: 54).

What we see developing is the idea of the whole woman who can be all things to all men, most importantly to her husband and her children. Glynis Cousin wrote, 'arguably they [women] have bought the idea of improving their womanly selves'. (1990, p. 39) Not only did women have to be proficient in so-called neutral practical skills, they had to be physically attractive, hence an emphasis on classes such as keep fit, slimnastics and of course beauty care. We have already seen the concentration on the acquisition of good taste. This extended into an appreciation of a smattering of culture along the lines of the nineteenth-century construct of the lady of leisure with her range of accomplishments. This included offering courses in subjects such as languages, art-appreciation, history and philosophy – the inculcation of the 'great tradition' of our cultural heritage. These subjects, referred to as liberal adult education in Britain and the liberal arts in the United States, had been in past times largely the preserve of the universities, the WEA and other voluntary organisations but were not excluded from the local authority provision.

I believe that Groombridge makes a false premise when he refers to women's subjects as being a part of liberal adult education. I suggest that there is little or no connection or linkage between the two areas. The common denominator is the woman herself who was expected to become competent in a wider range of subjects. The following quote from the same writer shows that he had to link women's subjects with more liberal provision in order to give the lie to the fact that a large part of adult education provision for women was unmistakably vocational. If this was not achieved then the justification for adult education being liberal education for the personal enrichment and development of the individual was in jeopardy. If adult education was considered vocational then it had implications for more than the individual which of course as far as women were concerned it clearly had. It had implications for the home life of men and children.

Although in a sense such classes [women's] have a vocational value, there is also a liberal and social element and an absence of examination pressures in education of this kind that differentiates it sharply from most male vocational training.

(Groombridge, 1960, p. 54)

Later in the same report, Groombridge displays an ambivalence which is apparent in other policy documents on adult education about the ideology and reasoning around provision for women: 'Women find classes a help in their work and it is, of course, always difficult to decide whether cookery and dressmaking, for instance, should or should not be regarded as vocational subjects for housewives' (ibid., p. 144).

I have no doubt that adult education provision for women has provided for their training in domesticity although policy-makers have continued to blurr the boundaries between the meaning of non-vocational and vocational education. Margaret Cole, a long serving member of the London County Council Educational Committee and an exponent of adult education was certainly clear about what she thought:

"non-vocational" ... is another tiresome and misleading term; it means in effect "classes which do not prepare you directly for earning a living". But since the bulk of women who go to evening institutes are taking classes in cookery, dressmaking, home management, etc., etc., the persistence of the phrase merely reflects the obsolete idea, long popularised by the males responsible for the census returns, that homemaking, being unpaid, was not a serious occupation.

(Cole, 1956, p. 68)

Writing a year earlier, E. Malcolm Firth, Principal of a London women's institute commented somewhat facetiously, 'Yes! Cookery was considered a recreational subject!' (Firth, 1955, p. 170) Cousin summed up the argument neatly:

Although few would argue that subjects like microwave cookery and keep fit actually fulfil the aims prescribed in a liberal education, these subjects are implicated in the debate about liberal education because of their presumed non-vocationalism. The range of subjects is, of course, only non-vocational in so far as it rarely leads to paid work. In another sense, LEA provision of this kind is profoundly vocational in that it is concerned with the jobs of wife and mother. This understanding has yet to find a place in the current preoccupations about vocationalism and liberal adult education. The false dichotomy between vocationalism and non-vocationalism ... is not false simply because the two overlap; it is false because non-vocationalism is a misnomer for much that is labelled non-vocational.

(Cousin, 1990, p. 38)

I would only take issue with her over one point. I believe that women would very clearly see that domestically orientated skill-based classes have few linkages with liberal education. Unfortunately men do not appear to take the same view with such certainty. Green et al. in their book on women and leisure found that the majority of household tasks tended to be seen as 'neither work nor leisure'. There was an element of both. The key factor was the autonomy of organising one's work, not the work itself. 'This highlights the inadequacy of seeking to define activities as either "work or leisure". In women's lives such boundaries as do exist are likely to be complex, blurred and shifting'. (Green et al., 1990, p. 10)

ADULT EDUCATION AS LEISURE

Nell Keddie argued, with specific reference to the Inner London Education Authority (ILEA) adult education curriculum, that it

is strongly located in the home and in women's activities and not in leisure activities – which are of necessity male-orientated since women's work rarely permits the clear boundaries between work and home-work that the term leisure usually implies.

(Keddie, 1980, p. 83)

I believe this statement has more universal relevance. One result of adult education being defined as non-vocational is that it has been assumed to be a leisure activity. I argue that at the being of this century leisure was a relatively new phenomenon for many men and women but increasingly ideological weight was given to the idea of leisure as a pleasurable activity for women in the same way that men had begun to have time for leisure and recreation (or re-creation) after a day's work. I maintain that leisure is an inappropriate concept for many women, particularly mothers of dependent children or those who care for elderly relatives. What leisure they do have is more fragmented, less demarcated and there is less of it.

Where no clear boundaries exist between work and leisure, women frequently sacrifice personal leisure in order to accommodate caring for the family, in which case their own time spaces for uninterrupted leisure became fragmented, with the attendant reduced options on how and where to spend it.

(Green et al., 1990, p. 23)

Much of what passes for leisure for women is related to their domestic responsibilities and is more home-based than for men, for example knitting and sewing. They also tend to engage in so-called leisure activities while still involved with domestic duties, and are often engaged in more than one activity when, for example, they are watching television and sewing and at the same time listening out for the children. Clarke and Critcher wrote:

Gender as a social division in leisure ... redefines time and space for women as compared with men. Women are expected – and come themselves to expect – to participate in those leisure activities defined as appropriate for women, at those times and in those places compatible with established female roles.

(Clarke and Critcher in Green et al., 1990, p. 16)

Women have less time for themselves than men (see Deem: 1986). There is no doubt that, as the adage says, women's work is never done. I would suggest that women also find it less easy to cut off from their domestic responsibilities than men from theirs and may feel guilty if they have leisure interests, unconnected with the home and which may require the spending of money, money which they feel could be used for more useful things. An ACACE survey found that 22 percent of the women who had not followed an adult education course of their choice had not done so because they had to look after children or other dependents. Only 4 percent of the men surveyed gave this as a reason. In addition 8 percent of the women compared to only 2 percent of the men said that their families would not let them study. (ACACE, 1982, p. 69)

A neo-marxist interpretation of leisure would suggest that it has a social control function whilst ameliorating the worst effects of the capitalist mode of production. As Ross Fergusson and George Mardle suggest, it also 'in diverse ways ... confirms the "naturalness" of the particular social world. This is particularly true of the culture and mass media – the epitome of industrialised leisure' (1981, p. 75).

Clare Manifold pointed out that these authors: 'anticipate a "curriculum for leisure" in the educational context which threatens to *trivialise, domesticate and contain social productive power* in the mass of the population in the same way as the society of leisure is the recasting of the society of unemployment' (Manifold, no date, p. 12; emphasis in original).

Although Fergusson and Mardle appear to address their remarks to men they have relevance to women and to the function of adult education. What they fail to mention is that leisure grounded in capital is 'ameliorative' and 'alienating' for women and is not leisure at all. It would appear that a common assumption among males, and I include policy-makers here, is that not only do women have leisure, they have more of it than men, a point which I have refuted. The Ministry of Education asserted in 1956:

> It may be, as principals of evening institutes [males ?]· often assert, that the men are tired out after a day's work and do not want to go out to recreative classes, whereas the housewife, who may have been in all day, gladly goes out to meet other people two or three evenings a week. (1956, p. 39; my interjection)

While this statement appears to suggest that men are perceived as working and women who stay at home do not work, it is certainly true that adult education allows an acceptable form of social contact for women with other women. The reality is, however, that men have greater opportunities, more money and a wider range of activities outside the home environment from which to chose from than women – the pub for example being just one option? Isn't it that men perhaps are less keen to engage in activities in what is in effect a single-sex female environment? '[M]any groups of women are expected to chose their leisure time activities mainly from within the limited range of home and family orientated activities which are socially defined as acceptable, womanly pursuits' (Green et al., 1990, p. 25).

ACACE made similar assumptions in 1982 to the Ministry of Education when in noting that more middle-class women than men were in full-time education it said that this was 'possibly because of the greater availability of leisure time and a desire to catch up with their husband' (ACACE, 1982, p. 16). Later, the authors of the report, in commenting on the fact that more women than men took part in general cultural and creative classes continued: 'We do not know, however, whether this genuinely relates to differences in interest or temperament between men and women, or whether men *simply do not have the time* because of the more pressing needs for work related courses' (ACACE, 1982, p. 55; my emphasis).

It appears that women see things differently. Bridget Barber, in a survey of adult education in Crowborough, Sussex, found that many women attending daytime classes felt that they should really have been at home at work whilst their husbands were out at work. According to Hughes and Kennedy:

> Some confirmation of this as yet relatively unexplored area is revealed in a recent survey amongst the audience of a South of England based television station TVS. This found that only 8–10% of women at home in the afternoon watched television. One respondent said, "It's a working day", and another "I feel I should be contributing in a working way".
>
> (Angela Lambert, Sunday Times, 30.10.83, quoted in Hughes and Kennedy, 1985, p. 149)

Women are constrained by guilt. 'Guilt is probably one of the most powerful factors that ties women to their children in the home – a socially induced guilt which illustrates the implicit assumption that a mother's place is in the home with her children?' (Green et al., 1990, p. 119).

Women appear to be ambivalent about adult education classes in the daytime because they take them away from their workplace and as such do not appear to be directly connected with their job. Again, I would argue that this does not invalidate my argument that it has direct links with their working lives. I suggest that it is not dissimilar to the training men receive off the job to enhance their work skills.

I have tried to indicate that not only is the concept of leisure different for men and for women but that those who make the decisions, in the main men, appear to have totally misread the situation, assuming that women who do not work outside the home have large chunks of non-obligated time. There is little basis for these assumptions. I want now to look at whether the word adult is a misnomer in relation to women and adult education.

WOMEN AND THE ADULT IN ADULT EDUCATION

I have suggested earlier that I believe 'adult' assumes a different meaning and comes at a different time for girls and boys. While it is very clear that the boundary between boyhood and manhood involves the assumption of different and greater responsibilities in the wider world, for example the responsibility of providing for a wife and family, a process which is delayed, there is not the same clear boundary to cross between girlhood and womanhood. Whilst women may leave the family home, they will usually exchange these horizons for another of the same kind, they will more than likely still be working in the service of men. The norm for the notion of an adult is a man and the male role. A woman is perceived as a deficient model of the same, never quite reaching the heights of adulthood. At the same time, I believe that girls have to grow up faster than boys and have traditionally been expected to take on jobs around the home at an earlier age than boys.

When the London adult institutes for women were established in 1913 they were open to all females from the age of fourteen, the official school leaving age. Yet in 1920, when institutes for men were opened, the minimum age was eighteen. Five years later, boys over the age of fourteen were given their own institutions, something which was never given to girls. This was partly because men do not wish to spend their non-work time in the company of boys, and certainly not with girls or women (Hughes, 1992, pp. 41–55). I suggest that this was a major reason why women came to have their own sex-specific curriculum, classes and even institutions. Whilst the benefits of women's only provision must be acknowledged we should be under no illusion that this was provided on male terms.

In 1947 the Ministry of Education issued a circular on *Homecraft*. Not only is the complexity of the subject made clear but the target group is both young girls and adult women. There was no natural break between the two stages; preparation for domesticity was continuous:

> Provision will take a variety of forms to meet a variety of demands and circumstances. Many girls contemplating marriage, conscious of their lack of experience to run a house, may welcome a short full-time course on selected topics of two or four weeks duration, or a part-time course with one or two meetings a week over a longer period. Part-time courses will probably best meet the needs of married women if they can spare the time, but many will be unable to do more than take advantage of lectures and demonstrations or of the help that can be given in well equipped and attractive advice centres by personal contacts supplemented by simple leaflets.
>
> (Ministry of Education, 1947, p. 4)

The rationale was clear: 'An incalculable sum of human happiness and efficiency depends on the knowledge and skill applied to the running of the home and the upbringing of children' (ibid., p. 1).

Whatever the reality in terms of student composition, policy-makers have remained concerned with the failures of the school system, the inadequate, or as termed in the Russell Report (1973), the 'disadvantaged'. A term which it was suggested

> should be constructed to include not only the physically and mentally handicapped but also those who, on account of their limited educational background, present cultural or social environment, age, location, occupation or status, cannot easily take part in adult education as normally provided.
>
> (DES, 1973, para. 52)

Women were not specifically identified in the report as being part of this category. Although there were clear differences in the kind of provision offered to different classes of women, for example make-do-and-mend as against classes which emphasised considerations of design and taste, I believe that as far as women were concerned gender was the major factor in the eyes of policy-makers, and not class. There was an overriding concern with the role of mothers in the process of the education and development of the next generation. There was just more confidence in the ability of middle-class mothers to perform these functions adequately and indeed well. It may well be that middle-class women were considered more adult than their working-class counterparts.

The report identified the emergence of two types of family, those with two earners and those with one or none. The latter were described as a large minority. The report observed that the two-income families were the most affluent, the better educated and more likely to spend their additional finance on leisure pursuits and non-essentials. While this may have been the case in some circumstances, it failed to take into account the many families where both parents were employed, often in low-paid work, for the sheer essentials of life. A two-tier system of education was envisaged – for those whom it was assumed needed to be taught certain basic skills connected with the making of a home, and for those who wished to improve and enhance their home life. I suggest that the rationale behind this attitude was clearly class-based and the onus was on women:

> The needs of these two groups are different but equally important ... This is seen, not only in classes related to home-making and domestic arts and crafts, but also in those giving instruction or coaching in outdoor activities that involve the family ... There is no reason to expect any reduction in the demands from the two groups in the population who now seek adult education related to the home and the family; that is, those whose earnings permit them to take seriously the graces of life, like foreign travel, or connoisseurship, or entertaining, and those who need to learn how to apply their owns time and skill to the improvement of the home and the material standard of living of the family.

> The needs of the affluent and the better educated are more likely to emerge as spontaneous demand than are those of the low earners. For the latter, a number of special

needs can be envisaged, some of which are found in present provision but not on anything like the scale required; at a simple level, skills in doing and making and maintenance about the home; at another level, access to creative and recreative pursuits that bring personal fulfilment and counter the dehumanising effects of a deprived environment; and yet another, knowledge about welfare and rights an sources of knowledge about welfare and rights and sources of help and advice; or again, access to skills that may open the way to "earning".

(DES, 1973, paras 31–2)

The report targeted mothers, particularly working mothers, who were probably assumed to be from the working class and considered the most lacking in parenting (mothering) skills. Parent education although couched in gender-neutral terms, was in reality, of course mothers' education. Educational home-visiting schemes, which became prevalent in the 1970s, I argue from direct work experience, have direct links with nineteenth-century philanthropy, when middle-class women went into working-class homes to teach the right way of being and doing. (Edwards, 1989) Whilst undoubtedly some mothers and children can benefit from this kind of intervention, it can for some women have an undermining effect.

Although the report appeared to argue for educational opportunities for women, the real priority, the education of the child, was clearly apparent. The education of working-class women in particular appeared to be in relation to benefits for the child.

The influences determining the ability to profit from schooling have been much studied and there is now a growing recognition of the critical importance of the surrounding environment, especially the home. When the values of the home are at variance with the values of the school, it is the latter that are commonly rejected.

(DES, 1973, para. 46.2)

The implication is that the values of the school were considered the correct ones and women had to be taught, or coerced, into modelling the home around these. They were to be the servants of the state and given little freedom to diverge from the norm. The report continued:

If investment in extended secondary and further education is to yield its fullest return, action upon the environment – that is, the adults whose world and its values surround the children – will be essential. The need here is not just for parent education as hitherto conceived, for that is based on a view of education as something of value for others, namely the children, and does not imply commitment to education as essential to oneself ...

Studies of intelligence and the development of intellectual ability have done away with the old concept of intelligence as an inborn fixed quantity and have shown that, to a considerable extent, it can be increased ... the full development of the school system needs support from the education of the adult in the child's environment.

As has been said of other schools, nursery schools and pre-school groups alone (however valuable and necessary) will be insufficient in themselves, since the most influential element in the pre-school environment is the mother. Unless she has opportunities to continue to approach self-fulfilment (as a person, not just as a mother) through her own experience of education, and to value education for this reason, it may well be that, by the time her children reach school, their progress towards intellectual maturity will already be slowing. The working mother is particularly important, perhaps with a special education need; and as many more women will be at work during the coming decades, the influence of working mothers on children at the starting point of the whole learning process will spread very widely. There will be a need for adult education that this too is a supportive influence.

(DES, 1973, paras. 46.2–46.4)

Jane Thompson commented:

It is noticeable that "working" fathers are not charged with the same responsibility for the pre-school education of their children, and that women as full-time workers and major breadwinners in single-parent households, are still subsumed within the primary concept "mother". (Thompson, 1983, p. 80)

I believe that women of all classes were linked together through gender issues, most particularly through mothering.

In some senses, in the eyes of men, the deciders, class was of secondary importance. All mothers needed to be educated as helpmates for their children, some, particularly working mothers, were more at risk of not fulfilling their functions. I believe that for policy-makers and managers of adult education women were in one sense invisible, the adult norm being male. Women were subsidiary to this never being wholly adult, particularly working-class women. I therefore find the term adult education particularly confusing and complex as a definition and as a description of a purpose.

I have tried in this chapter to suggest that some of the characteristics normally equated with adult education, for example, that it is non-vocational, that it is a leisure-time activity and that it is for adults, are not what they might seem to be in relation to women, when analysed from a feminist perspective. I have suggested that adult education for women has been primarily concerned with the home-based life of women as mothers. Although this role has grown in complexity as the century has progressed and standards and expectations have risen, the reasoning behind the provision remains the same.

Adult education has often been justified in terms of individual growth and development. I believe that as far as the education of women is concerned, the benefit relates to society at large, to men and children in particular and to women but little. Adult education for women helps provide men with what they want and in the process has helped define women into home-based roles, whose boundary stops at the front door or maybe at the school gate. One must acknowledge that some women have prised open the door of adult education and in some instances knocked it off its hinges providing an alternative curriculum and way of operating, e.g. women's studies courses and non-traditional women's classes. There is no doubt that the unthreatening and supportive ethos of much adult education has provided clear entry points and progression routes into other parts of the post-school educational system. It is not an isolated example to cite someone who moved from a cookery class through a fresh-start course and on to an Open University degree: Smith has argued that:

> Though women's participation in the educational process at all levels has increased this century, this participation

remains within marked boundaries. Among the most important of these boundaries ... is that which reserves to men control of the policy-making and decision-making apparatus in the educational system. (Smith, 1987b, p. 248)

In a book on adult education in Australia women are referred to as the 'invisible owners' (Tennant, 1991). Unfortunately, they are not the directors and one wonders what the future holds when we see so-called non-vocational and leisure education being squeezed off political agendas with the emphasis on the new vocationalism.

6 'The University' and the 'University of Life': Boundaries between Ways of Knowing
Rosalind Edwards

Throughout the 1980s and early 1990s, in many Western countries, women have increasingly turned to education: from the adult education courses discussed by Mary Hughes in the previous chapter, to more academic courses. At all levels and all modes of study, women's enrolment rates are outpacing those of men. (For example, for America see US Department of Education, 1988; for Britain see Department of Education, 1991). In particular, both governments and institutions of higher education have been encouraging women's return to education as mature students through 'access' and 'bridging' courses, and special admissions schemes. This contrasts with higher education institutions' historical tendency to keep women at bay at various levels (Oakley, 1981; Lie and O'Leary, 1990). Yet, despite the desire to expand the numbers in higher education, at the same time several governments have either introduced (for example, Britain) or extended (for example, Australia) student loan schemes and have imposed restrictions on the sector's public funding. Cuts in 'non-essential' areas of provision, such as day nurseries, as well as other logistical problems, such as timetabling and modes of study, impede mature women students' access to higher education (Sperling, 1991). Moreover, institutions of higher education themselves have not often thought through what such an expansion of 'non-traditional' student numbers might mean for the overall institutional ethos and epistemological base.

In this chapter I will be drawing upon the experiences of a group of mature mother-students in order to explore the meaning of 'knowing' as a student and as a mother and partner. I examine the interface between educational knowledge ('the

university') and family knowledge ('the university of life'),
revealing the tensions rooted in the institutionally and socially
constructed ethoses and values of 'academe' and 'family'
themselves. I argue that, because of these tensions and
conflicts, mother-students have to attempt to either separate
or connect their educational and family lives. Such attempts to
resolve the contradictions inherent in having both family and
higher education in their lives can mean that mother-students
have to 'rework' the meaning of formal education for themselves. They may also 'rework' the meaning of their family lives
– but that is not the subject of this particular discussion.[1] Here
I am mainly concerned with the way that higher education
constructs the relationship between its knowledge and 'family',
especially mothering, knowledge in the lives of mother-
students, and the ways that mother-students themselves
understand and work with this. Indeed, mother-students have
to work with, and come to some form of resolution between,
the two ethoses and 'ways of knowing' because the institutions
themselves do not have to address such issues.

STUDYING MATURE MOTHER-STUDENTS

As governments' and higher education institutions' interest in
mature students has heightened, research studies on this topic
have also proliferated. Such studies tend to approach the
subject from the perspective of 'education'. They mirror those
on home–school relations, as described in our introductory
chapter, in terms of the root of their agendas. The studies are
concerned with the interests of education institutions –
reaching and retaining more students – and with what is often
termed the 'external pressures and problems' (Woodley et al.,
1987, p. 119) of other aspects of students' lives, such as family,
on their ability to study successfully and to pass exams. To talk
of such 'externalities' reveals whose interests are paramount in
shaping these studies and where they are situated institutionally. Higher education infrequently considers its own
beliefs, values and practice as problematic (Thomas, 1990). By
contrast, this chapter takes just such a stance in examining the
bases of mothers' and higher education's knowledge, their
relationship to one another, and the implications for women
who become mature mother-students.

The women who took part in the research on which this chapter is based (Edwards, 1993) are a particular group: mothers of dependent children, who had someone they considered to be a long-term male partner, at least when they started a full-time social science degree course. Over the period of a year I carried out two or three in-depth interviews with 31 mothers of different races and classes, studying at five institutions (two universities and three polytechnics) in the south of England. Most of them were married, or living in cohabiting relationships that were akin to marriage, upon commencing their studies, but several were in long-term relationships where their partner did not live with them permanently. Twelve of the students were white working-class women and 10 were white middle-class. Nine women were from minority ethnic groups. The largest of this latter group were six Afro-Caribbean women who came to Britain either as young children or teenagers. All the women defined their own status as working-class, middle class, black, white or 'mixed' race.

Over the past 15 years or so, women's relationship to class has been a topic of constant debate.[2] Conventional stratification theory designates the family or household as the unit of stratification, with the head of the unit (usually male) determining the assigned class position of the subsumed rest of that unit. At an empirical level, fitting the students I interviewed into the conventional stratification system often proved difficult. Additionally, the women of 'mixed' race and all but one of the black women rejected social class as part of their identity and felt reality. For the white women, class was a part of their identity, although not necessarily in an uncomplicated way. Material and structural definitions of social class may be useful in identifying an important basis of economic power, but in the end they evade people's sense of themselves and the world in which they live. The women's own perceptions of their social status, as they lived it, served as a better guide to their understandings of the effects of gaining an education upon their lives (see next chapter also).

BOUNDED SPHERES OF KNOWLEDGE

Mature mother-students returning to formal education are, as many feminists have pointed out, entering a world of patriarchal knowledge, norms, values and structures (for example, Belenky et al, 1986; Smith, D.E., 1987a and 1989; Spender, 1981 and 1983; Sperling, 1991; Stanley and Wise, 1983; Thomas, 1990). Such feminist analyses often argue that within higher education institutions there is a separation of formal educational knowledge and the knowledge acquired through living. 'Public', objective, institutional and pedagogic episte-mologies are argued to be given validity over and above 'private', subjective, emotional and personal 'ways of knowing' – even if the former's very notion of 'objectivity' is question-able (Stanley and Wise, 1983). Students outside the 'white, male, middle-class' category thus are said to have to learn to treat their experiences as a faulty representation of theory, and theory as the 'real' reality. Liz Stanley and Sue Wise (1983) argue that women, generally, know about, and work with, two different worlds – the public (dominant) world of men and their knowledge and the private world of women and their knowledge.

Women, especially mothers, are said to have a special relationship with the private sphere of 'the family' because it is the primary site of both their work (domestic and repro-ductive) and of their social and personal identity (Oakley, 1981; New and David, 1985). Because of this, it has been argued that women are concerned with intimacy and care (Gilligan, 1982) and with endlessly piecing together the uncoordinated fragments of their own and others daily lives (Balbo, 1987). Mothers are thus continually working with routine, a patchwork of detail and intimate relationships – the creation of family life that Jane Ribbens has explored in Chapter 3. Sara Ruddick (1989) has termed this concern with, and attention to, particularity and detail 'maternal thinking'. She argues that maternal thinking is grounded in mothers' on-going experience rather than in instruction.

Higher education is a public institution that rejects the personal and subjective as academically valid because of the way it constructs its particular form of knowledge.'The family', in its turn, has been socially constructed as, and is both ideologically and popularly regarded as, a private domain into which public world concerns and values should not penetrate (Pateman, 1983; New and David, 1985). A boundary thus appears to be posited between the knowledge of 'the univer-sity' and the knowledge of 'the university of life', particularly that of the 'private' women's sphere. On the one side, the university: a 'masculinist' middle-class and white epistemological model that approaches human problems in a detached intellectualised fashion, alongside a belief that this embodies a neutral, and thus superior, form of reasoning. On the other side, the university of life: an emotional, subjective way of knowing that is particularly associated with female characteristics, and which is regarded by the university as 'unreliable' and 'biased'. Dorothy Smith has described the ways of being and of knowing within each sphere of 'education' and 'family' as 'opposing modes of organisational consciousness' (Smith, D.E., 1987a, p. 6).

THE MEANING OF 'KNOWING' IN FAMILY LIFE

By far the greatest number of women I interviewed shared a sense of the importance of their own part within their families as mothers and partners, the personal commitment involved in caring, and the need for attention to the concrete and the particular as part of this. Their family lives were, to borrow a phrase from Smith, 'a local and particular world' (Smith, D.E., 1987a, p. 6). For instance, in the cases where I asked women questions such as 'what does being a mother/wife/partner mean to you?', I was usually met with an initial bewildered silence, in a way I was not when I asked what being a student meant to them (see below). Family lives and relationships were difficult things for the women to conceptualise and talk about in abstract terms.

Knowledge of subjective minutiae is the 'way of knowing' in mothering and family life. Mothers' caring means that personal detail, emotions and empathy are the centre pins of their epistemological processes and frameworks in the domestic sphere. The women's accounts of their families were filled with particularised details about partners' and children's tidiness or untidiness and so on, and anecdotes about who said or did what to whom and when. Their knowledge about their families was experiential, and sensitive to individuals within them. Some of the mature mother-students who left their children with childminders during the day or those whose children were just starting school were, at first, worried that the minder or teacher did not really 'know' their child, their likes, dislikes and idiosyncrasies, in detail. Therefore, they would not be able to care for their children properly, or care about them. The women might also themselves, as mothers, lose touch with the detail of 'knowing'. Discussing whether or not to use a childminder when she returned to her third year of degree study, after taking a year out to have her second child, Paula (a black woman) said: 'I won't know what's happening to Andrew. How's he been all day, has he been neglected, was he lonely, is he feeling that nobody cares about him?'

Most of the women wanted to bring their children, and some of them their partners, to their place of study at least once because they wanted them to be able to visualise the place and the people in it. When they told their family that they were off to the university or polytechnic for the day, or spoke about things that had happened at the institution, they wanted them to be able to picture where they were. The inability to do this, in the case of those attending the one institution that did not easily allow children on site, caused the women not only practical inconvenience, but also went against what most of them felt was an integral part of being a mother to their children – that their children should really 'know' where they were in a concrete way.

The women held themselves responsible for the happiness and contentment of the other members of their family, especially their partners and children – in other words a sense of connectedness as described by Carol Gilligan (1982). These responsibilities for the well-being of the members of their families were felt by the women whether their partners lived with them permanently or not, and whatever their children's age. Within their families, happiness was to be achieved by the women paying emotional and physical attention to the details and routine of everyday life. There may be disagreements among feminists over whether this sort of care-giving is oppressive to women (as for Barrett and McIntosh, 1982), or humanising (as for Gilligan, 1982; Ruddick, 1989), or both (Abel and Nelson, 1990) – but there is no doubt that it forms the focus of many women's lives.

Motherhood is a particularly intense emotional commitment for the majority of women. This commitment is one that women themselves value and in the main enjoy, even if it is at times draining and frustrating (see Ribbens in Chapter 3, and also Boulton, 1983). Motherhood had literally changed the lives of the mature mother-students I interviewed in a myriad of ways. They often referred to the way that the births of their children had matured them because they had taken on the responsibilities mentioned above (again, see also Ribbens in Chapter 3). Importantly, several of the women spoke of being a mother changing not only the way they thought about things, but also the things they thought about. Politics, the world environment and so on, now became of interest and importance to them because they had children. Jenny (white working-class), who was 30 when she gave birth to her daughter, described the whole process graphically:

> I suppose it was having a baby that made me rethink my life, that I'd spent most of it in a bubble. And I think from that time I started to mature ... and it wasn't that kind of maturity of being able to do things. I think just mentally. And I often think now, what did I do with those first thirty years of my life? What did I used to think about, politically or anything? I just don't know ...Oh, I think having a baby definitely changed me completely. There's no doubt – or it started me on the road to rethinking.

One of the starting-points for learning and thinking about issues was their lives as mothers. In addition to this 'informal' learning process, the women had decided to enter 'formal' learning and to be a student at an institution of higher education.

THE MEANING OF 'KNOWING' IN HIGHER EDUCATION

The women were not returning to education because they were dissatisfied with their family lives, but because they were dissatisfied with their public world position both in terms of paid work and of social status. There was little evidence of the familial role and identity crises that some have suggested 'push' mothers and wives into returning to education (for example Lovell, 1980). Arlene McLaren (1988) describes such 'empty nest syndrome' assumptions as limited and inaccurate in her discussion of women students in adult education. They

do not take account of the policies and procedures of economic and educational institutions or changes in the social and
political environment. They ignore the way individuals make
choices within this context and construct their own realities
and understandings.

For the most part, the original 'push' into education came
from the women's paid employment, or prospective return to
paid employment. Many of them spoke of realising that they
would have to spend the rest of their paid working lives in jobs
they found unrewarding, both in monetary and personal
satisfaction terms.

Additionally, all the women spoke of wishing to return to
education in order to extend their understanding of society
in general. They also talked of doing the degree for their own
'self-esteem' in order to 'prove' themselves, occasionally add-
ing that they felt 'stupid' in the company of educated people
who appeared to be so much more knowledgeable. Higher
education itself was viewed as conferring prestige, related to it
being for 'intelligent' people. Universities, as against vocation-
ally-associated polytechnics, were especially viewed as presti-
gious institutions.[3] This view was held by both the mother-
students who attended universities (just over a quarter of the
women, mainly middle-class and all white) and those (the
majority) who attended polytechnics.

The mature mother-students put a great deal of store by the
acquisition of academic knowledge, both instrumentally and
personally. They felt that education gave them a different way
of looking at society and social life. The women referred to
academic knowledge as a particular way of knowing; a way of
'getting above' the social that was abstracted from their own
everyday lives. Jenny, a white working-class woman described
herself as now 'looking down' on the world, rather than being
a part of it, 'a bit like the greek gods'.

Later I address the differing extents to which the mother-
students felt that permeations of the subjective, emotional,
'local and particular' into academic knowledge was permissible. It should be noted, however, that even if they did this,
the women always stressed the broader view and 'objectivity'
on which academic knowledge lays such emphasis:

We are able, I think, as mature students, to be able to put
more reality into an academic piece of work. We can actually

absorb it and then relate it to reality. We're able to look at it
more objectively as well, much more. Because everything's
very subjective beforehand. (Helen, a white working-class
woman)

Academic knowing is also about individual achievement. This
was so for the mother-students, not only because they wanted to
'prove' themselves capable of degree level study, but also
because higher education individualises academic achievement.
In higher education students should discover knowledge themselves and work as individuals. Along with a conception of
objectivity, the mother-students also imbued this:

You only get a very small number of people who actually
exchange work. Actually I don't know whether the lecturers
like it as well. I don't think they do because I think they
think we ought to do things for ourselves. (Lorraine, a white
middle-class woman)

Success or failure was seen as in their own hands, rather than
in their relationship to others: 'You can attend lectures but I
mean when it comes down to it, you know, you've got to do it
on your own' (Michelle, a white working-class woman).

It is ironic that as part of their social science degrees the
women were learning that success or failure in schooling is
strongly skewed along sex, race and class lines, while simul-
taneously a hidden curriculum contained the notion that
success or failure in higher education depended on their
individual merits and application, regardless of sex, race or
class (see also Thomas, 1990).

STRADDLING TWO 'WAYS OF KNOWING'

Higher education means becoming knowledgeable in an
objective way and is about an individual achievement that is
not necessarily linked to caring and to others. This can be
counterposed with the greater meaning of knowing in family
life as grounded in the 'local and particular', in emotions,
subjectivity and in women's own caring about and for other
people. On one side of the boundary, their lives as students,
the mature mother-students were 'looking down' on the

world. They used decontextualised abstractions and theories to examine the specific, subjective and detailed. On the other side, their family lives as mothers and partners, they were firmly embedded in the world itself rather than distanced from it. Wider generalisations and understandings were also embedded in the emotional and intuitive (see Ribbens, forthcoming). Shifting between the two epistemologies could be uncomfortable.

Within many of the mature mother-students' accounts of their lives there were indications that this was the case. When they talked of the difficulties of breaking off from studying in order, say, to cook a meal, they spoke of the way that they would lose the threads of the topic they were concentrating on and how it would take them a long time to think themselves back into their studies when they returned to them.[4] Some of the women spoke of their shifts from the concerns of one 'world' to those of the other 'world' on arriving at the education institution or on arriving home:

> You'll be there [polytechnic] talking politics or something in the paper, you discuss that, but when you come home, you know, you have to switch that off, and nobody want to know about what Marx said or what Weber said. Who the hell is Marx and Weber to them, you know! They want where's my dinner or I fell today at school and somebody not talking to me ... and then when you are at college you can't talk about it [home] because nobody want to hear all about four kids and their – you know, that Sonia [daughter] did such a wonderful thing yesterday! Nobody wants to hear that, so you have to stop yourself from saying it. (Irene, a black woman)

The shift from the 'local and particular' to the 'conceptually ordered', with its required shifts in modes of being and knowing was felt, often unconsciously, by many of the mother-students I interviewed. As Smith describes it, the women were often operating with a 'bifurcated consciousness' (Smith, D.E., 1987a, p. 6).

The contrasting epistemologies of higher education and family life that exist by virtue of the nature of the two institutions, and as understood by the women I interviewed, has ramifications for their coexistence in mother-students' lives.

These will now be examined in two ways. Firstly, I look at ways in which family life experiences and 'local and particular' ways of knowing could be drawn upon in the women's formal studies, and the extent to which the women wanted to draw upon them. Secondly, I discuss the reaction of the women's partners and other members of their families to any attempts on the part of the women to draw upon their academic knowledge and 'conceptually ordered' ways of knowing within their family lives. I will show how these permeations of the understandings of one 'world' through to the other are linked to, and have implications for, the way that mother-students may come to view formal education.

FAMILY KNOWLEDGE IN THE ACADEMIC WORLD

Upon starting their degrees, the mature mother-students had looked forward to being able to explore their interests further within their courses. Their life experiences, including, as noted above, motherhood, were starting-points for thinking about issues and wanting to learn about them:

> I think as a black person actually going on to it [the degree course], it's because you want to know. Right. You want to know. You want to be able to put – you've had all this experience, all this knowledge, and you want to be able to put it in perspective. (Beverley, a black woman)

The majority of the women mentioned that because they had not gone straight from school to higher education they had gained useful experiences and wide perspectives.

Indeed, in the main, the mother-students talked about their experiences in the public world of paid and/or voluntary work in the health service, personal social services, adult education and so on, as being regarded as useful both by themselves and by lecturers in the universities and polytechnics they attended. They spoke of these experiences as useful when it came to understanding the social science issues they were studying and feeding-in to seminar discussions. When the women did choose to discuss these more public aspects of their lives in the formal academic setting, they mostly felt it was acceptable for them to do so. On the other hand, the women's private world experiences as mothers bringing up children and running homes were rarely felt by them to be valued. This is despite the fact that often their public world roles as, for example, nurses or secretaries, could also be termed caring work. There was a feeling that family-life experiences were somehow inferior even where they might have been relevant: 'We felt that by bringing in our home life, what was going on, we would be demeaning the conversation that was going on about a particular problem or Freud's theory or something like that' (Helen, a white working-class woman).

The mother-students responded to the sense that bringing their experiences of family life into academic learning was not really permissible in various ways. Several of them concurred with the view of family life experiences as not being academically valid:

> I don't like to ever harp on about having children. Not because I'm ashamed of it or anything, but I don't actually think people want to hear about – you know...I don't think people would want to know about that. (Victoria, a white middle-class woman)

Some women came to accept it once they had 'learnt the ropes'. Michelle (white working-class), for example, had talked in her initial interview at the beginning of her first year of degree study, of how she fed her life experiences into her learning. By the time of her second interview, however, during the summer break between her first and second years, she had shifted to regarding her experiences as irrelevant, saying that she kept them out of her academic learning.

Another group of the mature mother-students, however, said they did, to varying extents, speak about their family life experiences because they felt that these revealed an important perspective on issues – even though a few of them did not always think this was well received because it was not always perceived as academically valid:

> I would challenge things. My experience of being married, of trying to raise a family, of expecting my husband to play an equal part in it, would give me an insight into what the other people are saying, so I'd use that... I think it's no good just saying I don't agree with you. You've got to say why and what

it is in your experience that makes you disagree with what they've said. (Alexandra, a white working-class woman)

Some of these women drew on their experiences, but in a particular way. As mentioned previously, they and the women who said that they had overtly used aspects of their life-experience in seminar discussions, were careful to add that they recognised the need to place these 'within a wider context'. The women's perception of academic study as to do with objectivity and with the removal of personal bias made them wary as to how they drew upon their experiences:

> In terms of necessarily, not personal examples, but in terms of your personal experience giving you an understanding of the issues, I think I relate to it more that way rather than necessarily saying 'my experience of this was'. So it's a little bit more indirect. I mean you tend to try and feed it through the sort of *acceptable academic channels* maybe. (Angela, a white middle-class woman; my emphasis)

'Local and particular' knowledge thus has to be represented in a certain way in a 'conceptually ordered' world. These forms of communication perpetuate a marginalisation of women's family life experiences (Spender, 1985).

The apparent incompatibility between mother-students' everyday family life experiences and academic knowledge can also hold other implications for them. Women's exclusion from the academic arena has traditionally centred on their inferior intellectual capacities due to their reproductive, domestic, caring associations (Lie and O'Leary, 1990). It would seem that motherhood can still be viewed as incompatible with, and a major impediment to, academic learning. Stella (white middle-class) felt that acknowledgement of her mothering side was difficult for lecturers and others because it was often seen as irreconcilable with being able to do academic work:

> One thing sticks in my mind that one particular person said that I knew quite well – and when he taught me for the first time I happened to go along to his room when he was marking one of my essays and he said, this is really good, you write really well, and he sounded so surprised! And I said, what did you expect then! So I think maybe sometimes people, if you are a mother, people define you as that and

they don't really consider that you can do anything else! And that wasn't, that wasn't because he's a particularly insensitive person or whatever. But I do remember the note of surprise and I've never forgiven him for that!

For black mother-students there was also a sense that if they talked about their lives they could be 'sussed out' – a feeling that they were under scrutiny as blacks:

> I always believe that we are under constant scrutiny. Probably we are not. I don't know if we are. But constantly I have that feeling, you know. I don't know why I feel like that. I think the onus is on you to do even better to be accepted at their standard, you know what I mean? (Pat, a black woman)

Even when learning about topics that ostensibly addressed their lives, for some of the black and the white working-class mature mother-students there was a sense that what was presented to them was not their experience. This could lead the white working-class women (but none of the black women) to feel that where their own experiences did not fit what was being taught, then they, as working-class people, must be 'wrong', rather than the middle-class knowledge they were receiving being wrong:

> There have been things that have just ... I've thought no, that's absolute rubbish because you know, my experiences are very different to that. But I don't know whether I'd actually say that's absolute and total rubbish or whether I'd say well, maybe for other – I think it all again comes down to this fact of thinking that other people do things properly, you know, and if it doesn't apply to me then it's because I haven't done something properly! (Michelle, a white working-class woman)

The black women, however, tended not to question the legitimacy of their own experiences but could be left with the feeling that the subjects that were central to their lives and perceptions were not tackled deeply enough:

> Even if it's something about race or women, it's just like they're just touching the surface of it because they don't want to get down to the roots of the problem whatsoever. They just want to touch it and – like it takes half an hour for

them to discuss it and that's it, it's finished, you know. But when you tackle them to going into it more they say no, you know, we just want to talk about this particular area and that's it. (Anna, a black woman)

Although black women have been described as 'double tokens' in academic life (Reid, 1990), they are perhaps less likely to doubt the validity of their own experience because of their embeddedness in 'Afrocentric' communities and institutions. Patricia Hill Collins (1990) argues that few 'Eurocentric' institutions except 'the family' validate emotions and the ethic of caring that produce a different epistemological framework.

The ethos of higher education institutions overall, combined with a realisation that particular sets of experiences that form an important part of their identity are not really *de rigueur,* can reinforce the sense that mature mother-students are deviants, are Other, within a system with the norms of the white middle-class 'bachelor boy' student (Robinson, 1980). Women's life knowledge, especially that gained within the family sphere as mothers, is often not valued or acceptable as a legitimate way of knowing within academia. This was so for the mother-students I interviewed, irrespective of whether or not they themselves wished to use 'local and particular' knowledge in this way – and not all of them did.

PRIVATE BOUNDARIES

There was another reason why not all the mother-students would have wished to talk about, or have acknowledged, certain of their experiences within the formal academic setting, even had they been encouraged to do so. The idea of the privacy of family life was mentioned by several of them: Maureen, a black working-class woman, for example, talked of her personal experience as being 'my private affair'.

Thus, while what is regarded as acceptable academic knowledge in itself draws boundaries around the use of life experiences, there also appear to be boundaries that mother-students themselves may draw around aspects of their domestic and family lives. For the women, it was most often their relationships with men that were regarded as the ultimate privacy:

Your married life with your husband, things like that, I don't bring that up in the class. That's my business. On the other hand, things like unemployment or being on sickness benefit for a long time, the fact that I was divorced before I married Ivor and I spent some time as a single parent, you're talking in very general terms. You're just skimming off the top I suppose. (Anne, a white working-class woman)

It was also their relationships with their partners particularly, but also other members of their families, that could be affected by any permeations of academic ways of knowing into family life. These people, too, had perceptions of a boundary between academic knowledge and academic life and family knowledge and family life.

ACADEMIC KNOWLEDGE IN THE FAMILY WORLD

The women brought higher education into their family lives as partners, mothers and daughters in various ways and to varying extents. Not only do mother-students bring home their books and papers, but they may also bring home their newly acquired academic knowledge and understandings. The ability to define issues and to formulate and evaluate arguments are skills that higher education seeks to develop in students. Being able to talk with their families about what they were learning was seen by the majority of the women I interviewed as a form of caring about them, through 'sharing' their education, and as such allowed them to make a connection between their student and home lives.

While one group (just over half) of the mother-students' partners were said, by the women, to be willing to allow permeation of a 'conceptually ordered' way of looking at the world through to family life, many only allowed it in certain ways. This was often structured around a willingness to talk with the women about areas of learning which their partners felt that they knew about – and which, as will be seen, did not impinge upon the men personally. In the main these areas of expertise centred around 'public' issues, such as economics and some aspects of politics, including, in the case of the black women's partners, racism.[5] For example, June's (white

working-class) husband was happy to talk about some economic employment matters, but firmly rejected her attempts to
introduce sociological or psychological dimensions to issues:

> He used to say, "I don't want any sociology talk around
> here!" I used to explain something psychologically, you
> know, and he used to say, "I don't want to know." He used to
> think it was partly intruding I think.

June's reporting of her husband's words reveal the idea that
these particular educational understandings should not enter
family life and relationships. They are *intrusions* upon it. Apart
from not liking these sorts of analyses to be brought up within
the home, June also mentioned that her husband was deeply
shocked when she told him that she had talked about their
relationship as part of a seminar discussion on 'the family'.
The boundary between academic and certain aspects of family
life, it appears, should not be permeable in either direction.

The women's education could, however, eventually begin to
undermine their partners' superior status with regard to
knowledge. Kathleen Rockhill has referred to the way that
women gaining the 'symbolic power of education' is regarded
as a 'threat' by the men that they live with (1987b, p. 164). In
all, half of the group of women referred to above mentioned
this aspect of gaining knowledge as a conflictual factor in their
relationships. Helen (white working-class), for example, felt
that her boyfriend could not take any reversal in their
respective knowledges, and their relationship ended because
of this:

> He used to tell me about things because he's – he was a
> coach driver. And he used to go to all these different places
> and tell me about them. And, soon after I started the course,
> I started talking to him about things that I sort of learnt and
> discovered and what not. And I found that our roles were
> being reversed, that he didn't know about things that I knew
> about. I didn't know about things that he knew about, and I
> started to tell him things about different things. And I found
> him starting to switch off as soon as I started sort of talking
> about things that I'd learnt during that day or whatever, the
> lecture. Starting switching off. You know, that sort of glazed
> look...And when you can't talk to somebody about what

you've just learnt or heard or read or something, you can't discuss it, then there's nothing left really, is there?

Very few women did not feel their partners would be threatened by their becoming more knowledgeable about things. This threat could be so even where their partners were well-educated themselves.

Additionally, several of the white working-class women, in particular, mentioned how their partners would react angrily to any sociological or psychological analysis of their own actions, feelings or beliefs:

> My husband thinks I've changed ... if I want to talk to him about anything he always says I'm analysing him now, which is absolute crap but, you know. Whereas I wouldn't know where to start analysing him. I don't know. I know I sort of think things through more now. (Wendy, a white working-class woman)

It would appear that there was a fear that the insights the women gained from their studies might give them a power over their partners because they would be able to understand the men's emotions and motivations. Knowledge gained in the educational setting should also not be used in certain more personal and private ways, it seemed, and vice versa.

Some of the mother-students, after initial attempts at sharing their education, thus came to keep their academic knowledge separate from their partner relationships because of such perceived threats. They joined the other group of women (just under half) who had felt from the start that their partners did not want to discuss anything that they were learning, or perhaps even hear much at all about any aspects of their experiences as students. The majority of these women, like Helen, felt distressed by their partners' lack of interest. They did not all end their relationships because of this (in all, a third of the women's relationships with their partners came to an end), but came instead to keep their academic knowledge to themselves. Nevertheless, some of the women did not perceive their partners' lack of interest in their studies as unfair or hurtful. Indeed, they shielded their partners from any threat, even where there had been no indication that this was the case: 'I didn't actually want him to feel threatened in any way so I just didn't talk about it much' (Victoria, a white middle-class woman).

Additionally, only a few women felt they could discuss anything of what they were learning with their parents, even if their parents were willing, because the concepts involved were just 'beyond' them. Some, however, spoke of endeavouring to re-educate their parents on issues such as racism, sexism, political affiliation, and so on. Conflict and arguments ensued:

> And I said to Dad, I'm glad you don't subscribe to this awful tabloid press idea of seeing women as objects...And my mother, she said, how can you say that? Those girls have a right to earn money in the way they want to. And I said, yes, but it's just legitimating the whole thing of women being seen as objects. And she got really on her high horse and said, don't you come up here with all this clever talk. (Alexandra, a white working-class woman).

On the other hand, although their children's interest, if old enough, in discussing issues was welcomed by the mother-students (and the process of studying itself particularly could be shared if the children were taking exams themselves) any lack of acknowledgement on the part of their children was viewed as their just being disinterested because children have other concerns. Moreover, the women could often feed their education into their mothering in other ways, such as their relationship to their children's school (see next chapter) and by incorporating things they had learned in the way they dealt with or understood their children. Maureen, a black working-class woman said she tried to show her son the importance of education:

> I'm with the psychology teacher, and they say at a particular age the children never see the reverse point of view, they can't see your point of view. Yeah, from that, that's why I'm so patient in that respect.

These more indirect permeations of an academically inspired way of knowing about things also crept into the women's other family relationships, but not with so much ease. Along with an academic epistemology came a particular language to explain and describe the world. Academic 'jargon' gradually became part of their own language and a few of the women felt that their partners could also find this threatening because they would not be able to follow what the women were saying. The women's changing language, their 'clever talk' (as Alexandra's mother put it), could be an issue in their relationships with their parents, particularly for those from working-class backgrounds – even if they did not attempt any parental re-education:

> My own family, my mother and my sisters and my brothers, there was a bit of conflict there ... And I think one of the real issues was that my language changed, it developed. I was using different words which became natural to use, and maybe sounded slightly pompous. (Janice, a white working-class woman)

The black women were not so likely to face this problem in this context (though, like the white women, they could do so with friends) because their parents were not all living in Britain.

REWORKING EDUCATION

The value placed on particular aspects of mature mother-students' life experiences can make them feel that they do not fit into the higher education system. Not only are higher education and family life epistemologies two different forms of 'knowing', but one epistemology is socially privileged.[6] This is especially so with regard to mother-students' domestic life experiences. For mother-students who wish education and family to connect and feed into each other in their lives, in terms of what they are learning, this is thereby made a particularly difficult task. For those who wish to keep their family life experiences separate from their educational learning experiences there is less difficulty because the ethos of higher education institutions encourages this approach. This is so even for a subject area (social sciences) that might be thought to be more congruent with others aspects of students' life experiences and knowledge.

Nevertheless, this is not to say that higher education was a complete disappointment to the mother-students I interviewed. Mary Belenky and colleagues (1986), borrowing terms from Gilligan's (1982) work, make a distinction between 'separate knowing' and 'connected knowing'. The former is an orientation towards the detached in learning and the latter is towards the relational. They see higher education itself as concerned with, and rewarding, separate knowing, and as having the authority and power to require adherence to these 'agreed-upon ways for knowing' (Belenky et al., 1986, p. 134). Belenky and colleagues, however, state that some of those in their study of women in learning situations were able to rework, to 'jump outside' of, this frame of reference. They began to integrate personal, 'real life', and academic knowledge – a state that comes at the pinnacle of their typology of 'women's ways of knowing'.

Many of the mature mother-students I interviewed did indeed rework their educational experience, although this tended to be outside of formal academic requirements. Higher education does not easily admit the subjective and personal as a valid epistemological framework. As a socially privileged form of knowledge it does not have to question this stance. Thus the students were left to grapple with and resolve the tensions between the two ways of knowing. Reworking education was one form of resolution. As will be seen in the next chapter, this reworking can extend beyond mother-students' own personal learning to their children's.

Learning about race and racism as part of their social science degrees was mentioned by most of the black and 'mixed race' women as giving them a wider understanding that enabled them personally, if not academically, to put their own experiences in context in a way that was important to them. Additionally, while most of the women had felt that their life experiences prior to doing a degree had widened their perspectives when it came to studying social issues, a third, mainly black or mainly white working-class, felt that meeting other students had brought them into contact with groups of people from different cultures and/or different social and sexual orientations whom they would not necessarily otherwise have come across (for example, in the networks Jane Ribbens describes in Chapter 3). It was the personal relationships with such people, rather than any abstracted learning about them, that these women felt really broadened aspects of their outlooks:

> I made some really good friendships from it [the course], and I learned not just about studying about people.

Particularly about things like racism and homosexuality. And I really began to understand it, whereas before I – you know, like racism, I had a very narrow view of it. And homosexuality, I didn't talk about it. I mean because I've got a good [student] friend who is gay and, you know, we talk about it in depth. So I feel I've gained a good understanding of it in a completely different way. (Jenny, a white working-class woman)

These women redefined their formal education by trans-ferring notions of identification as caring from the private, women's, side of the academic/family boundary, into the academic area. Notions of concrete experience and empathy with others were allowed significance and were valued. They were seen as enhancing more abstract knowledge. The comment of Gayle (white working-class) illustrates the rework-ing undertaken by many of those interviewed:

It turned out at the end not to be what I thought it was about, which was sort of encouraging creative thought and, you know, bringing your own life and experiences into your studies and, you know, making parallels and links. And it wasn't about that at all. I mean it was training to be an administrator basically. But then I don't actually feel cross about that anymore because I think I gained an awful lot from doing that. I mean if they didn't give it value, well, you know, okay. I mean I actually developed my own ideas, and that was one of the most valuable things for me on the course.

Thus, despite any feeling that their life experiences had been asked for in the promotional literature put out by the institu-tions, but was either not used or was misrepresented, the majority of the women valued and enjoyed studying for a degree.

Not all the mother-students reworked the meaning of formal education in this way. For some of the women it was this very removal from the personal and everyday that they found satisfying. The opportunity to discuss issues on different terms, and to a depth that they would not normally do in everyday conversations, was something some women mention-ed as particularly enjoyable. Jennie (white working-class), for instance, was reflecting on her recent graduation: 'You miss most the opportunity to talk about things that you don't talk about in everyday life. That's really what you miss, sitting around theorising.'

Indeed, it was this academic overview that, as will be seen in the next chapter, gave many of the women confidence when dealing with others in the public sphere – and which those who reworked the value of formal education could also tap into. There is thus some irony here, in that while higher education constructed a boundary between the mother-students' family knowledge base and its own, it also gave them the confidence to cross such boundaries, especially in other contexts.

CONNECTIONS AND SEPARATIONS ACROSS THE BOUNDARY

Higher education and family require (and were, implicitly or explicitly, perceived by the women I interviewed as requiring) very different things of mother-students. The 'way of knowing' as a student in higher education and the 'way of knowing' as a female partner and mother are socially constructed. These epistemological constructions are ideologically built around different value bases and assumptions that can be in conflict: the one, objective, impersonal, unemotional and abstract; the other, subjective, personal, emotional and anecdotal. I am not making the argument that mothers cannot, or never, think or conceptualise in an abstract fashion. The vast majority of the mother-students I interviewed graduated with 'respectable' degree passes. Moreover, the social construction of academic knowledge as objective is itself just that – a construction. Knowledge is produced within specific political conditions and it articulates with established power relationships. Women and their experiences, particularly as mothers, have been left out of the discourses that construct the knowledge and means of explaining the world that are considered valuable (Edwards and Ribbens, 1991). Nevertheless, mature mother-students can, do – and have to – deal with the situation in which they move between competing, contradictory and hierarchically ordered epistemological frameworks. The women had to work with these institutionalised social constructions, and to work with them in a context in which academic ways of knowing are socially privileged. They negotiated this in two main ways.

Most of the mother-students I interviewed wanted, and usually worked towards, integrations and connections across the bounded ways of knowing within their families and their lives as students. These women did not want to act, feel or think differently in the education institution to the way they did at home, and vice versa. Their family experiences were seen as feeding into their academic learning. The knowledge that these women gained in higher education was fed back into their relationships with members of their families. These were the women who came to rework and redefine gaining a higher education as a broader and a personal process, while retaining a sense of its objectivity.

Some of the mother-students, however, wanted (and other women came to work with) keeping the boundary between the two intact. They felt that their family life experiences were not relevant to their academic learning, and/or that they were private matters. These women spoke of feeling, acting and thinking differently in the separate worlds, and of actively keeping them apart – especially where they regarded their partners as threatened by any interconnections. Some of these women also came to rework the meaning of education, but often they viewed it as an abstract, separate way of knowing that was not part of their 'real life'.

The mother-students' race and class could affect their views of the reception of the experiences of the 'university of life' within 'the university', for example, in worries about being under scrutiny or having the wrong life experiences. They were not, however, so significant when it came to permeations of 'the university' through to the 'university of family life' in terms of their partners' reactions to this. While only the white working-class women spoke of their partners' aversion to any academically inspired analysis of their motivations, in all other respects the mother-students reported the same sorts of threats to their male partners whatever their race or class. Nevertheless, such factors did play more of a part in their relationships with their parents, especially over language for white working-class women, and, as will be seen in the next chapter, had some relevance to all the mature mother-students' children, through schooling.

LESSONS FOR HIGHER EDUCATION

There are implications in the findings of this study for teaching mature mother-students, and indeed all students, within higher education. These implications spill over and affect the institutional ethos and epistemological base of higher education.

Mother-students are not traditional students coming to higher education straight from school after taking their exams. Moreover, they have responsibilities other than studying, in the form of their families. For women who want to separate their family responsibilities, particularly their mothering knowledge base and experiences, higher education institutions reflect and reinforce this way of allowing education and family to co-exist in their lives. On the other hand, mother-students who desire connections between their family and educational knowledge and experiences (the majority of the women I interviewed, at least at some stage of their degree courses) can find this difficult within the institution (as well as at home). Women pursuing the adult education courses Mary Hughes has described (Chapter 5) may well find such connections both easier and institutionally supported (see Sperling, 1991).

Belenky and colleagues (1986) argue that higher education needs to take students' knowledge rather than discipline-based knowledge as its starting-point. They argue for an approach that treats the student as an independent subject rather than as an object; a process that would: 'emphasise connection over separation... accord respect to and allow time for the knowledge that emanates from firsthand experience' (Belenky et al., 1986, p. 229). Such an approach is said not to be opposed to objectivity, but attempts to meld it with subjectivity. While many of the mother-students I interviewed would have welcomed and valued this way of learning, it must be borne in mind that some of them were not keen to integrate their family life experiences with their studies. Additionally, because of the threat to their relationships with their partners, others of them came to feel that any connections in the opposite direction were not possible. Some flexibility with regard to the extent of the connectedness of the personal with the academic thus needs to be allowed for.

Jenny Shaw (1986) has also argued for a 'democratisation of knowledge'. She urges a changed relationship between teaching and research, with research skills utilised in the investigation of contemporary issues being at the core of the undergraduate curriculum.[7] Jane Ribbens (1991) has shown the way in which personal, autobiographical, experiences can be integrated into and enhance academic learning. Providing opportunities for all students to go deeply into areas that are of importance to them, providing them with the techniques to do this, would allow mature mother-students and others who wish to do so, to render visible their domestic and other experiences. It would also allow the pursuit of issues of sex, race and class, where women saw these as of importance in their lives, while not penalising those who, for whatever reason, do not wish to cross the boundary and make their 'private' lives 'public'. It is not only mature mother-students and other students who may benefit from such methods; they would enhance lecturers' intellectual development as well (Sperling, 1991).

Curricular and epistemological changes such as those outlined above may also mean that it is not only mother-students who have individually to adjust and work towards a resolution between two modes of 'knowing', but that institutions of higher education will, in their turn, have to learn to 'cope' with the mature mother-students and other non-traditional students entering their portals, and accept the validity of other epistemological frameworks.

NOTES

1. For those interested in this aspect, see Edwards (1993).
2. See Nicola Charles (1990) for a summary of the complexity of the debate.
3. Many Western countries either have ended (for example Sweden) or are taking steps to end (for example, Britain and Australia) the binary divide in higher education, replacing it with a unified system.
4. A shift that even some experienced academic women find difficult. See, for example, Dorothy Smith's (1987a) and Hilary Land's (1989) accounts of combining motherhood and academic life. See also Sylvia Ann Hewlett's (1987) account for other difficulties.

5. See Marilyn Porter (1983) for similar findings about 'areas of expertise' that are defined by men as male concerns.
6. Indeed, mothers are not allowed their own expertise even in mothering. Academics and professionals (often men) must validate it (Hardyment, 1984).
7. In practice, substantive topics and research methods are often kept separate (Gubbay, 1991); an example of the disciplinary boundaries that many feminists eschew.

7 Shifting Status: Mothers' Higher Education and their Children's Schooling

Rosalind Edwards

As we have argued throughout this book in relation to children's schooling, the educationalists' agenda has crossed the home–school boundary – home life has been converted into schooling within professional discourse and activities. Parental involvement in their children's education has come to dominate the educational research and policy agenda. In particular, contained within the literature on home background and children's educational achievement is a focus upon the role of a mother's own level of education as correlating with her childrearing and participation in her children's education (New and David, 1985; Walkerdine and Lucey, 1989). A mother's education is viewed as important for her children's advancement at school not only through direct influences, such as helping with homework, but also through indirect influences, such as having books around the house and so on. This view of mothering has a long history. Many of the nineteenth-century feminists who advocated higher education for women as a means of improving their position in the public world of paid work also felt educated women would make better mothers, utilising their education in rearing their children (Banks, 1981). Later, in the 1960s, higher education was often still viewed both by and for the women entering it as enhancing their future roles as mothers responsible for their children's development (as Ann Oakley recounts in her autobiography (1984)).

Thus mothers' education has often been and still often is seen in terms of being good for their children rather than for themselves. Like other aspects of mothering, it is examined unidirectionally, in relation to children's educational performance – from the standpoint of educational professionals rather than that of mothers (Smith, D.E., 1987a; and see Smith, T.E., 1989, for an example of this approach). This chapter is concerned, as are Jane Ribbens' chapters, with the discourses of the 'other side' of the home–school boundary, rather than with measuring children's educational achievement or 'parental' attitudes and participation in terms of educationalists' definitions. Much of this type of educational research is primarily orientated around children in their home and school environments, as affected by mothers, rather than a broader context that takes into account the placing of mothers within the wider social structure, and mothers' own understandings of this.

The context examined here is the shift in status felt by mothers in their dealings with schools and the formal public world generally upon gaining a social science degree level education: 'In industrial and post-industrial societies, formal education is one of the important determinants of individual social status and of the individual's ability to contribute to society' (Smith, T.E., 1989, p. 88).

I build upon my previous chapter to examine the ways that being a student – undergoing a status transition – can affect mothers' views on, and understanding of, their children's upbringing and education, and their relationship to their children's schools. Gaining access to higher education gave the women the feeling of holding a different position in a social system structured by differentiation and inequality from that which they had occupied before becoming a student.

The first part of this chapter looks at the meanings the mature mother-students attached to the relationship between their parents and their schools in their childhood. The women's perceptions are, of course, retrospective, and filtered through understandings gained by studying. There is, however, a certain congruence between the parental home–school relationships recalled by the women I interviewed and those of the grandmothers interviewed by Ribbens (Chapter 3). Moreover, these retrospective interpretations of the past provide important pointers to the mother-students' present understandings about parent's relationship to their children's schooling and how they view their children's education. As Connell and colleagues (1982) point out, links between families and schools cannot be understood at just one point in time.

Each family has a history, including a history of a relationship to schooling. Predominant in the women's accounts of their childhood are boundaries between home and school for themselves and their parents, created by differences in social status, as well as notions of parents 'pushing' or 'not pushing' their children educationally.

The mother-students whose perceptions form the starting point for the discussion here (sample as in the previous chapter) had between one and three children of various ages, but six women had four children or more. All had at least one child in full-time education, apart from three women who had not had any children when they started studying but had become pregnant and given birth to a child during the course of their degrees. The children mainly lived with their mothers; in two cases care was shared with the women's ex-husbands (both women having new partners). The mother-students were thus conducting a relationship with their children's schools at the same time as they were involved in education themselves as students.

The second half of the chapter looks at the ways in which the women felt that higher education had affected their childrearing, their interactions with their children's teachers and others in the public sphere, and their views of what education means for their children. Again, social status (here as conferred by higher education) and 'pushing' of children are themes. As will be seen, higher education, and studentship within it, is a resource or an identity that is a source of status, which mothers can draw upon in their relationships with public world professionals. Indeed, it will be argued that without such access to 'public world' sources of status, it is difficult for mothers to feel that they can have an equal place alongside schools and a voice in their children's schooling. There are, however, tensions between the view of higher education as conferring a shift in status that emerges from the students' accounts of their ability to operate in the public world generally, and the implications for their informal social relationships. The mother-students' increased involvement in their children's schooling is not without tensions for the education system either.

RETROSPECTIONS ON EDUCATION AND HOME–SCHOOL
RELATIONS

Stratified social factors such as class appeared important to the
women themselves when they entered secondary school.
Although (as detailed in the previous chapter) ten of the 22
white mature mother-students identified themselves as middle-
class in adulthood, six of these women regarded themselves as
having had working-class childhoods. Thus 18 white women in
all can be said to come from working-class backgrounds.
(None of the women described themselves as working-class
and from a middle-class background.) As was noted previously,
only one black woman saw class, as well as race, as part of her
identity and as having an important role in her life. That the
women's own perceptions of their social status is important for
any understanding of the effects of education on their lives,
has been pointed to in the previous chapters. Its importance
will become apparent again in what follows.

It was in early adolescence that the white women reported
they became aware of social class differences. This was
particularly so in the case of white working-class girls who went
to grammar schools.[1] Gillian's account of how social class
differences came to her attention is fairly typical:

> I didn't fit in at all with the school. My friends were at the
> secondary modern ...There was one other girl who lived
> quite close to me who went to the same grammar school,
> and she came from a big house and was extremely snobby.
> We didn't relate to each other at all. And I mean my mum
> used to sort of get nervous if we went past their house, you
> know ...I used to bring kids home from school occasionally,
> but when I went to their house, you know, they went to the
> toilet inside, upstairs or downstairs. It wasn't an easy thing to
> ask people to cross the yard. No, it wasn't, it wasn't a nice – I
> mean it exposed me to a lot of snobbiness ... And it's so easy
> to get alienated at school because of that.

Grammar schools were at the pinnacle of the secondary
education status hierarchy. Working-class children who attended them were often moving outside their own worlds and
communities. They moved away from their peer groups, or
'moved up' above themselves. The feeling of being out of

place was common amongst grammar school children from working-class backgrounds (Douglas, 1969)[2] Indeed, 'getting above yourself' in terms of education was a theme of many of the black and the white working-class women's accounts. It was one of the reasons given by the women for their lack of educational attainment in childhood, and it is a topic that will be returned to in examining the women's perceptions in adulthood.

Low expectations of them on the part of their teachers was also mentioned by over a quarter of the mature mother-students as a reason for lack of achievement. The black women schooled in Britain saw this entirely in terms of race, whereas the white women felt it most often in terms of sex but also in terms of class:

> There was a problem. The teachers didn't want the majority of the black students to do O-levels[3] ... I have nothing to thank the education system for, right, at that age. (Maureen, a black working-class woman);

> I don't ever remember any teacher saying to me, you know, you could go and do O-levels, or have you thought about talking to your parents? ...I think if I hadn't gone to that school and they hadn't trained us so much like that [as office workers], perhaps I might have gone off, you know, into something else that would have been more suitable for me, I think. Because, you know, that was my destiny as far as they were concerned! Just fodder. (Judith, a white middle-class woman from a working-class background)

Thus, while their teachers may have valued education itself, several of the women felt that as children they were not valued in relation to education within their school life. Education was not for the likes of them, as female, as black, and/or as working-class. Indeed, such attitudes were implicit, or even explicit, in much British education policy throughout the 1950s and 1960s, especially in terms of white working-class girls needing an education that fitted them for wife- and motherhood rather than for any public world role (David, 1980).

Facets of these attitudes appeared to be mirrored in the expectations of some of the women's parents too. Their brothers' education was mentioned by many of the mother-students who had them, as being regarded as more important by their parents. Even for those who did not have brothers, their parents expected that girls would marry and have children, and therefore needed only enough education to get them a job that would fill in the time until this happened, and which they could pick up again later on. Indeed, most of the white women did this and were quite happy to do so at the time. While the black women also mentioned that their parents and other carers expected them to find a man and have children, without exception they all stressed how much importance was attached to getting a good education by their parents, grandparents and so on: 'That's what I was taught at home, back in the West Indies, by my godparents, that for you to achieve and reach anywhere you have to have that, a good education' (Beverley).

For many of those in the education profession, parental valuing of education is regarded as being demonstrated by their support of their children's schooling. Reinterpreted in the discourse of the other side of the boundary this can often be spoken about in terms of dilemmas over the extent to which children should be 'pushed'. Being 'pushed' or 'not pushed' by parents to achieve educationally, either as a good or a bad thing, was talked about by all the mother-students. In the main, not being pushed was valued:

> [My parents] never pushed me. I mean they were really great because they encouraged me all the time. They always said, well, just do your best and if you, you know, that's all you can do...They just thought that the fact that I was happy and getting on reasonably well was okay. (Victoria, a white woman from a working-class background)

All but one of the four white women from middle-class backgrounds regarded themselves as having been pushed, but the pressure was felt to be too much by two of them. While a few white women from working-class backgrounds spoke of their parents' disdain for education beyond that which was absolutely necessary, most of them felt that, like the black women's parents, their parents did value education and had pushed them up to a point beyond which they were either not encouraged to go, or it was left very much up to them. (A childhood situation that resonates with that is described by Arlene McLaren, 1988, for women students in adult education.)

The encouragement usually stopped at minimal qualifications because that is where their parents' own understandings of the possibilities of the education system ceased (and teachers did not appear to often hold out alternative scenarios for them). Very few of the women's parents had stayed on at school beyond school-leaving age, and most of their parents had few, if any, qualifications:

> Educationwise, I mean it was nothing great, but [my parents] did read and write. You know, they could get by ... They were both workers and they didn't really understand the education system. (Maureen, a black working-class woman)

> I mean [my parents] were both really poorly educated ... They were very much aware that there was that gap. And they were also – they were aware and, guilty isn't the right word, but they, both of them, felt that they couldn't give to us the practical help at home that they would have liked to have done. I think they felt that, you know, that they were lacking ... I mean I won quite a lot of prizes at school and always my parents would go and my dad would say, she's done it all on her own, you know. We can't help her. We can't do anything. So, you know, they were very aware. (Jackie, a white woman from a working-class background)

It was not that the women felt that their parents were unintelligent. Over a third of them stressed that their mothers and/or their fathers had been 'bright' and could have gone on to better things if free universal education had been available to them and/or the Second World War had not disrupted their schooling. Parents were, however, not 'educated' people in the formal sense.

For the black and the white working-class mother-students as children (and also as adults, in fact) 'educated' people were often an unknown factor, moving outside their own social circles. The women often mentioned how their parents regarded teachers as people with authority and power – whom they were not quite sure how to relate to: '[My mother] wouldn't have known her way – how to manage relationships with school. She wouldn't have known how to go into the school and create the right impression' (Jennie, a white woman from a working-class background).

The world of education was a status-bound and alien world where class and race played an important part. The white women from middle-class backgrounds spoke of their parents as regarding themselves as social equals to teachers – indeed, half were in fact teachers, as was one black woman's father. In the main, however, the black women, along with the white women from working-class backgrounds, regarded their parents as feeling socially inferior to educated people in some way and as not having an understanding of the (British) education system, or feeling confident or competent educationally.

Education and schools were part of a world into which, largely, the women's parents fitted uneasily. In a variety of ways, their relationship to this world was one of exclusion – as it was for the women as children. The women's own understandings of the education system, as social science students in higher education, however, led them to feel a different placing and status to that of their parents in relation to schools and to other public institutions. It was a placing they had actively chosen, in that they had decided to become mother-students and gain access to higher education, and which they valued. Yet, as will be seen, they could feel uncomfortable about this change of status, and also continued to be concerned with issues of 'pushing' children educationally.

THE STATUS OF HIGHER EDUCATION

The shift in placing the mature mother-students felt was based, to a large part, on the status that higher education holds. The education system reflects the hierarchical nature of wider society, and higher education is at the pinnacle of the educational ordering. It is a valued and a scarce resource. For the mother-students, higher education meant present or potential status. As we saw in the previous chapter, it was about becoming knowledgeable in an objective way and about individual achievement – but it also meant being and feeling different in many ways: as students in higher education, as mothers, and as members of the population generally.

Apart from wanting knowledge because they were interested in the subject and to 'prove' themselves (chapter 6), the women also felt that higher education would give them status in the eyes of others and would lend more weight to their opinions. They talked of the intellectual status they, and others, accorded to educated people, especially those who had degrees. There was a recognition that a degree education was not available to all, and a sense that gaining one would some-how place them apart from the general population:

> Doing a degree, it's like joining an exclusive club. (Jackie, a white working-class woman – first year student);
> Because having done it, then you feel like you've accom-plished something, especially like it's only ten percent of the population. I say here I go again, I'm in the minority! But positive, in a positive way. (Irene, a black woman – graduate)

Gaining a higher education was, therefore, a shifting of the women's status in some way – and several of them said that just being a student in itself gave them a prestige that had not been accorded to them previously, either as mothers/partners and/or paid workers: 'I mean it gives you status being a student – from housewife to student in one leap' (Jennie, a white working-class woman).

Studying for a degree set the women apart from others. It particularly set them apart from mothers in general:

> Perhaps when they're [children] older they'll think oh well, mummy wasn't like somebody else's mummy and just watched sort of all the soaps all day long. Which I must admit I'm very tempted to do because I love them! But maybe they'll think back then and think well, I think it's really good that mum was different. (Victoria, a white middle-class woman).

The black and the white working-class mature mother-students often regarded themselves as now being able to talk and reason, as Sandra (black) put it, 'on a different level' – a level that was one many of their friends could not relate to. They could end up feeling themselves to be 'cut off' from the women they had previously regarded as the same as themselves:

> especially when I went out during the summer holidays to work, I mean the people that I met like in the offices where I temp'd, it was just awful...It's really petty and I'd think, God, I couldn't stand this. You know, I just wouldn't fit. It's this

feeling that you don't fit any more...If I'd stayed like most women – I mean I don't feel I've got anything in common with most women of my age, or a certain group. There are a whole section of women that I meet that I feel I've got absolutely nothing in common with. (Jenny, a white working-class woman)

Although white middle-class women also saw themselves as thinking about issues in a different way, they were now able to join their friends who had degrees: 'The fact that most of the people I knew were graduates and made assumptions that I was, and I felt I had been lacking something' (Angela, a white middle-class woman).

This 'different level' of thinking, the women's gaining an education, as was mentioned in the previous chapter, could be fed through into their mothering.

GAINING A HIGHER EDUCATION AND CHILDREARING

Dorothy Smith (1987a, and with Griffiths, 1987) argues that in the last fifty years mothers have been inculcated with an understanding of themselves and their responsibilities that is all encompassing *vis-à-vis* their children's fate in schools, irrespective of the resources they have at their disposal in order to carry this out. She argues that the power of educational discourse has subordinated mothering to its authority. Many of the mature mother-students combining family life and studying for a degree did, indeed, take for granted a view of their own education as benefiting their children in this way:

I've wanted to study to have a reasonably good standard of education, which I think's important in life anyway. Because what you have you pass on to your children. I mean I see it as a bit of an investment. (Paula, a black woman)

I mean I don't know whether we'll have bright or thick children or what, but it will be quite nice to give some education to my children. (Madeline, a white middle-class woman)

They saw themselves as 'passing on' their education to their children in several ways, including direct discussion and acting as a role model. They could, in these and other ways, incorporate their education into their childrearing.

The overwhelming majority of the mother-students said that they did at least try to discuss issues that they were learning about at the university or polytechnic with their children, even from an early age. Those that did not speak of this were those with babies. Discussion of social issues was broadly seen as 'educating' their children, and their degree studies were felt to have been important in this perception. For example, several women mentioned that when they did sit and watch television with their children they would now often choose to watch an informative type of programme so that they could discuss it with them:

> They did have a series about the life, you know, birth, talking about the miracle of life. And I didn't do any studies. I sat there with all of them. We all sat round the box watching babies born and all that! ...So I use programmes like that to discuss things... Doing the degree makes you more aware about how important parent involvement is. You see, it makes you more aware. (Irene, a black woman).

The women felt their children had become much better informed because of this type of discussion, and mentioned that it might also have some effects upon their children's current and/or future education. Just under half the mother-students referred to the way in which their own education had enabled them to help their children with homework. They saw themselves as role models for their children; because they went off to do their 'homework' within the home their children were encouraged to do theirs in the same way. Even in cases where children were too young to have homework, or even to be at school, the women spoke of their children copying them:

> If I pick up a book, they'll want to pick up a book, which is quite good. So if I want to do some reading or writing I'll always bring up a book, because I know they're going to run and get a book as well. Every time I get paper to write, they want paper to write as well, you know! (Anna, a black woman)

T.E. Smith's (1989) work suggests that these students' view of themselves as role models holds true. He also argues that, due to mothers giving more time and attention to their children than do fathers, this influence is stronger than that of educated fathers – again, a view also held by many of the women.

In these ways the mother-students' education could be integrated into their everyday lives with their children, and was particularly stressed in the case of bringing up their younger (pre-teenage) children. Only one woman did not feel her own education had this effect: 'You're in a rut by the time you've – you know, the age mine are, you've made your mistakes and go on making them I suppose'. (Jennie, a white working-class woman)

The rest of the women, however, regardless of the age of their children, felt that it did have some effect. They spoke of being more aware of the way they brought up their children, daughters particularly, in terms of assumptions or stereotypes on the basis of sex, and of the broader discussions referred to above.

In some ways the mother-students could be said, as a result of their gaining a higher education, to have moved towards the more 'pedagogic' type of discourse and attitude towards childrearing that has the seal of approval from educational and childrearing experts. The black women were particularly likely to stress this type of relationship with their children when they talked of the effects of their education upon their children. Valerie Walkerdine and Helen Lucey (1989), in Britain, and Annette Lareau (1989), in America, have characterised mothers feeling it incumbent upon themselves to transform their every action into a basis of pedagogy as a more middle-class feature of childrearing. They have documented middle-class women's production of correct learning environments in the home for their children. If this line of thought is followed, it could be argued that the black and the white working-class mother-students who spoke in these terms were, as part of the hidden curriculum contained in their social science degrees, taking on white middle-class styles of childrearing. The power and status of the educational discourse could be said to have encapsulated the women's childrearing practices. As will be shown, however, the situation is more complex than this – not least because of the women's desire for connections between their academic learning and their home life, and its thwarting in so many areas other than in their relationships with their children (as discussed in Chapter 6). The women's perceptions of the meaning of education for their children, and of their role as 'pushers', also demonstrate other complexities. The mother-students did not absorb meanings passively and unreflexively, they actively negotiated meanings for themselves.

REWORKING CHILDREN'S EDUCATION

The reworking of education described in the previous chapter did not apply only to the mature mother-students' own learning, but also to their children's. The 'ethic of care' explored in the previous chapters as an integral part of many mothers' 'way of knowing' meant that while the mother-students may have embraced a more pedagogic attitude towards their children and 'educationalised' the home environment, this was not always based upon narrow definitions of formal school-based educational success, such as achievement based on test scores and exam passes, only.

Many of the women, though, did speak of the way higher education was now seen as a 'normal' or 'natural' thing to do by their children. If this is true, as several studies suggest it is (Redpath and Harvey, 1987; Raffe, 1988), then the increased number of mother-students in higher education bodes well for the future supply of students! Both their children and themselves regarded higher education as attainable, and understood it in a way that was not possible for the women and their own parents in childhood:

> [My children] must be aware of the route to higher education if they want to. Yeah, they must be aware of how to do things. They know the procedures. And I am now in a position to help them through the procedures. (Anne, a white working-class woman)

This appeared to be so even for two of the eight students whose partners already had a degree-level education (mainly white middle-class). This was perhaps because the women's studying was visible to their children within the home in a way their partners' education had not been; because the women took their children to see the institutions if they could; and because it was they, as mothers, who in the main brought up their children and therefore the women felt more responsible for setting their children's horizons. The majority of the mother-students spoke of wishing their children to go on to higher education. Some of them mentioned that they worried that the pressures which they were under, because they were combining education and family life, would be noted by their children and attached purely to being a student, thus putting them off the whole idea. There were, however, important caveats to this educational desire for their children for a number of the mother-students.

White working-class women, but also several white middle-class and black women, were very aware of not 'pushing' their children too hard educationally – as they had themselves, in the main, valued not being pushed too intensely by their own parents. For example, Carol was a white woman from a working-class background who had married a man from a middle-class professional background. She had been motivated to do a degree in part because she felt educationally inferior to him. Carol found herself torn between valuing this lack of 'push' and valuing her husband's views on the matter:

> I can't really make up my mind whether I really want to push [my son] along more or whether to just let him progress, you know, by just going to playschool. I've got quite a dilemma about it ... Because there's more to life than just learning and doing well, there's being happy and caring about other people as well.

[Has (your husband) got any preference?]

> He quite likes the idea of him learning and going to a school, proper kind of thing where they teach them from as young an age as possible ... He's had that discipline and seems to have done quite well from it ... But then, you know, I had a happy childhood. Although he says he had a happy childhood. It's very difficult.

The stress that the educationalisation of the home environment and the pushing of their children on the part of parents, often middle-class, can result in, both for children and parents, has been revealed by Lareau (1989) and Klaus Ulich (1989). These mother-students were also aware of this aspect of wanting their children to achieve educationally. As well as class differences, there may well be gender differences at play here, linked to the mothers' concern with, valuing of, and responsibility for, the happiness and well-being of their families. It may also be linked to their own current educational experiences.

A quarter of the mother-students, again mainly composed of white working-class women, felt that doing a degree had led them to come to see the education of their children as not just about gaining formal qualifications, but as a much broader, more personal, development. In the same way that they and others of the women had to virtually redefine what education was about for themselves because their life experiences were either not used or misrepresented in their academic learning (Chapter 6), the women could extend this redefinition to their children:

> I want him to do whatever he feels happy doing. Maybe I might have been, you know, a bit more ambitious for him before and think I want him to do really well in the education system. But I think now well, he can do as he pleases. (Lorraine, a white middle-class woman)

> Maybe my perception of education has changed. Well, I'm more interested in what's going on around ...Doing the degree, I have aspirations for them, but I'm also knowing that it's up to them. You know, this idea you'll be pushing, pushing them and say, oh, you have to do it. You see? Instead of saying oh, they have to get their A-levels, go on and do the degree and do that, I don't think they have to do that. It's up to them to choose what they want to do. And being a mother, I'm always wanting what's more important for my children is their happiness. (Irene, a black woman)

Such feelings may also be linked to the fact that the students had made 'unusual' decisions for themselves. They had chosen to enter higher education. They might thus have come to see their children as able to take control of their lives by making such choices – but not necessarily through formal educational achievement.

Nevertheless, gaining access to the 'élite' status of having a higher education was felt by the mother-students to have served them well personally, particularly in their relationships with their children's school and in their dealings with the formal public world generally.

MATURE MOTHER-STUDENTS' CONFIDENCE IN HOME–SCHOOL RELATIONS AND IN THE PUBLIC SPHERE GENERALLY

Ribbens (Chapter 3) suggests it may be that mothers who are most confident about their own definitions of their children's educational needs are those with higher levels of education. Less educated mothers may tend to perceive education as something that is defined by, and contained within, the educational setting (Newson and Newson, 1977; Atkin, Bastiani and Goode 1988). Ribbens notes that the educated mothers she interviewed were more confident about extending that definition into the education system. Others, too, have stated that while women, particularly as mothers, feel little confidence, especially outside the home, educated women are less likely to feel this way (Thompson, 1983). Lareau (1989) has found working-class mothers to be more likely to defer to teachers' expertise and to feel themselves as lacking competence educationally. They are thus hampered in their interactions with teachers and other professionals. Middle-class mothers, with a college education, are said by Lareau to have 'symbolic access' to the world of educational and other professionals. She says they have a sense of equality in their interactions with teachers. The boundary between home and school was greater for working-class mothers than it was for middle-class mothers, although both classes of mothers felt a greater status differential between themselves and teachers than did middle-class fathers.

The mother-students felt that gaining a degree-level education had given them confidence. One of the aspects of this that the black and the white working-class women were most likely to mention was that, as social science students, higher education gave them, as well as a general knowledge of how society works, a specific understanding (gained both personally and academically) of how the education system works. They thus felt themselves to be much more confident in their dealings with teachers and with the education system generally. For example, Val (black) requested a copy of her child's school's working party report on implementing the national curriculum[4], which she said she would never have seen herself feeling knowledgeable enough to do before. Wendy (white working-class) felt herself able to go and talk to her son's teacher about his lack of reading progress and to request his school reading books be sent home – again, something she felt she would have not been able to prior to studying for a degree. The women – whatever their class or race – saw themselves as being able to talk to teachers on more equal terms than previously. Moreover, if the teachers knew they were students (often having this mentioned to them by the women's children), the women perceived the teachers as respecting them and their opinions much more (even if they did not like the values behind this change of attitude particularly):

> I've been up there on parents' evenings and they really look down their nose at you. Really offhand. In fact one of them was downright rude and turned his back on me …[now it's] oh, she can read, she's worth talking to. It makes me really cross. (Anne, a white working-class woman)

The mother-students' accounts of their confidence to intervene or become involved in areas of their children's education, were aspects of home–school relations in which the women had pointed to their parents as having a lack of understanding. Jennie, referred to earlier as saying that her mother 'wouldn't have known how to manage relationships with school', continued on to say of herself: 'I think I know how to. You know what I mean? The things you say to teachers to make them feel that you know what's going on!' Additionally, where the students recalled a status differential between their own parents and their teachers, they saw this changing for themselves as parents who were students in higher education. Indeed, several of them planned to train to become teachers once they had graduated.

Interest in children's schooling and progress, alongside a pedagogic attitude to childrearing, is often assessed by teachers and other educationalists as indicative of parental support for education. While middle-class parents may be more involved in their children's education, as defined by teachers, this participation does not mean unequivocal support and backing for teachers and the education system (Lareau, 1989). Paradoxically, part of this type of involvement includes using the system to the best advantage, which can also involve challenging it. The mother-students could indeed use the education system in ways they would not have had either the confidence or the knowledge to do prior to their own forays into higher education. Janice (white working-class), for example, pushed a reluctant local education authority to provide special tuition for one of her children who had learning difficulties in a way she felt she would not have been able to do before, and Paula (black) was able to ensure her child went to the particular school she wanted her to attend.

The black and the white working-class mother-students' confidence in dealing with the education system was not just on the level of knowing what it requires of parents and children, but was also on the level of who loses out within the education system. As social science students, the whole area had been 'demystified' for them:

> I mean when my first, my two big ones went to school, I mean I didn't have the sense where education, you know, where I would sort of – you know, you go to like open day and school and the teacher fob you off with all sorts of cock and bull stories. Before time I believe them ... But now I don't give a damn. When people talk about West Indian children in this country not learning its got nothing to do with the children ...They [teachers] weren't interested in whether the kids learnt. They see them walk through the door, oh a black face, another problem. (Val, a black woman);

> I mean I'm very interested in the sociology of education and things to do with class, social class and stratification and things like that. And I think a lot of it is you think, Christ, you know, they're [children] not in with much of a chance in the education system as it is (Michelle, a white working-class woman).

Thus these students acquired confidence in their dealings with the education system could cause them to lose confidence in it. Around half of the black and the white working-class women felt a need to supplement or change their children's education in some way. For example, the two women quoted above (Val and Michelle) were, respectively, hiring a private tutor and considering whether private education was financially feasible for their children. As Smith (1987a) remarks, the education system produces inequalities, but this is not an official part of its aims. The education system, like many other public institutions, depends on ignorance of this. Parents' knowledge of this is threatening to the institution in its present form.

The new confidence and status felt by the mother-students also extended beyond their children's schooling into other aspects of the public sphere. They spoke of a generally increased ability to express their views, both in informal social and formal public world situations. The white middle-class women were more likely to stress the former and the black and the white working-class women more likely to mentioned the latter, perhaps because white middle-class women have already learnt the ideological 'co-ordinating relations' that those in authority operate with (Griffiths and Smith, 1987). As many of those analysing and explaining women's lives have pointed out, it is principally mothers who hold responsibility for linking and co-ordinating the physical and emotional needs of family members with the varying requirements of public world organisations and agencies (for example, Graham, 1984; New and David, 1985; O'Donnell, 1985). The women in this study felt that they now occupied a different position in this mediating work with teachers, doctors, welfare agencies and so on:

> I suppose in certain situations I know what to do in some respects. I can put on a front when I want to get on with it, whereas before I might just have not done anything. Even simple things like going to the doctor, you know. I might have thought I should just take the doctor's word and not question anything. You know, just accept what they say. But right now I don't really feel that way. If the doctor tells me something and I'm not happy I'll tell him I'm not happy. (Paula, a black woman)

> We're also able to, if we do have to use – have to go to, say, to a local authority or something like that, we can also use

our knowledge what we've gained by manipulating the situation. Instead of you being the client and them being sort of the employer or whatever, you can now manipulate that situation where it's a one to one basis. Because in the past, specially with social security or something like that, you were there [points down], and this is much more one to one. You negotiate, you know, what's going on. You get more confident as well in handling authority and in handling people in authority as well. (Helen, a white working-class woman)

As with their children's teachers, several of the mother-students felt not just that their attitude to those in official public capacities had changed, but that they were viewed differently when it became known that they either had, or would have, a degree. A few of the women remarked upon how sad it was that 'motherism'[5] made it necessary to have a degree in order to gain status:

There's a whole different way – you know, they look at you in a different light...there's that, which is very pleasing. But it makes you think well, it's wrong. I shouldn't've had to do this to feel that I'm an equal or whatever. But education still does have this very strong status thing I suppose attached to it, doesn't it? ...But it's sad you have to go and do a degree to get that confidence and feel that you're a fully paid-up member of society. Because you didn't get – I didn't get that when I was at home with the kids. (Judith, a white middle-class woman)

It would appear that mothers, as holders of 'ways of knowing' generated in the private world of 'the family', have little status in the public sphere unless they can also lay claim to a place of status in the public world. As graduates of, or students within, higher education the women felt they were listened to, and what they had to say accorded greater weight, than it had been when they were just 'somebody's mum' or 'the woman behind the typewriter'. In the women's own eyes as well, higher education had status and put them in a different position when dealing with 'public' people such as teachers. There were, however, tensions for many of the mother-students in gaining access to this status.

CONTRADICTIONS IN STATUS THROUGH HIGHER EDUCATION

The mature mother-students felt that they had gained confidence through being a student in higher education. They regarded the status higher education gave them in others' eyes as making a difference to the way they approached, and the way they were treated by, teachers and others in the public world. The power balance between themselves and those in 'authority' was perceived as having shifted. The students felt that doing a social science degree had led them to understand and to question the place and 'expertise' of the people operating 'the system'. They felt that the status differential between themselves and public institutions and professionals was no longer the same. They had shifted it by virtue of their higher education.

When talking of their new confidence and status, however, the mother-students often were careful to add that while their knowledge meant that they were no longer 'down there' in their negotiations with those in authority, it did not mean that they were now 'above' these and other people (again this was stressed most by the black and the white working-class women):

> I think I'm more confident. I do things – it's like I used to be nervous about phoning up people, you know, sort of complaining about things and that sort of thing, whereas now I do it anyway. It doesn't worry me any more, that sort of thing. I think I always thought sort of before, God they're better than me. I mean I don't think I'm better than them by any means, but now I think that they're not better than me. (Wendy, a white working-class woman)

The status they gained through higher education left the mother-students in a different position from those who were still 'down there' – and those people were their former peers. Now it was the women themselves who might be regarded as 'up there' by their friends and acquaintances, and they could feel uncomfortable about this.

While most of the white middle-class mother-students had friends who had studied, the majority of the black and the white working-class women did not have many friends who had any experience of further or higher education. Being regarded as 'snobbish' or 'standoffish', and being 'ostracised' because of their education was a possibility spontaneously mentioned by three-quarters of them, but by only one-third of the white middle-class women. As was noted earlier, the women felt different from 'normal' mothers and from their former peers. In the previous chapter it was shown that gaining a higher education could cause conflict with the women's partners, parents and other relatives. Several mother-students spoke of feeling 'alien' and an 'outcast' within their own families of origin because of their studies. Other studies of young British and American black women students (Tomlinson, 1983; Scotland, cited in Smith, 1982) and white working-class males (Jackson and Marsden, 1966) who have succeeded educationally confirm this sense of isolation, and also reveal the ambivalence that accompanies it.

The very image and status, and the supposed objectivity of academic knowledge allowed the women to perceive themselves as holding, and to view others as perceiving them as holding, a different and confident place in their mediating work with the public world. Yet within the students' accounts there was a tension between the status of higher education and not 'getting above' themselves or viewing themselves as 'better' than others. While they valued and wanted the status that higher education gave them, they could find it difficult to deal with some of the ramifications of this. Their means of doing so centred around the sorts of separations and connections referred to in the previous chapter. Again, in this case, friendship and education could be actively kept apart where interconnections were threatening.

CONCLUSION

Gaining a higher education gave the mature mother-students a different status, identity or set of resources to bring to their encounters with teachers and other professionals in public institutions. The majority of working-class and black mothers are deprived of such an identity or such resources, and thus often approach teachers from a different position in the status hierarchy than that of many middle-class mothers. When teachers, educational researchers and policy-makers call for greater home–school liaison and more parental involvement in their children's education they usually mean a change, an 'improvement', in working-class parents' (mothers') behaviour, values and attitudes (Epstein, 1990), rather than any greater social shifts and changes in parents' socioeconomic conditions. Studying for a social science degree, however, had not just changed the mother-students' attitudes in relation to their children's education; according to the women themselves, it had significantly changed their status in relation to the education system and their understanding of the way it worked. Such changes were not just shifts in class status, as would be indicated by Lareau's (1989) analysis of the way the defining characteristics of social class shape the resources parents have to comply with teachers' requests for parental involvement and support. They were also gender-based shifts, with the mother-students gaining a prestige from higher education that motherhood, on its own, could not confer. The women felt that teachers listened and spoke to them as students or graduates, rather than as mothers.

This would suggest that mothers may need access to status identities and resources that confer status, such as higher education (perhaps particularly in the social sciences), if they are to feel able to conform to teachers' expectations of the meaning of parental involvement and support for their children's education. In a sense we are brought full circle here, back to the quotation with which Miriam David began the second chapter of this book: 'educate a man and you educate a person, educate a woman and you educate a family'. The argument here, however, is not only that educating mothers is good for home–school relations and 'parental' involvement, and therefore, if dominant educational beliefs are followed, for their children's educational achievement. The mature mother-students' education was not exclusively utilised for the purposes of mothering within the private sphere. It gave the women a place of status for themselves in the public sphere – the ability to draw upon an identity and resources from outside of the domestic context and the role of mother. Moreover, this is not simply a matter of any type of access – rather it is a question of the status of such identities and resources in relation to those of teachers and others with whom mothers mediate with on behalf of their families in the public sphere. As we have seen, though, this may be double-edged – both for the education system and professionals within it, who will be subject to greater demands and criticism, and for the mothers themselves, who may feel alienated from their partners, friends and relatives, and may take on even greater responsibilities and obligations in terms of their children's educational achievement.

NOTES

1. From the introduction of universal free secondary education in the late 1940s until the late 1960s, children at British state schools sat an academic test at the age of 11 (the 11+). If they passed this test they were selected for entry to grammar schools – intended for academically 'bright' children. White middle-class children formed the bulk of these schools' intake.

2. See also Irene Payne (1980) for a personal account of a white working-class girl at a grammar school that contains the issues concerning snobbery and lack of parental understanding of the education system that are discussed in this section of the chapter.

3. Until 1987, a two-tier system of national public examinations operated, taken towards the end of compulsory secondary schooling at the age of 15/16. O-levels were taken by 'brighter' pupils, while CSEs were taken by children regarded as academically less able.

4. The national curriculum is a common core curriculum prescribed for schools under state control. It was introduced in Britain under the Education Reform Act 1988, and was a new legislative phenomenon in its concern with the content of schooling (David, 1989a).

5. The term 'motherism' has been used by Victoria Hardie (1989) to describe the practical and psychological ways that mothers and mothering are socially devalued.

8 Conclusions

INTRODUCTION

In this conclusion, we address five issues. First we reiterate what we, as feminists, set out to do and why we decided to present the issues in the ways we have presented them. Second, we evaluate our methods of working, particularly the use of our concepts in a case-study approach and the contexts in which we used them. Third, we present our findings in terms of illustrations and critiques of our concepts in the context of our methods. Fourth, we consider the contributions that our studies and analyses have made in various substantive and theoretical areas. Fifth, finally we present what *we* have learnt and how this might contribute to a future agenda for practice and policy.

WHAT WE SET OUT TO DO

Our aim, as we presented it in the introduction, was to explore the relations between families and education in a *new* way and especially from a *feminist* perspective. As feminists, we chose to focus on women as mothers at various levels in education, and to make mothers' voices heard in the context of the realities of their family-based lives. We wanted to look again at the various relations between home and school, parents and education – especially their children's education – parents and adult education – particularly their own education as adults. We also wanted to look at both policy and practice, or rather the 'rules' and prescriptions in government or public policies and alternatively the experiences and activities of mothers in relation to schools and as adults in education.

We chose these issues advisedly. There is a wealth of material on families, parents and education that has accumulated over the years, especially from the perspective of education and educationalists. Moreover, issues about parents and education are high on the public policy agenda at the time we write. In the British context, the government has produced, as a central part of its domestic policies, the Citizen's Charter which includes the Parent's Charter for Education as a key component. One of the first aspects of the Charter to be enacted was the Education (Schools) Act, 1992. This gave parents more power to decide about schools for their children both in terms of parental choice of school and in terms of governors' choice of inspectors of schools. The White Paper on Education, published in the summer of 1992, entitled *Choice and Diversity: A New Framework for Schools,* took further the notion of the key part to be played by parents in educational decision-making, at the expense of local bureaucracies. But none of this has been about the *gender* of parents as mothers or fathers, nor has it been explicitly about the power relations between men and women in the family. It has all been from the perspective of policy-makers aiming to 'improve' educational provisions or achievements.

We, as feminists, wanted to look at the other side of the coin. We wanted to explore the subtle meanings of policy especially for women as mothers and mothers' experiences of school and education for themselves and for their children. Despite the burgeoning feminist literature, theories and analysis, there is, as we have argued before, a curious lack of feminist analysis of mothers' experiences in relation to children and their education. The main work conducted has been of a rather theoretical nature in North America (Smith, 1987a). Lareau (1992) has very recently tried to put a gender gloss on her empirical studies of parental involvement in elementary education. There have been only two similar approaches in Britain. (Walkerdine and Lucey, 1989; Anderson, 1989) This was the lacuna we hope we have now opened up to further investigation.

We chose to look at these issues in a particular set of contexts. First, we wanted to explore afresh how public understandings are constructed through policy developments and evaluations. We looked at public policy developments in home–school relations or family and education as a way of beginning to understand the differences between public and private constructions of knowledge and their potential effects on mothers' understandings. Similarly we chose to look at the construction of public policy around women as 'adults' in education, using adult education as a case-study example, as a prelude to understanding women's own perspectives and ways of knowing about education.

Second, we wanted to explore mothers' experiences in two different kinds of setting, both related to their wider policy contexts. We wanted to explore mothers' experiences in relation to their family-based childcare and formal education both for their children and for themselves. We chose to focus on these boundaries at the level of both home–school relations and student–institution relations.

We aimed to show how an analysis which looks across the boundaries with regard to the relationships between family and education generally and home–school and student–institution relations in particular reveals an issue – or agenda – that has been obfuscated by present policy and academic analysis and research. The boundaries analysis, as we have approached it, reveals issues concerning power in policy and practice. Moreover, and more importantly, it reveals the gendered nature of these power relations.

Using a boundaries analysis we have shown how boundaries do exist and occur, but in subtle and shifting ways produced by interactions and issues that come from both sides. Being a mother can mean different ways of knowing about and experiencing the world as compared to more official understandings. Policy understandings and educational institutions are constructed upon 'public' world ways of knowing and a professional agenda, and cannot or rather do not relate to the realities of women's family-related lives. In addition, being a child means different things in family and educational settings.

We wanted to contribute to feminist theoretical and analytical developments, by looking at an area that is of vital significance to gender relations but has been oddly neglected. We also wished to contribute from a different perspective to educational developments, including educational policy analysis and evaluation. In addition we wanted to add a feminist perspective to sociological theory, by pointing to women's crucial role within the family, and its significance to general theoretical developments, around notions of authority. Similarly, we aimed to contribute significantly to the debates within the sociology of the family and those in social policy analysis concerned with issues of maternal authority or responsibility.

CONCEPTS AND CONTEXTS

Our perspective is that of feminists. By this we mean that we have tried to make gender visible and explicit in a range of different contexts by more than merely the addition of issues pertaining to gender. This has meant making issues of gender central rather than peripheral to our analyses and attempting to ensure that these issues are relevant to all of our understandings. We have been concerned to highlight and understand issues from what Smith (1987a) has called 'the standpoint of women'. However, as we have shown, in our analyses of both policy and mothers' experiences, this might more aptly be termed the *standpoints* of women; moreover, a particular group of women – *mothers*.

Mothers have differential resources available to them in their mediating work with educational institutions, most often related to their position in society as structured not only by gender, but by social class and race. Also, within gendered contexts cross-cut by class and race, mothers create and bring their own differential understandings and perceptions to bear. This becomes visible through a feminist approach that pays attention to, values and cares about women's – mothers' – experiences.

Our analyses of policy, practice and experience from this feminist perspective have allowed us to weave both structural and subjective approaches within our book as a whole. Our chapters examining a range of educational policies and those exploring case studies of mothers' various experiences in relation to varying educational settings are complementary and integral to each other. At the general socio-political level, mothers are placed in particular ways by educational policies and institutional practices. There are, usually unstated, assumptions and requirements about their roles and responsibilities in family life and in their mediating work with educational institutions in relation to their children. Within this general setting, individual mothers continually, in each of their particular situations, understand, respond and make choices. In this final chapter we are attempting to elucidate and assess a particular way of examining and understanding the relationship and links between the two levels through the notion of boundaries.

We took as our organising principle the notion of *boundaries* which we have adopted from a range of other analyses, not only confined to feminist analysis. We use this as the basis for beginning to analyse different perspectives in both institutions and policy analysis. What we meant by *'boundary'* is that there are different ways of viewing the world dependent upon ones social position. This is perhaps not dissimilar to the idea explored by Shakespeare in *A Midsummer Night's Dream* in the playlet: the 'wall' between Pyramus and Thisbe. This kind of concept not only has implications for how different social 'actors' 'see' the world from their position but also for how different kinds of knowledge and ideas come to be constructed in interaction with each other. However, the notion of *boundary* only serves as an organising principle to imply that there are different ways of viewing the world from different perspectives. Boundaries are not fixed and immutable from this framework. They serve to illustrate differences. They may be permeable and flexible, but they may also be patterned.

The notion of boundary allows us to examine more clearly the interface between mothers and education. First, it allows us to look carefully at the constructions in education policy and practice of mothers' particular kinds of work in relation to educational institutions and practices. In other words, the notions of 'partnership' and liaison imply particular kinds of educational work from mothers. So too do the normal or regular practices of educational institutions. Many schools, and their headteachers in particular, refer to the parental body as '*my* parents'. This in itself implies a range of particular expectations for the activities and actions of the parents as a group as assumed by the teachers and educationists in general.

Second, the notion of 'boundaries' alerts us to the shifting nature and characteristics of mothers' responsibilities as constructed by different groups and institutions. It also allows recognition that these ideas are constructed not only by officials and policy-makers but also by the social 'actors' themselves. In other words, mothers do not absorb the meanings of their work and roles unreflexively, but are active in creating, constructing and responding to the meanings constructed in the social conditions in which they live.

Third, we have found some similarities between our notion of boundary and that being suggested by Ruth Merrtens and her research team at the University of North London who are exploring notions of parental involvement in primary education (Merttens and Vass, 1991). She has discussed these ideas as being about 'ruling the margins', a lovely pun on the idea. She has focused on the 'margin' between the home and school itself, thinking about the problematic nature of the distinctions between home and school, and where the 'division' should lie in terms of parents' and teachers' responsibilities for their children's education at home or at school. However, we have tried to use the notion to imply that there are differing perspectives on both gender and power in these boundaries, not only issues of home/school or parent/teacher/educator relations.

We have used the concept of boundary in association with the other concepts that are often more commonly relied upon in feminist types of analysis. In particular, there is the pair of notions that have become crucial to some aspects of feminist analysis; namely *public/private*. There are other notions, too, that help to elucidate our ideas and which are used in association with the idea of boundary, namely, family with education; mother with institution; vocational with non-vocational; authority with responsibility; and adult and child. In other respects, we might consider these the *context* for our analysis.

For instance, we have seen as a crucial aspect of our analysis the notions of public versus private. However, we concur with those feminist analyses which do not regard the ideas of public and private as being unproblematic. On the one hand, ideas about the *public* can be seen as being about public institutions, such as those created through public policies. On the other hand, the idea of public can refer more generally to the kinds of knowledge and ways of 'knowing' that have developed out of these kinds of distinction.

Similarly, the obverse of these ideas, the notion of the *private* also is not unproblematic. It might, for instance, refer to ideas about family and home as not being in the public domain but entirely within the private. However, as our analyses illustrate, the notion of the family and mothers' work within the family are *not* entirely private matters but are the subject of regulation by official and governmental organisations, as well as more informal rules and understandings. They also imply gendered *power* relations.

Indeed, our boundaries approach shows how the different understandings about the world are largely managed by women in the early stages of education, so that children learn about different ways of understanding the public and private worlds through interactions with mothers. Mothers are the mediators for children of their relationships with the 'public' as well as the 'private' worlds. A number of feminist writers, in different contexts, have begun to show how important this kind of mediation is. It can also be illustrated by the more general work on caring (Lewis and Meredith, 1990). The extent to which women's mediation affects, in particular, gendered notions of citizenship has also been discussed (Lister, 1990; Sassoon, 1992). This is a key part of learning to be a 'citizen' in Western societies with all that is entailed in learning about gender and power.

The *contexts* in which we have used our boundaries approach are twofold; we have looked at the boundaries in terms of policy on mothers and education and practices for others in relation to different educational institutions. In terms of policy we have explored the construction of understandings about *home–school* relations in the developments of educational policy over a thirty-year period, during which notions of parental involvement became paramount. In terms of practice we have explored the ways in which mothers' family-related lives have influenced their relations and understandings with educational processes and institutions. We have also looked at the observe of this and shown how, for instance, ideas about homework are influenced by as well as influence public and educational understandings. This has enabled us to show especially how power has operated in terms of gender.

In other words, we have used a *case-study* method to explore the concepts within what we consider to be a number of critical *contexts*. We have not tried to be exhaustive in our methods but rather have attempted to elucidate the concept of 'boundary' in a series of contexts. We hope that they will help to illustrate the utility of our ideas and open up the possibility of other areas of fruitful investigation.

OUR FINDINGS

We have shown how, buried within family–education and home–school relations, is a particular placing of mothers who are in fact essential to those relations, but whose aims, thinking, effort and time, within varying material conditions, are obliterated. The currency of professional and policy talk about 'parental involvement', 'home–school liaison' and 'home–school partnership' especially presupposes mothers' time, skills and effort. Yet they neither recognise them, nor do they recognise the gendered nature of the distribution of power in this involvement, liaison and partnership. Stepping across the boundary of policy and practice, to a stance in the gendered and 'powered' world of mothers, shows that these concepts are not lacking in tension, as implied within the language, but involve complex shiftings of power. They are imbued with both collaboration and dissent, with resistances and accommodations, with contradictions and compromises. These issues only become clear when we cross conceptual boundaries and look from the bases of mothers' experience and understandings.

The history of education policy-making, especially as we have shown it in Chapters 2 and 5, with respect to primary education and adult education, and the conventional analysis of such policy-making, have rolled on without reference to the gendered nature of their assumptions. The nature of women's status in society, especially as mothers, as 'consumers' of education, either on behalf of their children or for themselves, has been ignored.

An understanding of mothers' actual experiences of the relationship between their placing as carers within the family and the education system, at all levels, in particular, has received little attention at macro (family–education) or micro (home–school and student–institution) layers of analysis. We also explored these in Chapters 3 and 4 and 6 and 7. They reveal these relationships as being situations based on differential power and in which 'family' and 'education' and individual 'homes' and 'institutions' are, in fact, gendered power relationships.

In Chapter 2 Miriam David explored the ways in which policy has been developed around 'home–school' or parent/family and education relations from the understandings of social scientists. We investigated the ways in which social scientists predicated their knowledge on particular public ways of viewing the 'family' and its relations with the education system. We also showed how those kinds of understanding tended not to include either a gender or a race perspective, but were based upon 'common' public world knowledge of the roles of men and women within and outside the family. The general assumption, however, was that men and women had very different roles within both the privacy of the family and in the public world, with mothers responsible for the care and education of children at home and at school. However, the boundary between home and school or rather mothers and educators has not remained fixed over the forty to fifty year period under review. It has changed and developed over the amount of 'professionalism' expected of either mothers or educators with respect to their children's schooling.

Additionally, we explored how our social-scientific know-ledge began to develop varying perspectives with the involve-ment of feminists and others in these endeavours. Nevertheless, policy tended not to incorporate this burgeoning literature into its changing orientations. Indeed, notions of gender and race remained curiously absent from the public discourse on family and education, and especially from the increasingly prescriptive policy-notions about parental roles, such as parental involvement or participation and parental choice. Home–school relations as understood in the public arena kept a firm boundary around these ideas. Nevertheless, *mothers'* work, with respect to young children at home and at school, increased greatly, through policy prescriptions, over this forty to fifty year period. At the same time, however, there have been major changes in family life, such as the increase in divorce, separation and the creation of lone-parent families, most usually mother-headed families, which mean that mothers' lives are likely to be far more complex than in the past. The 'requirement' of greater involvement of mothers in their children's education may therefore be far less straight-forward than policy prescriptions suppose.

In Chapter 5 Mary Hughes reviewed and evaluated the traditional assumptions and policy issues in post-school educa-tion from a feminist perspective. We have selected here a case study of what is known, in Britain, as *Adult Education*. Adult education has, in Britain, been seen as a *women's service*, providing traditional, domestically oriented subjects for women in the family as students. Hughes has argued that, for women students, adult education is largely a vocational activity and *not* non-vocational as it has been traditionally defined, particularly by policy-makers. Policy-makers have seen adult education as providing courses for women to pursue which would build upon their domestic and home-based activities, but arguably, in their leisure time. We have seriously questioned the idea of a *leisure* activity for women, especially mothers of dependent children. We have also argued that the concept of leisure for women, especially at home, is problematic and certainly has a different basis than for most men.

Additionally, we explored the meaning of the notion of *adult* in the policy context of adult education especially in relation to women and mothers in particular. We argued that policy-makers tended to specify a less clear boundary between an adult woman and a female child than between a boy and a man as far as policy, provision and expectation is concerned. Whilst it may be that the term adult appears to be gender-blind, especially with respect to policy prescriptions for adult education, we have argued that for some women students in adult education, especially those who are, or are potentially, mothers, the term adult is a misnomer. There is a cycle of dependency entailed within courses in adult education for such female students that has closer links with child rather than adult status.

Our analysis reveals the need to take a different stance, one that takes up a viewpoint from the 'other side' of the concepts and theories of the dominant educational and sociological discourses. Rather than an 'ungendered' (but in fact masculinist) and an 'above experience' stance, between us we look at actual situations and explore the relations that organise them.

In particular, the relationships between family and education and home and school have been analysed in a way that renders both their reliance on mothers and those mothers' own understandings and experiences invisible. Moreover, where mothers have been seen as necessary in the family–education and home–school linkage, they have been regarded as without agency.

However, we have also shown how mothers, in fact, do not merely accept the 'rules' and 'regulations' as prescribed by policy and educational institutions but are active in creating their own meanings and understandings. One *key* finding is that maternal responsibility for children's education is taken to imply a variety of processes and activities by mothers themselves. This is usually taken to mean something more than 'being responsible'. As Ribbens has shown so carefully in her chapters, it has taken on the meaning of 'authority'. Mothers' role in family-based activities becomes crucial to their understandings of how much power or control over their children's destinies they are able to assert.

Ribbens has shown, in Chapters 3 and 4, that if we listen to mothers talking on their own terms about their young children, they do express much concern about their lives and 'progress' in school. These concerns occur, however, within quite a different framework from that which is relevant to teachers and educationalists. Mothers see children from the concerns of their own lives as individual women and also as the parents who generally take primary responsibility for their children's experiences as family members and as 'social beings' who take part in a variety of interactions, outside the home as well as inside it. In the pre-school years, women have largely taken the responsibility for all these aspects of their children's lives, and may or may not have paid some attention to 'education' alongside these other concerns.

These various sets of concerns may take some part in shaping the ways that mothers regard the issue of school choice – in particular, how far they place significance on the school as an extension of the local community or as a more strictly defined educational institution. They also affect whether they expect there to be continuity or a break between children's experiences at home and at school. Yet even where they feel they do have any control as to which particular school their child attends, the point of entry to school is highly significant. This is true not only for the child and mother as individuals, but also for a major shift in their relationship together. It is the point when another, generally female, adult comes to hold a position of authority in the child's life, often regardless of the mother's views of her suitability so to do. Lightfoot (1978) has described these first

teachers as 'the other woman' in children's lives. There are
thus major issues here concerning the possibilities of mothers'
own experiences of power and authority being compromised
in relation to the educational system, as well as a welcome
relief from their continuous maternal responsibilities. Within
the context of compulsory schooling, the mothers' concerns
with children as 'family' members and as participants within
complex webs of informal ties may receive little recognition.
And the possibilities are almost non-existent for the recognition – let alone valuation – of any notions of education,
learning or knowledge other than as these are defined within
the formal education system itself. Yet it is within this formal
system that a highly significant aspect of children's social
identities and future life chances will be shaped – as the
mothers themselves are only too well aware.

Given these ambiguities and possible contradictions for
mothers about their children's entry into and participation
within the formal educational system, it seems inevitable that
there will be the potential for conflicts and tensions between
all mothers and schools. Nevertheless, there may be much
goodwill expended towards the management of these
tensions, since it appears to be children's lives that are centrally at issue. Women may thus take a variety of approaches in
their interactions with teachers and schools and may shift
boundaries in complex ways around alliances of, for example,
children, fathers, teachers and other educationalists. Within
the state school system, three particular approaches were
discussed – first, treating home and school as separate spheres;
second, treading a gentle line in hoping for the good opinion
of the school and fostering a supportive relationship; and
third, working the system more assertively and more know-
ledgeably to seek maximum benefit for the child. Three other
possible approaches can be seen where the child is *not* educated within the state system. First, we saw the confidence
inspired by having purchased entry into the chosen school
leading then to a distant but positive relationship to, second, a
contrasting situation of very close ties and constant interactions between home and school designed to ensure continuity for the child's experiences in both situations. Third and
finally, keeping the child outside the formal education system
altogether reveals the extent of the assumptions which are

normally taken for granted, about who defines education and the sorts of impact children's school lives may have on family lives. In all of these situations, it is *mothers* who generally handle the daily and detailed implications and consequences of the interface between two quite different sorts of institution in which children are participating.

Taking this rather different perspective on the family–school linkage, to view the meanings of the boundary as this is experienced in varying ways by mothers, reveals just how far existing research has occurred within a set of assumptions and language that allows only one side of the boundary to be fully understood. The almost complete dearth of research on the implications of homework for family lives is a case in point.

It is clear that we have thrown up more new questions than we may have answered. In relation to the different ways in which mothers view schools, for example, we know very little about why women use variable approaches in mediating this relationship for their children. Ulich's (1989) discussion of the nature of educational knowledge in Germany suggests there may be *national* differences as to how far educational content is defined as separate from everyday knowledge. Clearly particular *educational philosophies* also vary as to how they define educational knowledge. As Ribbens's discussion, in Chapter 4, of the Steiner school shows, no clear boundary is defined there between everyday and educational knowledge, with the result that a Steiner school seeks to influence and define how children should spend their time throughout their waking time, whether at home or at school. *Individual schools* also vary in how they construct knowledge bases and in their attitudes towards encouraging parents to be in close contact. There were variations in this respect even within Ribbens's small sample within two local education authorities.

There are also some indications of generational differences as Wadsworth (1991) suggests. The grandmothers interviewed in Ribbens's sample certainly appeared to take a more distant and deferential view of education than their daughters. Nevertheless, it is difficult to disentangle general cultural changes in attitude towards authority, and the particular experiences of individual daughters, some of whom had been upwardly mobile from their families of origin (which is part of the wider cultural pattern anyway). It may also be the case that we need to distinguish between absolute and relative changes over time (as we distinguish between absolute and relative social mobility).

As Ribbens discussed in Chapter 5, a comparison between Janet and her own mother revealed that Janet's attitude to her son's schooling was indeed one of greater involvement, a higher level of contact with the school and a greater confidence about her own ability to participate in his educational activities at home (showing an absolute change between generations). Nevertheless, in comparison with the other mothers interviewed in the present generation, it is clear that Janet's relationship with the school was more difficult than for many women, just as her own mother's had been in her generation (demonstrating an absence of a relative change over time).

In Ribbens's small sample it is not possible to trace definite patterns over why the *mothers themselves* took different approaches to their dealings with schools, but some themes may be discerned even between those women living in broadly similar socio-economic circumstances. *Income differences* were still relevant among this group, for example in being able to buy either private education or extra resources in state schools. There is also wider evidence of this (Johnson, 1987; Fox, 1985; Darling-Hammond, et al., 1985).

Besides financial factors, the women's own experiences of the educational system and level of educational qualifications appeared to be relevant at times. As Atkin et al (1988) observe, the sharing of ones' children with the educational system is justified partly by reference to the view that teachers are professionals, but is also a source of ambivalence from parents because this professionalism makes teachers very powerful. If mothers view themselves as having access to some aspects of teachers' professional power then this will go some way to reducing teachers' power. Mothers' educational qualifications may serve to reduce that part of teachers' professional power which is based on the extended personal experience within the educational system which comes from participation in higher education.

In addition, however, whether or not the women had any sort of experience of exerting *control and authority outside the domestic context* appeared to be a factor in their confidence in dealing with schools. This points to the possibility that women

feel more able to deal confidently with schools if they themselves have some experience of authority outside of the role of
mother, in some more formal public setting. In other words
issues of locality, race, gender and class (taken from educational qualifications, income and experience of authority in
the workplace) have relevance in how these boundaries are
experienced. Unless mothers have access to place and status in
the public world, as things stand, they can find it difficult to
make their voice heard.

While our own research has highlighted some possible
dimensions relevant to these questions of how mothers themselves construct and negotiate variable home–school relations,
these can only be tentatively sketched out at present until
further research sheds more light on these issues. Furthermore, not only do we need further research in order to
illuminate what is going on in these *maternal mediations of
home–school relations* but we also need to continue to listen
closely to mothers in order to begin to see what other agenda,
knowledge and understandings may be involved, and so what
further questions we have so far failed to recognise.

Edwards also discussed how these meanings are constructed
by the mothers themselves in her two chapters. She showed in
particular that from across both conceptual and factual boundaries mothers construct their own understanding of their
responsibilities for their children's education. This understanding may well be related to mothers' own educational
experiences, resources and identities. In Chapter 6, Edwards
outlines the different and incompatible epistemological bases,
the socially constructed ways of knowing, of motherhood and
academe, revealing the way that mature mother-students, as
women with their feet in two worlds, had individually to resolve
the tensions. We trace the various ways that they did this,
creating varying patterns and understanding of the coexistence
of the two in their lives. It was the mature mother-students who
had to work with and attempt to resolve the inherent tensions
between the epistemologies of family and education, not the
educational institutions. This is because of the gendered nature
of the status and power relationship between the two worlds
and ways of knowing within them.

Despite the lack of status accorded to the mother-students
private world epistemological bases within educational, and
other public world, institutions, the mothers felt that their

status as students within higher education, with access to its way of knowing, meant that they were now in a different placing in their mediating work as mothers with these institutions. As Edwards shows in Chapter 7, having access to an educationally valued resource or identity allowed the mothers to feel that they could have both a more equal place in the home–school partnership and a legitimised voice in their children's schooling. Once again, though, within this publicly defined and gendered agenda, the mothers could create their own definitions and agendas. They could rework the meaning of education for their children and of home– school relations, albeit fraught with contradictions for both the education system and themselves.

OUR CONTRIBUTIONS

In summary, we believe that we have made a number of contributions to knowledge, to feminist literature and theory and to public policy and practice. In the first place, our contributions have been around issues of power and gender, but especially about the triangular relations of power. We have focused, unlike the majority of previous feminist work, on not just gender relations but those of women as mothers. We have tried to illustrate, through our series of case studies, just how different women's relations are from those of men especially in respect of children's care and education. As we have tried to show, these are not just defined differently by the policies of government and other public agencies, the practice of schools and communities, as demonstrated through social scientific research, but by mothers themselves. This has previously been ignored or rendered invisible in the literature, even feminist research and studies, theories and politics. By using feminist approaches together with our boundary analyses, in case studies, we have illustrated different ways of knowing and understanding and how mothers construct their own worlds.

Our second major contribution is to educational studies. We regard these case studies as contributions to policy-relevant rather than policy-driven research. We have tried to show how mothers do not just accept passively the ways in which policy prescriptions, public constructions, educational agencies define their roles. Rather home–school or family–education relations at all levels of the education system are constructed and transformed by mothers' own views and definitions. Different classes of mothers, mothers from varying racial backgrounds, have various views of the values of education and schooling for their children and themselves. So how such relations are constructed depends upon mothers' own values and definitions. We have, however, found differing patterns, especially that mothers' own educational qualifications and experiences influence and are important to their constructions of such relations. We have also tried to go beyond the exciting new analyses of Merttens and her colleagues to illustrate not only the problematic nature of the margins between home and school but how these boundaries are imbued with implications about power and authority, especially in terms of gender. These influence how mothers are expected to take school or educational issues into the home and how they are also meant to take home and domestic issues into the school.

Our third contribution builds upon these notions of gendered power relations. We hope that we have also begun to contribute to sociological theory in terms especially of definitions of power and authority. Traditional sociology, and especially sociological theory, has tended to ignore feminist debates about gendered power and authority. We have tried to start a discussion about the different nature of *maternal authority* as opposed to conventional debates about paternal or patriarchal authority or delegated and professional authority. Maternal authority, more than paternal or patriarchal authority, rests in the private sphere. But mothers have a special and crucial role, as we hope we have illustrated, in helping children to learn how to become citizens.

Our fourth contribution has been to begin to consider, in terms of social policy theory, notions of time and leisure and responsibility from a feminist perspective. Many feminists and others have usefully begun to consider different approaches to the nature of women's time and concepts of leisure. (Balbo, 1987; Land and Rose, 1985). We hope we have added to that debate by illustrating the complexity of these issues and considerations. However, *time* is an important concept from the point of view of social policy considerations. Time influences the differential ways in which women's work, especially *mothers' work*, is defined in relation to policy debates and our discussion of them.

Fifth, we have illustrated the argument made by Janet Finch (1986 and 1991) with regard to qualitative research being the ideal vehicle for demonstrating the effects and implications for people's lives of social policies and practices. Moreover, she argues that theory and data are closely intermeshed which means that the researcher cannot just be a technician but has to take a moral stance (1986). In a more recent essay (1991), she explores these research issues from a feminist perspective. We have aimed to develop this feminist approach through our qualitative case studies.

A FUTURE AGENDA

Finally we believe we have found that a feminist set of case studies, from our vantage point, has begun to aid the process of developing clearer understanding and knowledge, which may then begin to influence new understanding and a transformed agenda for future actions. Given that we are all feminists, professionals, academics and mothers who are in mid-career, we have concentrated our attention on these issues of family–education relations. Despite our clear professional and educational differences and careers to date we have all found ourselves in agreement on the problematic issues to do with current home–school or family–education relations. We are aware, as Snitow (1992) for the US and Coward (1992) for Britain have argued, that feminists are increasingly disillusioned with political action only in the public sphere. We wish to concur and argue for the view that *home* may be as subversive or as questioning of public knowledge and public agendas as public feminist activities. This returns us to the original arguments of the second wave of the feminist movement, that *the personal is political*. We also want to find ways to ensure that mothers are not made to feel guilty about their choices in the private sphere of the home or even in the public arenas. Motherhood is not only pleasurable in and of itself but is crucially important for future generations, for changes in the balances between home and school, public and private, family and education. Rearing children and constructing the under-standing and knowledge on which we all come to 'know' the world is as importantly done by mothers in circumstances of their own choosing as it is done by constricting, controlling and confining public agendas which do not acknowledge these issues.

Bibliography

Abbott, P. and Sapsford, R. (1990) 'Health visiting: policing the family?', in Abbott, P. and Wallace, C. (eds) *Sociology of the Caring Professions*, Falmer Press, London.

Abel, E.K. and Nelson, M.K. (1990) 'Circles of care: introductory essay', in Abel, E.K. and Nelson, M.K. (eds) *Circles of Care: Work and Identity in Women's Lives*, State University of New York Press, Albany, NY.

Acker, S., Megarry, J., Nisbet, S. and Hoyle, E. (eds) (1984) *The World Year Book of Education*, Kogan Page, London.

Adler, M., Petch, A. and Tweedie, J. (1989) *Parental Choice and Educational Policy*, Edinburgh University Press.

Advisory Council for Adult Education (ACACE) (1982) *Continuing Education: From Policy to Practice*, ACACE, Leicester.

Aldous, J. (1978) *Family Careers: Developmental Change in Families*, John Wiley, New York.

Allatt, P. and Yeandle, S. (1992) *Youth Unemployment and the Family*, Routledge, London.

Anderson, B. (1989) 'The gender dimension of home–school relations', in Macleod, F. (ed.) *Parents and Schools: The Contemporary Challenge*, Falmer Press, London.

Arendt, H. (1969) 'On violence', *International Encyclopedia of the Social Sciences*, vol. 12, pp. 43–7, New York, cited by Friedman, R.B. 'On the concept of authority in political philosophy', in Flatham, R.E. (ed.) *Concepts in Social and Political Philosophy*, Macmillan, New York.

Atkin, H. and Bastiani, J. with Goode, J. (1988) *Listening to Parents: An Approach to the Improvement of Home–School Relations*, Croom Helm, London.

Backett, K. (1982) *Mothers and Fathers: A Study of the Development and Negotiation of Parental Behaviour*, Macmillan, London.

Bainham, A. (1990) *Children – The New Act: The Children Act 1989*, Family Law, Bristol.

Balbo, L. (1987) 'Crazy quilts: the welfare state debate from a woman's point of view', in Sassoon, A.S. (ed.) *Women and the State: The Shifting Boundaries of Public and Private*, Hutchinson, London.

Banks, O. (1976) *The Sociology of Education*, Batsford, London.

Banks, O. (1981) *Faces of Feminism*, Martin Robertson, Oxford.

Barker, M. (1981) *The New Racism*, Junction Books, London.

Barrett, M. (1980) *Women's Oppression Today*, Verso, London.

Barrett, M. and McIntosh, M. (1982) *The Anti-Social Family*, Verso, London.

Bastiani, J. (ed.) (1987) *Parents and Teachers, vol. 1: Perspectives on Home–School Relations*, NFER-Nelson, Windsor.

Beattie, N. (1985) *Professional Parents: Parent Participation in Four West European Countries*, Falmer Press, London.

Belenky, M., Clinchy, D.M., Goldberger, N.R. and Tarule, J.M. (1986) *Women's Ways of Knowing: The Development of Self, Voice and Mind*, Basic Books, New York.

Bell, C. and Newby, H. (1976) 'Husbands and wives: the dynamic of the deferential dialectic', in Barker, D.L. and Allen, S. (eds) *Dependence and Exploitation in Work and Marriage*, Longman, London.

Bell, L. (1992) *My Child, Your Child: Child Care Structures and Patterns of Exchange Between Mothers in a Hertfordshire Town*, unpublished PhD, London University.

Bell, L. and Ribbens, J. (1993) 'Isolated housewives and complex maternal worlds? The significance of social contacts between women with young children in industrial societies', *Sociological Review* (forthcoming).

Bernstein, B. (1970) *Class Codes and Control, vol. 1: Theoretical Studies Towards a Sociology of Language*, Routledge & Kegan Paul, London.

Bernstein, B. (1972) *Class Codes and Control, vol. 2: Applied Studies Towards a Sociology of Language*, Routledge & Kegan Paul, London.

Bernstein, B. (1974) *Class Codes and Control, vol. 3: Towards a Theory of Educational Transmissions*, Routledge & Kegan Paul, London.

Best, R. (1983) *We've All Got Scars Now*, Indiania University Press, Bloomington.

Beveridge, Sir W. (1942) *Social Insurance and Allied Services, Cmd 6404*, HMSO, London.

Blatchford, P., Battle, S. and Mays, J. (1982) *The First Transition: Home to Pre-School: A Report on the 'Transition From Home to Pre-School' Project*, NFER-Nelson, Windsor.

Blaxter, M. and Paterson, E. (1982) *Mothers and Daughters: A Three-Generational Study of Health Attitudes and Behaviour*, Heinemann, London.

Blunden, G. (1984) 'Vocational education for women's work in England and Wales', in Acker, S. et al. (eds).

Boh, K. (1989) 'European family life patterns: a reappraisal', in Boh, K. (ed.).

Boh, K. (ed.) (1989) *Changing Patterns of European Family Life: A Comparative Analysis*, Routledge, London.

Boudon, R. and Bourricaud, F. (1982) *A Critical Dictionary of Sociology*, Routledge, London.

Boulton, M.G. (1983) *On Being a Mother: A study of Women and Preschool Children*, Tavistock, London.

Bowlby, J. (1953) *Child Care and the Growth of Love*, Penguin, Harmondsworth.

Brannen, J. and Moss, P. (1991) *Managing Mothers: Dual-Earner Households After Maternity Leave*, Unwin, London.

Bronstein, P. and Cowan, C.P. (eds) (1988) *Fatherhood Today: Men's Changing Role in the Family*, John Wiley, New York.

Brophy, J. and Smart, C. (1981) 'From disregard to disrepute: the position of women in family law', *Feminist Review*, no. 9, pp.3–16.

Brown, A. (1991) 'Participation, dialogue and the reproduction of social inequalities', in Merttens, R. and Vass, G. (eds).

Brown, G. and Harris, T. (1978) *Social Origins of Depression: A Study of Psychiatric Disorder in Women*, Tavistock, London.

Brown, P. (1990) 'The "Third Wave": Education and the ideology of parentocracy', *British Journal of Sociology of Education*, vol. 11, no. 1, pp. 65–85.

Bruner, J. (1980) *Under Five in Britain*, Grant McIntyre, London.

Cahill, S. (1990) 'Childhood and public life: reaffirming biographical divisions', *Social Problems*, vol. 37, no. 3, pp. 390–402.

Central Advisory Council for Education, England (1967) *Children and Their Primary Schools*, (The Plowden Report), HMSO, London.

Charles, N. (1990) 'Women and class – a problematic relationship', *Sociological Review*, no. 1, pp. 43–89.

Cheal, D. (1991) *Family and the State of Theory*, Harvester Wheatsheaf, New York.

Chodorow, N. (1978) *The Reproduction of Mothering: Psychoanalysis and the Sociology of Gender*, University of California Press.

Clarke, J. and Critcher, C. (1985) *The Devil Makes Work: Leisure in Capitalist Britain*, Macmillan, London.

Cleave, S., Joweh, S. and Bate, M. (1982) *And So To School: A Study of Continuity From Pre-School to Infant School*, NFER - Nelson; Windsor.

Cohen, B. (1990) *Caring for Children: The 1990 Report*, Family Policy Studies Centre, London.

Cole, M. (1956) *Servant of the County*, Dennis Dobson, London.

Collins, P.H. (1990) *Black Feminist Thought: Knowledge, Consciousness and the Politics of Empowerment*, Harper Collins Academic, London.

Collison, P. (1963) *The Cuttleslowe Walls*, Faber, London.

Connell, R.W., Ashenden, D.J., Kessler, S. and Dowsett, G.W. (1982) *Making the Difference: Schools, Families and Social Division*, George Allen & Unwin, London.

Coote, A., Harman, H. and Hewitt, P. (1990) *The Family Way*, Institute of Public Policy Research, London.

Cousin, G. (1990) 'Women in liberal education', *Adults Learning*, vol. 2, no. 2, pp. 38–9.

Coward, R. (1992) *Our Treacherous Hearts: Why Women Let Men Get Their Way*, Faber, London.

Crittenden, B. (1988) *Parents, the State and the Right to Educate*, Melbourne University Press, Carlton, Victoria.

Crompton, R. and Sanderson, K. (1990) *Gendered Jobs and Social Change*, Unwin Hyman, London.

Cross, C. (1989) 'Foreword', in Glenn, C. *Choice of Schools in Six Nations*, U.S. Department of Education, Washington.

Cunningham-Burley, S. (1985) 'Constucting grandparenthood: anticipating appropriate action', *Sociology*, vol. 19, no. 3, pp. 421–36.

Dale, J. and Foster, P. (1986) *Feminists and State Welfare*, Routledge & Kegan Paul, London.

Dale, R., Eslang, G., Fergusson, R. and MacDonald, M. (eds) (1981) *Education and the State, vol. 2: Politics, Patriarchy and Practice*, Falmer Press, London.

Dalley, A. (1988) *Ideologies of Caring: Rethinking Community and Collectivism*, Macmillan, London.

Daniels, W.W. (1980) *Maternity Rights: The Experience of Women*, Policy Studies Institute, London.

Darling-Hammond, L., Kirby, S.N. and Schlegel, P.M. (1985) *Tuition Tax Deductions and Parent School Choice: A Case Study of Minnesota*, National Institute of Education and the Rand Publication Series, The Rand Corporation, San Francisco.

David, M.E. (1980) *The State, the Family and Education*, Routledge & Kegan Paul, London.

David, M.E. (1985) 'Motherhood and social policy – a matter of education?', *Critical Social Policy*, no. 12, Spring, pp. 28–44.

David, M.E. (1987) 'On becoming a feminist in the sociology of education', in Walford, G. (ed.) *Doing Sociology of Education*, Falmer, London.

David, M.E. (1989a) 'Education', in McCarthy, M. (ed.) *The New Politics of Welfare: An Agenda for the 1990s?*, Macmillan, London.

David, M.E. (1989b) 'Prima donna inter pares: women in academic management', in Acker, S. (ed.) *Teachers, Gender and Careers*, Falmer Press, London.

David, M.E. (1993) *Parents, Gender and Education Reform*, Polity Press, Cambridge.

Davidoff, L., L'Esperance, J. and Newby, H. (1976) 'Landscape with figures: home and community in English society', in Mitchell, J. and Oakley, A. (eds).

Davidoff, L. (1990) 'Adam spoke first and named the orders of the world: masculine and feminine domains in history and sociology', in Corr, H. and Jamieson, L. (eds) *The Politics of Everyday Life: Continuity and Change in Work and the Family*, Macmillan, London.

Deem, R. (1986) *All Work and No Play: The Sociology of Women's Leisure*, Open University Press, Milton Keynes.

Deem, R. (1989) 'The new school governing bodies: are gender and race on the agenda?', *Gender and Education*, vol. 1, no. 3, pp. 247–61.

Deem, R. (1990) 'The reform of school governing bodies: the power of the consumer over the producer?, in Flude, M. and Hammer, M. (eds) *The Education Reform Act 1988: Its Origins and Implications*, Falmer Press, London.

Delphy, C. and Leonard, D. (1992) *Familiar Exploitation: A New Analysis of Marriage in Contemporary Society*, Polity Press, Cambridge.

Department of Education and Science (1973) *Adult Education: A Plan for Development* (The Russell Report), HMSO, London.

Department of Education (1991) *Mature Students in Higher Education 1975–1988*, HMSO, London.

Devereux, W.A. (1982) *Education in Inner London 1870–1980*, Inner London Education Authority, London.

Dingwall, R. and Eekelaar, J. (1986) 'Judgements of Solomon: psychology and family law', in Richards, M. and Light, P. (eds).

Dinnerstein, D. (1977) *The Mermaid and the Minotaur: Sexual Arrangements and Human Malaise*, Harper Colophon Books, New York.

Douglas, J.W.B. (1967) *The Home and the School*, Panther Books, London.

Edwards, R. (1989) 'Pre-School home visiting projects: a case study of mothers' expectations and experiences', *Gender and Education*, vol. 1, no. 2, pp. 165–81.

Edwards, R. (1993) *Mature Women Students: Separating or Connecting Family and Education*, Falmer, London.

Edwards, R. and Ribbens, J. (1991) 'Meanderings around "strategy": a research note on strategic discourse in the lives of women', *Sociology*, vol 25, no. 3, pp. 477–89.

Eekelaar, J. (1991a) 'Parental responsibility: State of Nature or Nature of the State?', *Journal of Social Welfare and Family Law*, no. 1, pp. 37–50.

Eekelaar, J. (1991b) *Regulating Divorce*, Clarendon Press, Oxford.

Ehrensaft, D. (1983) 'When women and men mother', in Trebilcot, J. (ed.) *Mothering: Essays in Feminist Theory*, Rowman & Littlefield, Savage, Maryland.

Elshtain, J.B. (1981) *Public Man, Private Woman*, Princeton University Press, Princeton, NJ.

Elshtain, J.B. (1989) 'The family, democratic politics and the question of authority', in Scarre, G. (ed.) *Children, Parents and Politics*, Cambridge University Press, Cambridge.

Epstein, J.L. (1990) 'School and family connections: theory, research and implications for integrating sociologies of education and family', *Marriage and Family Review*, vol. 15, no. 1, pp. 90–126.

Faludi, S. (1992) *Backlash: The Undeclared War Against Women*, Chatto & Windus, London.

Femiola, C. (1992) *Day Care in the Home: A Study of the Issues Relating to the Quality of Care Provided by Nannies*, Wandsworth Parents Information Centre, London.

Fergusson, R. and Mardle, G. (1981) 'Education and the political economy of leisure', in Dale et al. (eds).

Finch, J. (1984) *Education and Social Policy*, Longman, London.

Finch, J. (1986) *Research and Policy: The Uses of Qualitative Methods in Social and Educational Research*, Falmer, Brighton.

Finch, J. (1989a) 'Kinship and friendship', in Jowell, R., Witherspoon, S. and Brook, L. (eds) *British Social Attitudes: Special International Report*, Gower, Aldershot Hants.

Finch, J. (1989b) *Family Obligations and Social Change*, Polity Press, Oxford.

Finch, J. (1991) 'Feminist research and social policy', in Maclean, M. and Groves, D. (eds).

Firth, E.M. (1955) 'Adult education according to women: an intimate history', *Adult Education*, vol. 28, no. 3, pp. 168–80.

Fox, I. (1985) *Private Schools and Public Issues*, Macmillan, London.

French, M. (1986) *Beyond Power: On Women, Men and Morals*, Abacus, London.

Friedan, B. (1981) *The Second Stage*, Summit Books, New York.

Friedman, R.B. (1973) 'On the concept of authority in political philosophy', in Flatham, R.E. (ed.) *Concepts in Social and Political Philosophy*, Macmillan, New York.

Gamarnikow, E. and Purvis, J. (1983) 'Introduction', in Gamarnikow, E. et al. (eds).

Gamarnikow, E., Morgan, D., Purvis, J. and Taylorson, D. (eds) (1983) *The Public and the Private*, Heinemann, London.

Gaskell, J.S. and McLaren, A.T. (eds) (1987) *Women and Education: A Canadian Perspective*, Detselig Enterprises, Calgary, Alberta.

Giddens, A. (1991) *Modernity and Self-Identity: Self and Society in the Later Modern Age*, Polity Press, Cambridge.

Gieve, K. (ed.) (1989) *Balancing Acts: On Being a Mother*, Virago, London.

Gilligan, C. (1982) *In a Different Voice: Psychological Theory and Women's Development*, Harvard University Press, London.

Glatter, R. (ed.) (1989) *Educational Institutions and Their Environments: Managing the Boundaries*, Open University Press, Milton Keynes.

Glenn, C. (1989) *Choice of Schools in Six Nations*, U.S. Department of Education, Washington.

Golby, M. (ed.) (1990) *The New Governors Speak: Exeter Papers in School Governorship*, Fairway Publications, Tiverton, Devon.

Golby, M. and Lane, B. (1989) *The New School Governors: Exeter Papers in School Governorship*, Fairway Publications, Tiverton, Devon.

Golby, M. and Brigley, S. (1989) *Parents as School Governors*, Fairway Publication, Tiverton, Devon.

Gordon, L. (1986) 'Feminism and social control: the case of child abuse and neglect', in Mitchell, J. and Oakley, A. (eds) *What Is Feminism?*, Basil Blackwell, Oxford.

Gordon, T. (1990) *Feminist Mothers*, Macmillan, London.

Graham, H. (1982) 'Coping: or how mothers are seen and not heard', in Friedman, S. and Sarah, E. (eds) *On the Problem of Men*, Women's Press, London.

Graham, H. (1983) 'Caring: a labour of love', in Finch, J. and Groves, D. (eds) *A Labour of Love: Women, Work and Caring*, Routledge & Kegan Paul, London.

Graham, H. (1984) *Women, Health and the Family*, Harvester, Brighton.

Graham, H. (1985) 'Providers, negotiators and mediators: women as the hidden carers', in Olesen, V. and Lewin, E. (eds) *Women, Health and Healing: Towards a New Perspective*, Tavistock, London.

Green, E., Hebron, S. and Woodward, D. (1990) *Women's Leisure: What Leisure?*, Macmillan, London.

Gregory, P.R., Allebon, J. and Gregory, N.M. (1984) 'The effectiveness of home visits by an educational welfare officer in treating school attendance problems', *Research in Education*, no. 32, pp. 51–65.

Griffin, C. (1987) *Adult Education as Social Policy*, Croom Helm, London.

Griffiths, A.I. and Smith, D.E. (1987) 'Constructing cultural knowledge: mothering as discourse', in Gaskell, J.S. and McLaren, A.T. (eds).

Groombridge, B. (1960) *Education and Retirement*, National Institute of Adult Education, Leicester.

Grubb, W.N. and Lazerson, M. (1978) *Broken Promises: How Americans Fail Their Children*, Basic Books, New York.

Gubbay, J. (1991) *Teaching Methods of Social Research*, report of a conference, School of Economic and Social Studies, University of East Anglia.

Gubrium, J. and Holstein, J. (1990) *What is Family?*, Mayfield Publishing, Mountain View, California.

Habermas, J. (1976) *Legitimation Crisis*, Heinemann, London.

Hall, C. (1992) *White, Male and Middle-Class*, Polity Press, Cambridge.

Halsey, A.H. (ed.) (1972) *Educational Priority*, vols 1–6, HMSO, London.

Halsey, A.H., Floud, J. and Anderson, C.A. (eds) (1961) *Education, Economy and Society*, Free Press, Glencoe.

Halsey, A.H., Heath, A. and Ridge, M.J. (1980) *Origins and Destinations*, Oxford University Press, Oxford.

Hamilton, D. and Griffiths, A. (1984) *Parent, Teacher, Child*, Methuen, London.

Hamner, J. and Statham, J. (1987) *Women and Social Work: Towards a Woman-Centred Practice*, Allen & Unwin, London.

Hamner, J. and Maynard, M. (eds) (1897) *Women, Violence and Social Control*, Macmillan, London.

Handelman, D. (1987) 'Bureaucracy and the maltreatment of the child: interpretive and structural implications', in Scheper-Hugher, N. (ed.) *Child Survival: Anthropological Perspectives on the Maltreatment of Children*, D. Reidel, Dordrecht.

Hardie, V. (1989) 'The world became a more dangerous place', in Gieve, K. (ed.).

Hardyment, C. (1984) *Dream Babies: Child Care From Locke to Spock*, Oxford University Press.

Harrington-Brown, L. and Kidwell, J.S. (1982) 'Methodology in family studies: the other side of caring', *Journal of Marriage and the Family*, vol. 44, no. 4, pp. 833–9.

Harris, C. (1977) 'Changing conceptions of the relation between family and societal form in Western society', in Scase, R. (ed.) *Industrial Society: Class, Cleavage and Control*, Allen & Unwin, London.

Heleen, O. (1988) 'Involving the "hard to reach" parent: a working model', *Equity and Choice*, vol. 4, no. 3, pp. 60–3.

Henderson, R.W. (1981) 'Home environment and intellectual performance', in Henderson, R.W. (ed.).

Henderson, R.W. (ed.) (1981) *Parent–Child Interaction: Theory, Research and Prospects*, Academic Press, London.

Hendrick, H. (1992) 'Child labour, medical capital and the school medical service 1890–1918', in Cooter, R. (ed.) *In the Name of the Child: Health and Welfare 1880–1940*, Routledge, London.

Hewlett, S.A. (1987) *A Lesser Life: The Myth of Women's Liberation*, Sphere Books, London.

Higgins, J. (1978) *The Poverty Business*, Blackwell/Robertson, Oxford.

Hochschild, A. with Machung, A. (1989) *The Second Shift: Working Parents and the Revolution at Home*, Piatkus, London.

Hoem, J. (1988) 'The Swedish family: aspects of contemporary developments', *Journal of Family Issues*, no. 9, p. 397. Cited by Eekelaar, J. (1991a).

Hood-Williams, J. (1990) 'Patriarchy for children: on the stability of power relations in children's lives', in Chisholm, L., Bucher, P., Kruger, H-H, and Brown, P. (eds) *Childhood, Youth and Social Change: A Comparative Perspective*, Falmer Press, London.

Hooper, C-A, (1991) 'Child sexual abuse, child protection and the politics of motherhood', paper presented to the Social Policy Association conference, University of Nottingham, July.

Hoy, W.K. and Miskel, C.G. (1989) 'Schools and their external environments', in Glatter, R. (ed.).

Hughes, M. (1992) 'London took the lead: Institutes for women', *Studies in the Education of Adults*, vol. 24, no. 1, pp. 41–55.

Hughes, M. and Kennedy, M. (1985) *New Futures: Changing Women's Education*, Routledge & Kegan Paul, London.

Hughes, M., Wikeley, F. and Nash, T. (1990) *Parents and the National Curriculum: An Interim Report*, School of Education, University of Exeter.

Ingleby, D. (1986) 'Development in social context', in Richards, M. and Light, P. (eds).

International Council for Adult Education (ICAE) (1990) *Voices Rising: A Bulletin About Women and Popular Education*, ICAE, Toronto.

Jackson, B. and Marsden, D. (1966) *Education and the Working-Class*, Penguin, Harmondsworth.

Jaques, E. (1976) *A General Theory of Bureaucracy*, Heinemann, Portsmouth.

Jamieson, K. and Toynbee, C. (1988) *Shifting Patterns of Parental Control 1900–1980*, paper presented to the British Sociological Association conference, University of Edinburgh.

Johnson, D. (1987) *Private Schools and State Schools: Two Systems or One?*, Open University Press, Milton Keynes.

Johnson, D. (1989) 'Boundary issues: what's new in home–school relations', *Management in Education*, vol. 2, no. 4, pp. 19–20.

Johnson, D. (1990) *Parental Choice in Education*, Unwin Hyman, London.

Johnson, D. and Ransom, E. (1980) 'Parents' perceptions of secondary schools', in Craft, M., Raynor, J. and Cohen, L. (eds) *Linking Home and School*, Harper & Row, London.

Joshi, H. (ed.) (1989) *The Changing Population of Britain*, Basil Blackwell, Oxford.

Jowett, S. (1990) Working with parents – a study of policy and practice, *Early Child Development and Care*, no. 58, pp. 45–50.

Keddie, N. (1980) 'Adult education: an ideology of individualism', in Thompson, J.L. (ed.).

Keddie, N. (1981) 'Adult education – a woman's service' (unpublished paper).

Kelly, L. (1988) *Surviving Sexual Violence*, Polity Press, Oxford.

Kerchoff, A. (1972) *Socialization and Social Class*, Prentice-Hall, Englewood Cliffs, NJ.

Keys, W. and Fernandes, C. (1990) *A Survey of School Governing Bodies*, vol. 1, NFER, Windsor.

Kiernan, K. and Wicks, M. (1990) *Family Change and Future Policy*, Family Policy Studies Centre, London.

Knijn, T. (1989) *Changing Motherhood in the Netherlands: Class Related Attitudes and Practices*, paper presented to International Colloquium on Gender and Class, 18–20 September, University of Antwerp.

Kohn, M. (1963) 'Social class and parent–child relationships: an interpretation', *American Journal of Sociology*, vol. 58, no. 4, pp. 471–80.

La Fontaine, J.S. (1990) 'Power, authority and symbols in domestic life', *International Journal of Moral and Social Studies*, vol. 5, no. 3, pp. 187–205.

Land, H. (1976) 'Women: supporters or supported?', in Barker, D.L. and Allen, S. (eds) *Sexual Divisions and Society: Process and Change*, Tavistock, London.

Land, H. (1983) 'Who still cares for the family?', in Lewis, J. (ed.) *Women's Welfare, Women's Rights*, Croom Helm, London.

Land, H. (1989) 'Girls can't be professors, Mummy', in Gieve, K. (ed.).

Land, H. and Rose, H. (1985) 'Compulsory altruism for some or an altruistic society for all?', in Bean, P., Ferris, J. and Whynes, D. (eds) *In Defence of Welfare*, Tavistock, London.

Laosa, L. (1981) 'Maternal behaviour: sociocultural diversity in modes of family interaction', in Henderson, R. (ed.).

Lareau, A. (1989) *Home Advantage: Social Class and Parental Intervention in Elementary Education*, Falmer Press, London.

Lareau, A. (1992) 'Gender differences in parent involvement in schooling', in Wrigley, J. (ed.) *Education and Gender Equality*, Falmer Press, London.

Lewis, C. and O'Brien, M. (eds) (1987) *Reassessing Fatherhood: New Observations on Fathers and the Modern Family*, Sage, London.

Lewis, J. and Meredith, B. (1989) *Daughters Who Care: Daughters Caring For Mothers At Home*, Routledge & Kegan Paul, London.

Lewis, S., Izraeli, D.N. and Hootsmans, H. (1992) *Dual-Earner Families: International Perspectives*, Sage, London.

Lichtner, M. (1991) 'Labour market strategies and adult education in Europe', *Studies in the Education of Adults*, vol. 23, no. 2, pp. 145–53.

Lie, S.S. and O'Leary, V.E. (eds) (1990) *Storming the Tower: Women in the Academic World*, Kogan Page, London.

Lightfoot, S.L. (1978) *Worlds Apart: Relationships Between Families and Schools*, Basic Books, New York.

Lister, R. (1990) 'Women, economic dependency and citizenship', *Journal of Social Policy*, vol. 19, no. 4, pp. 445–69.

Lovell, A. (1980) 'Fresh horizons: the aspirations and problems of intending mature students', *Feminist Review*, no. 6, pp. 93–104.

Lukes, S. (1978) 'Power and authority', in Bottomore, T. and Nisbet, R. (eds) *A History of Sociological Analysis*, Heinemann, London.

Macbeth, A. (1984) *The Child Between: A Report on School–Family Relations in the Countries of the European Community*, Commission of the European Communities, Luxembourg.

Macbeth, A. (1989) *Involving Parents: Effective Parent–Teacher Relations*, Heinemann Education, Oxford.

Maclean, M. and Groves, D. (eds) (1991) *Women's Issues in Social Policy*, Routledge & Kegan Paul, London.

McLaren, A.T. (1988) *Ambitions and Realizations: Women in Adult Education*, Peter Owen, London.

Manicom, A. (1984) 'Women teachers and feminist education', *Journal of Education*, vol. 12, no. 2.

Manifold, C. (undated) 'What links are there between education and the family: part two', Birkbeck College, London.

Mark, P. (1985) 'Authority', in Kuper, A. and Kuper, J. (eds) *Social Science Encyclopedia*, Routledge, London and New York.

Marston, C. (1991) 'The enclosure act: the significance of family boundaries, in Ribbens, J. (ed.) (1991b).

Mayall, B. (1990) 'Childcare and childhood', *Children and Society*, vol. 4, no. 4, pp. 374–85.

Mayall, B. and Foster, M.-C. (1989) *Child Health Care: Living With Children, Working with Children,* Heinemann, Oxford.

Mee, L.G. and Wiltshire, H.C. (1978) *Structure and Performance in Adult Education,* Longman, London.

Melhuish, E. and Moss, P. (1991) *Childcare in Europe,* Routledge, London.

Melhuish, E. and Moss, P. (eds) (1991) *Day Care for Young Children: International Perspectives,* Routledge, London.

Merriam, S.B. and Cunningham, P. (1979) *Handbook of Adult and Continuing Education,* Jossey Bass, New York.

Merttens, R. and Vass, J. (1987a) 'IMPACT – a learning experience', *Primary Teaching Studies,* pp. 263–71.

Merttens, R. and Vass, J. (1987b) 'Parents in schools: raising money or raising standards?', *Education,* vol. 3, no. 13, pp. 23–7.

Merttens, R. and Vass, G. (eds) (1991) *Ruling the Margins: Issues in Parental Involvement,* Falmer Press, London.

Miles, R. and Phizacklea, A. (1984) *White Man's Country: Racism in British Politics,* Pluto Press, London.

Ministry of Education (1956) *Further Education – Homecraft,* Circular 117, HMSO, London.

Mitchell, J. and Oakley, A. (eds) (1976) *The Rights and Wrongs of Women,* Penguin, Harmondsworth.

Morgan, D.H.J. (1975) *Social Theory and the Family,* Routledge & Kegan Paul, London.

Morgan, D.H.J. (1985) *The Family, Politics and Social Theory,* Routledge & Kegan Paul, London.

Morgan, D.H.J. and Taylorson, D. (1983) 'Class and work: bringing women back in', in Gamarnikow, E., Morgan, D., Purvis, J. and Taylorson, D. (eds) *Gender, Class and Work,* Heinemann, London.

Moss, P. (1990) *Childcare in the European Communities 1985–1990,* Women of Europe Supplements no. 31, August, Commission of the European Communities.

Moss, P. and Melhuish, E. (1991) *Current Issues in Day Care for Young Children: Research and Policy Implications,* HMSO, London.

Munn, P. (1991) 'Mothering more than one child', in Phoenix, A., Woollatt, A. and Lloyd, E. (eds).

Murcott, A. (1983) "It's a pleasure to cook for him": food, mealtimes and gender in some South Wales households', in Gamarnikow, E. Morgan, D. Purvis, J. and Taylorson, D. (eds).

Nault, R.L. and Uchitelle, S. (1982) 'School choice in the public sector: a case study of parental decision making', in Manley-Casimir, M. (ed.) *Family Choice in Schooling: Issues and Dilemmas,* Gower, Aldershot.

New, C. and David, M. (1985) *For the Children's Sake: Making Childcare More Than Women's Business,* Penguin, Harmondsworth.

Newman, M. (1979) *The Poor Cousin: A Study of Adult Education,* Allen & Unwin, London.

Newson, J. and Newson, E. (1977) *Perspectives on School at Seven Years Old,* George Allen & Unwin, London.

Oakley, A. (1974) *The Sociology of Housework,* Allen Lane, London.

Oakley, A. (1980) *Women Confined: Towards a Sociology of Childbirth,* Martin

Robertson, Oxford.

Oakley, A. (1981) *Subject Women*, Martin Robertson, Oxford.

Oakley, A. (1984) *Taking it Like a Woman*, Jonathan Cape, London.

Oakley, A. (1986) *From Here to Maternity: Becoming a Mother*, Penguin, Harmondsworth. (First published in 1979 under the title *Becoming A Mother*, Martin Robertson, Oxford).

O'Donnell, L. (1985) *The Unheralded Majority: Contemporary Women as Mothers*, Lexington Books, Lexington, Massachusetts.

Ogelsby, K.L. (1991a) 'European aspects', *Adults Learning*, vol. 2, no. 3, pp. 159–61.

Ogelsby, K.L. (1991b) 'Women and education and training in Europe: issues for the 1990s', *Studies in the Education of Adults*, vol. 23, no. 2, pp. 133–44.

Pascall, G. (1986) *Social Policy: A Feminist Analysis*, Tavistock, London.

Pateman, C. (1983) 'Feminist critiques of the public/private dichotomy', in Benn, S.L. and Gaus, J.F. (eds) *Public and Private in Social Life*, Croom Helm, London.

Payne, I. (1980) 'A working-class girl in a grammar school', in Spender, D. and Sarah, E. (eds) *Learning to Lose: Sexism and Education*, Women's Press, London.

Petch, A. (1986) 'Parental choice at entry to primary school', *Research Papers in Education*, vol. 1, no. 1, pp. 26–47.

Phoenix, A. (1987) 'Theories of gender and black families' in Weiner, G. and Arnot, M. (eds) *Gender Under Scrutiny: New Inquiries in Education*, Hutchinson, London.

Phoenix, A. (1991) *Young Mothers?*, Polity Press, Cambridge.

Phoenix, A., Woollett, A. and Lloyd, E. (eds) (1991) *Motherhood: Meanings, Practices and Ideologies*, Sage, London.

Plowden, B (1987) 'Plowden twenty years on', *Oxford Review of Education*, vol. 13, no. 1, pp. 119–25.

Porter, M. (1983) *Home, Work and Class Consciousness*, Manchester University Press.

Prout, A. (1988) '"Off school sick": mothers' accounts of school sickness absence', *Sociological Review*, vol. 36, no. 4, pp. 765–89.

Purvis, J. (1991) *A History of Women's Education in England*, Open University Press, Milton Keynes.

Radford, J. (1991) 'Immaculate conceptions', *Trouble and Strife*, no. 21, Summer, pp. 8–12.

Radin, N. (1988) 'Primary caregiving fathers of long duration', in Bronstein, P. and Cowen, C.P. (eds).

Raffe, D. (ed.) (1988) *Education and the Youth Labour Market*, Falmer Press, London.

Rapp, R., Ross, E. and Bridenthal, R. (1979) 'Examining family history', *Feminist Studies*, no. 5, Spring, pp. 174–95.

Raywid, M.A. (1985) 'Family choice arrangements in public schools: a review of the literature', *Review of Educational Research*, vol. 55, no. 4, pp. 435–67.

Redpath, B. and Harvey, B. (1987) *Young People's Intentions to Enter Higher Education*, HMSO, London.

Reid, P.T. (1990) 'African-American women in academia: paradoxes and barriers', in Lie, S.S. and O'Leary, V.E. (eds).

Ribbens, J. (1989) *Bringing Up Our Children: Whose Practice and Whose Reality?*, paper presented to the British Sociological Association Conference, Plymouth Polytechnic.

Ribbens, J. (1990) *Accounting for Our Children: Differing Perspectives on 'Family Life' in Middle Income Households*, unpublished Ph.D., C.N.A.A./South Bank Polytechnic.

Ribbens, J. (1991a) 'Mothers as mediators: negotiating child-rearing within and outside the home', talk given to the Family Studies Group of the British Sociological Association.

Ribbens, J. (1991b) *The Personal and the Sociological: The Use of Student Autobiography in Teaching Undergraduate Sociology*, Oxford Polytechnic, Oxford.

Ribbens, J. (forthcoming) *Mothers and Their Children: Towards a Feminist Perspective on Childrearing*, Sage, London.

Rich, A. (1977) *Of Woman Born*, Virago, London.

Richards, M. and Light, P. (eds) (1986) *Children of Social Worlds: Development in a Social Context*, Polity Press, Cambridge.

Riley, D. (1983) *War in the Nursery*, Virago, London.

Robinson, E (1980) 'Course design and structure', in Equal Opportunities Commission *Equal Opportunities in Higher Education*, report of an EOC/SRHE (Equal Opportunities Commission/Society for Research Into Higher Education) conference at Manchester Polytechnic, EOC, Manchester.

Rockhill, K. (1987a) 'Gender, language and the politics of literacy', *British Journal of the Sociology of Education*, vol. 8, no. 2, pp. 153–69.

Rockhill, K. (1987b) 'Literacy as threat/desire: longing to be SOMEBODY', in Gaskell, J. and McLaren, A.T. (eds).

Ruddick, S. (1982) 'Maternal thinking, in Thorne, B. and Yalom, M. (eds) *Rethinking the Family: Some Feminist Questions*, Longman, New York.

Ruddick, S. (1989) *Maternal Thinking: Towards a Politics of Peace*, Women's Press, London.

Sargant, N. (1991) *Learning and Leisure: A Study of Adult Participation in Learning and its Policy Implications*, NIACE (National Institute of Adult Continuing Education), Leicester.

Sassoon, A.S. (1992) 'Equality and difference: the emergence of a new concept of citizenship', in McLellan, D and Sayers, S. (eds) *Democracy and Socialism*, Macmillan, London.

Scarre, G. (ed.) (1989) *Children, Parents and Politics*, Cambridge University Press, Cambridge.

Scott, G. (1990) 'Parents and preschool services: issues of parental involvement', *International Journal of Sociology and Social Policy*, vol. 10, no. 1, pp. 1–13.

Scottish Education Department (1975) *Adult Education: The Challenge of Change* (The Alexander Report), HMSO, London.

SCUTREA (1990) *Towards 1992: Education of Adults in the New Europe*, Proceedings of the 20th Annual Conference of SCUTREA, (Standing Committee for University Teaching and Research in the Education of Adults), Sheffield.

Segal, L. (1985) *Is the Future Female? Troubled Thoughts on Contemporary Feminism*, Virago, London.

Sevenhuijsen, S. (1991) 'Justice, Moral reasoning and the politics of child custody, in Meehan, E. and Sevenhuijsen, S. (eds) *Equality, Politics and Gender*, Sage, London.

Sharistanian, J. (1987) 'Conclusion: the public/domestic model and the study of contemporary women's lives', in Sharistanian, J. (ed.) *Beyond the Public/Domestic Dichotomy: Contemporary Perspectives on Women's Public Lives*, Greenwood Press, Westport. Connecticut.

Shaw, J. (1981) 'In loco parentis: a relationship between parent, state and child, in Dale, R. et al.

Shaw, J. (1986) 'What should be done about social science in higher education', in Finch, J. and Rustin, M. (eds) A Degree of Choice? *Higher Education and the Right to Learn*, Penguin, Harmondsworth.

Silver, H. (1990) *Education, Change and the Policy Process*, Falmer Press, London.

Silver, H. and Silver, P. (1991) *America's Educational War on Poverty*, Falmer Press, London.

Smith, C.H. (1982) 'Black female achievers in academe', *Journal of Negro Education*, no. 51, pp. 318–57.

Smith, D.E. (1987a) *The Everyday World as Problematic: A Feminist Sociology*, North Eastern University, Boston.

Smith, D.E. (1987b) 'An analysis of ideological structures and how women are excluded: considerations for academic women', in Gaskell, J.S. and McLaren, A.T. (eds).

Smith, D.E. (1989) 'Sociological theory: methods of writing patriarchy', in Wallace, R.A. (ed.) *Feminism and Sociological Theory*, Sage, London.

Smith, T.E. (1989) 'Mother–father differences in parental influence on school grades and educational goals', *Sociological Inquiry*, vol. 59, no. 1, pp. 88–98.

Snitow, A. (1992) 'Feminism and motherhood: an American reading', *Feminist Review*, no. 40, pp. 32–52.

Sokoloff, B. (1987) *Edith and Stepney: The Life of Edith Ramsey. Sixty years of Education, Politics and Social Change*, Stepney Book Publications, London.

Spender, D. (1981) 'Education: the patriarchal paradigm and the response to feminism', in Spender, D. (ed.) *Men's Studies Modified: The Impact of Feminism on the Academic Disciplines*, Pergamon, Oxford.

Spender, D. (1983) 'Theorising about theorising', in Bowles, G. and Duelli Klein, R. (eds) *Theories of Women's Studies*, Routledge & Kegan Paul, London.

Spender, D. (1985) *Man Made Language*, Routledge & Kegan Paul, London.

Sperling, L. (1991) 'Can the barriers be breached? Mature women's access to higher education', *Gender and Education*, vol. 3, no. 2, pp. 199–213.

Stacey, J. (1986) 'Are feminists afraid to leave home? The challenge of conservative pro-family feminism', in Mitchell, J. and Oakley, A. (eds), *What is Feminism?*, Basil Blackwell, Oxford.

Stacey, M. and Davies, C. (1983) *Division of Labour in Child Health Care: Final Report to the S.S.R.C. 1983*, University of Warwick.

Stacey, M. and Price, M. (1981) *Women, Power and Politics*, Tavistock, London.

Stanley, L. and Wise, S. (1983) *Breaking Out: Feminist Consciousness and Feminist Research*, Routledge & Kegan Paul, London.

Stillman, A. and Maychell, K. (1986) *Choosing Schools: Parents, LEA's and the 1980 Education Act*, National Foundation for Educational Research, Slough.

Stolz, L.M. (1967) *Influences on Parent Behaviour*, Stanford University Press.

Sutherland, G. (1984) *Ability, Merit and Measurement: Mental Testing and English Education 1880–1940*, Clarendon Press, Oxford.

Tennant, M. (ed.) (1991) *Adult and Continuing Education in Australia: Issues and Practices*, Routledge, London.

Thomas, K. (1990) *Gender and Subject in Higher Education*, S.R.H.E./Open University Press, Milton Keynes.

Thompson, J.L. (ed.) (1980) *Adult Education For a Change*, Hutchinson, London.

Thompson, J. (1983) *Learning Liberation: Women's Response to Men's Education*, Croom Helm, Beckenham.

Titmuss, C. (1981) *Strategies for Adult Education: Practice in West Europe*, Open University Press, Milton Keynes.

Tivers, J. (1985) *Women Attached: The Daily Lives of Women With Young Children*, Croom Helm, London.

Tizard, B. and Hughes, M. (1984) *Young Children Learning, Talking and Thinking at Home and at School*, Fontana, London.

Tizard, B. et al. (1988) *Young Children at School in the Inner City*, Lawrence Erbaum, London.

Tomlinson, S. (1983) 'Black women in higher education – case studies of university women in Britain', in Barton, L. and Walker, S. (eds) *Race, Class and Education*, Croom Helm, Beckenham.

Tomlinson, S. (1991) *Teachers and Parents: Home–School Partnership*, Institute for Public Policy Research, London.

Tomlinson, S. and Hutchinson, S. (1990) *Bangladeshi Parents and Education in Tower Hamlets*, A.C.E., London.

Tong, R. (1990) *Feminist Thought*, Unwin Hyman, London.

Tulkin, S. (1975) 'An analysis of the concept of cultural deprivation', in Bronfenbrenner, U. and Mahoney, M.A. (eds) *Influences on Human Development* (2nd edn) Dryden Press, Hinsdale, Illinois.

Tunnard, J. (1991) 'Rights and duties', *Social Work Today*, vol. 23, no. 14, 28 November, p. 21.

Ulich, K. (1989) 'Eltern und schuler: die schule als problem in der familienerziehung', *Zeitschrift für Sozialisations Forschung und Erzietungssoziologie*, vol. 9, no. 3, pp. 179–94.

Ungerson, C. (1988) *Policy is Personal: Sex, Gender and Informal Care*, Tavistock, London.

University of Glasgow (1986) *Parental Choice of School in Scotland*, Department of Education, University of Glasgow.

Urwin, C. (1985) 'Constructing motherhood: the persuasion of normal development', in Steedman, C., Urwin, C. and Walkerdine, V. (eds) *Language, Gender and Childhood*, Routledge & Kegan Paul, London.

U.S. Department of Education (1988) *Digest of Education Statistics 1988*, National Centre for Education Statistics, Washington.

Valentine, C. (1968) *Culture and Poverty: Critique and Counter Proposals*, University of Chicago Press, Chicago.

Ve, H. (1989) 'The male gender role and responsibility for childcare', in Boh, K. (ed.).

Wadsworth, M.E.J. (1991) *The Imprint of Time: Childhood, History and Adult Life*, Clarendon Press, Oxford.

Walford, G. (1991) 'Choice of school at the first City Technology College', *Educational Studies*, vol. 17, no. 1, pp. 65–75.

Walkerdine, V. and Lucey, H. (1989) *Democracy in the Kitchen: Regulating Mothers and Socialising Daughters*, Virago, London.

Wallman, S. (1978) 'The boundaries of "race": processes of ethnicity in England', *Man*, vol. 13, no. 2, pp. 200–17.

Wallman, S. (1979) 'Introduction: the scope for ethnicity', in Wallman, S. (ed.) *Ethnicity at Work*, Macmillan, London.

Warnes, A.M. (1986) 'The residential mobility histories of parents and children, and relationships to present proximity and social integration', *Environment and Planning*, no. 18, pp. 1581–94.

Weber, M. (1973) 'The types of authority and imperative co-ordination', in Flatham, R. (ed.) *Concepts in Social and Political Philosophy*, Macmillan, New York.

Werbner, P. (1988) 'Taking and giving: working women and female bonds in a Pakistani immigrant neighbourhood', in Westwood, S. and Bhachu, P. (eds) *Enterprising Women: Ethnicity, Economy and Gender Relations*, Routledge, London.

Westwood, S. (1980) 'Adult education and the sociology of education: an exploration', in Thompson, J.L. (ed.).

White, A. (1990) 'New Man – the same old story?', Guardian, 20 June.

White, I. (1992) 'Parent Power', *Social Work Today*, vol. 23, no. 18, 16 January, p. 22.

Williams, F. (1989) *Social Policy: A Critical Introduction. Issues of Gender, Race and Class*, Polity Press, Cambridge.

Williamson, B. (1991) 'Continuing education in Europe: opportunities and constraints', *Studies in the Education of Adults*, vol. 23, no. 2, pp. 211–27.

Wilson, E. (1977) *Women and the Welfare State*, Tavistock, London.

Wolfendale, S. (1983) *Parental Participation in Children's Development and Education*, Gordon & Breach, New York.

Woodhead, M. (1990) 'Psychology and the cultural construction of children's needs', in James, A. and Prout, A. (eds) *Constructing and Reconstructing Childhood: Contemporary Issues in the Sociological Study of Childhood*, Falmer, London.

Woodley, A., Wagner, L., Slowey, M., Hamilton, M. and Fulton, O. (1987) *Choosing to Learn: Adults in Education*, SRHE/Open University Press, Milton Keynes.

Woods, P. (1988) 'A strategic view of parent participation', *Journal of Education Policy*, no. 3, pp. 323–34.

Young, M. and Willmott, P. (1957) *Family and Kinship in East London*, Routledge & Kegan Paul, London.

Young, M. and Willmott, P. (1973) *The Symmetrical Family*, Routledge & Kegan Paul, London.

Index